Transport Strategies for Net-Zero Systems by Design

OECD
BETTER POLICIES FOR BETTER LIVES

Please cite this publication as:
OECD (2021), *Transport Strategies for Net-Zero Systems by Design*, OECD Publishing, Paris, *https://doi.org/10.1787/0a20f779-en*.

ISBN 978-92-64-59144-8 (print)
ISBN 978-92-64-86878-6 (pdf)

Photo credits: Cover © Jan Kamensky.

Corrigenda to publications may be found on line at: *www.oecd.org/about/publishing/corrigenda.htm*.

Foreword

Meeting the temperature goal of the Paris Agreement will require transformational, rather than incremental, changes. Efforts to decarbonise the economy without limiting the growth in energy and materials demand is a race against the clock: as shown by the IPCC, while we reduce emissions per unit via efficiency improvements, emissions increase via growing energy and materials demand. Limiting the growth of energy and materials demand will also help avoid risky reliance on unproven carbon dioxide removal technologies in the medium-term and make it easier to harness the synergies between strong climate action and wider economic, social and environmental benefits in the near-term.

Approaches to reach net-zero targets that focus mostly on improving efficiency via technological solutions limit our ability to radically cut emissions while improving people's lives. Such approaches try to fix systems that are unsustainable by design, and miss the opportunities that redesigning systems can unleash. There are indeed enormous untapped opportunities to harness if we focus our policy efforts on designing systems that improve people's well-being with less energy and materials, and hence far lower GHG emissions.

This report builds on the 2019 report, *Accelerating Climate Action: Refocusing Policies through a Well-being Lens* and explores policy packages focused on systems redesign in the context of the surface transport sector. It identifies three key dynamics at the source of high emissions: induced demand, urban sprawl and the erosion of active and shared transport modes, the combination of which leads to car dependent systems and citizens.

The report calls for policy reprioritisation so that policies and regulations with the potential to reverse such dynamics are at the centre of climate action. These include street redesign, spatial planning aimed at increasing the proximity of people to places of interest, and policies to accelerate the development of networks of sustainable transport modes. Policies such as carbon pricing and incentives for vehicle electrification, core in current climate strategies, remain fundamental and their effectiveness and public acceptability can significantly increase after policy reprioritisation towards systems redesign.

Climate strategies focused on redesigning systems can bring the transformational change needed to meet net-zero goals on time while improving people's lives. Moving towards these strategies imply a mind-set shift, it implies thinking of ends (e.g. accessibility) rather than means (e.g. mobility), and innovating at the systems level and in the way we do policy-making. Such innovation is essential to transition towards better systems for better lives.

Acknowledgments

This report is part of the work programme of the OECD's Environmental Policy Committee and benefited from feedback and inputs. The work was carried out by Aimée Aguilar Jaber and Mariana Mirabile from the mitigation team of the OECD's Environment, Transitions and Resilience (ETR) Division. Simon Buckle, Head of the ETR Division provided inputs, support and guidance at different stages. The report was produced under the overall guidance of Rodolfo Lacy, the Director of the Environment Directorate of the OECD and benefited from the input of delegates to its Working Party on Climate, Investment and Development, OECD colleagues and external experts. This report also substantially benefitted from the generous support of the Japanese government.

Authors are grateful for the valuable comments and inputs from OECD colleagues from the Environment Directorate: Daniel Nachtigall, Brilé Anderson, Emily Neeson, Sirini Jeudy-Hugo, Katia Karousakis, Xavier Leflaive, Edward Perry, Dirk Röttgers, Matilda Saarinen; from the International Energy Agency: Luca Lo Re; Daniel Crow; from the International Transport Forum: Stephen Perkins; Joshua Paternina Blanco; Tatiana Samsonova.

Authors would also like to thank Joss Colchester (Systems Innovation), William Hynes (OECD, New Approaches to Economic Challenges), and OECD colleagues from the Centre on Well-being, Inclusion, Sustainability and Equal Opportunity (WISE) and the Observatory of Public Sector Innovation (OPSI), whose work greatly inspired the Well-Being Lens process presented in this report, as well as to Jack Harich (Thwink), Hannah Härtwich (Systems mapper), and Antoni Oliva (22Sistema) for their feedback and support on systems dynamics.

Special thanks to the experts having contributed to the report, namely Oliver Chaplin (United Kingdom Department for Business, Energy and Industrial Strategy), Ralph Chapman (Victoria University of Wellington); Yves Crozet (CERRE), Jose Iracheta Carroll (INSUS), Peter Jones (UCL Bartlett School of Planning), Giulio Mattioli (Universität Dortmund), Salvador Rueda (Fundación Ecología Urbana y Territorial), Vicente Torres (Urbvan), Eduardo López Moreno (UN-habitat) and Samie Raichs Tovany (UN-habitat).

Authors are are also grateful to Sama Al Taher Cucci (ENV/OECD) and Beth Del Bourgo (ENV/OECD) for their communications support, Elodie Prata-Leal for her support in formatting the report, Jennifer Allain for her support in editing the report, and to Jan Kamensky for the cover image.

Table of contents

Tables

Figures

Boxes

Executive summary

An important limitation for scaling up climate change mitigation is that efforts all too often aim at optimising individual components within our economic and social systems rather than transforming the systems themselves, which are unsustainable by design. IPCC scenarios indicate that focusing on policies that transform systems so that- in their functioning, or by design-, they **improve well-being, while requiring less energy and materials, and produce less emissions** can be more effective to achieve net-zero goals on time.

System redesign has rarely been the focus of climate action. In the case of transport, for decades, CO_2 emission mitigation action has mainly focused on optimising vehicles' emission performances (a component) in car-dependent urban and transport systems.

The OECD Well-being lens process can help policymakers reprioritise climate action towards system redesign and accelerate the transition towards net-zero systems. The process builds on systems thinking and consists of three steps: i) *envision* the outcomes a well-functioning system achieves; ii) *understand* why the current systems' functioning is not achieving such outcomes and how it could be designed to lead to better results; and iii) *redesign* the system via policies packages focused on reversing unsustainable dynamics to transition towards better functioning systems.

The Well-being lens process triggers two mind-set shifts, that are needed to meet net-zero targets on time: i) from means (e.g. GDP) to ends (well-being); and ii) from parts (e.g. vehicles) to systems functioning (e.g. car-dependency). The first shift allows *envisioning* an increase in well-being (health, equity, etc.) through low-demand systems (rather than considering high demand as a condition for high life quality). For policy-making, this means that managing or reducing demand becomes a central policy lever. The second shift sheds light on the importance of *understanding* the systems' dynamics driving unsustainable results. For policy-making, this means focusing climate action on reversing such dynamics and redesigning systems.

The rest of this summary describes the results from applying the Well-being lens process to the passenger surface transport sector, with a focus on urban areas and their commuting zones.

Envision the systems that we need

Well-functioning transport systems allow people the possibility of accessing places with ease (accessibility) in a sustainable and healthy manner. In these systems, people walk, cycle and use micro-mobility for the majority of their trips, and high emitting and space-intensive modes (e.g. automobiles) are used for less frequent trips. These systems are characterised by: i) proximity between people and places; and ii) investment and public space allocation to sustainable modes of transport so that these are the convenient modes, and thus people choose them. By their design, these systems can yield low mobility and emissions, more equitable and safe access to opportunities and healthier lifestyles.

In contrast, in current transport systems many people use motorised vehicles for the majority of their trips. These choices are determined by: i) long distances between people and places, and ii) the allocation of public space and investment to private motorised vehicles (cars, motorbikes); thus increasing their convenience and the number of people that choose them. These systems result in high mobility and emissions, coupled with unequal and unsafe access to opportunities and unhealthy lifestyles.

Understand the systems we have

The choice to drive a car or a motorbike is not solely the result of people's individual preferences (i.e. exogenous to the system) as is often argued. Such choice is determined largely by transport and urban systems organised around car driving, which leads to **induced demand, urban sprawl, and the erosion of shared and active modes of transport.** These three dynamics are at the source of high emissions and a number of negative impacts on people's wellbeing, such as air and noise pollution, congestion, road injuries and fatalities, reduced travel options and unequal access to opportunities.

The systems we create are a result of what we do, which is in turn determined by what we measure and the mental models that "filter" what we see. For decades, transport policies have focused on supporting mobility (erroneously conflated with well-being) instead of accessibility, which is the combination of mobility and proximity. A mobility focus has led to reducing proximity, which mobility-oriented policies compensate with yet more mobility, locking territories into unsustainable dynamics. An analytical, rather than systemic, mind-set has also reduced the problem to identifying the part in the system (e.g. combustion cars), causing the undesired result.

Mobility-oriented and analytical mind-sets translate into decoupling strategies, which focus on improving or replacing (mainly private) combustion engine vehicles. Meanwhile efforts to reduce the number of vehicles, the distances travelled, or car use, are perceived as going against people's freedom and well-being; thus, if undertaken, efforts are kept at the margin of climate strategies

Redesign our systems by changing policy priorities

Policies with the potential to transform the system's functioning include the following.

Street redesign and improved management of public space can **reverse induced demand** by reallocating public space and investment to low carbon and space efficient modes, and balancing space use between transport and other uses; leading instead **to disappearing traffic.** Barcelona's Superblocks are an example of street redesign and reallocation planned to transform the whole of the Barcelona Municipality.

Spatial planning aimed at increasing proximity can **reverse urban sprawl.** Urban development and renewal strategies guided by accessibility principles could allow urban areas and their hinterlands to become networks of 15-minute cities in which people can move across the territory, but no longer need to travel long distances to meet their everyday needs. This requires changes in governance, planning and regulation.

Policies to mainstream shared mobility are fundamental to accelerating the development of sustainable transport networks. Strengthening public transport networks is key to avoid the often-observed public transport low-cost, low-revenue, low-quality trap. In parallel, support to mainstream shared bicycles and micro-mobility, and the expansion of on-demand micro-transit services is key to make these modes convenient options for daily trips.

Numerous synergies exist between the policies described above, market-based instruments and incentives to improve vehicle technologies, the efficiency and feasibility of which can significantly increase after policy reprioritisation towards systems redesign.

1 Introduction

This chapter sets the scene and explains the relevance of the analysis presented in this report. It explains how diverse pathways to net-zero differ in the level of certainty they bring for achieving net-zero targets on time, as well as in the synergies and trade-offs they offer with other environmental and social goals. It also explains what transformational pathways to net-zero are and why these are needed.

Planetary emergencies such as climate change require bold and rapid action. The scale of the challenge "demands a step change in both the breadth and scale of ambition" (UK Department of Transport, 2020[1]). An important limitation for scaling up the ambition is that most climate action today focuses on incremental change in the systems that underpin our modern economies and societies. In other words, climate action all too often aims at optimising individual components within these systems rather than transforming the systems themselves, which are unsustainable by design.

A focus on optimising parts leads to net-zero pathways and climate strategies that place an overriding focus on technological change to drive the transition; assigning a marginal role to reducing demand through transforming systems, and leading to incremental, rather than transformational, change (see Box 1.1). Strategies in the transport sector are good examples of this, as most strategies to reach net-zero carbon dioxide (CO2) emissions prioritise policies that will improve vehicle performance in car-dependent systems. The expectation is that technological change (mostly at the level of the vehicle) will offset emissions related to large and growing demand for mobility.

Following such an incremental approach to designing pathways to net-zero (and the strategies to implement them), entails high risks for reaching net-zero targets on time, and thus the Paris Agreement's temperature goal. It also leaves huge untapped potential for addressing other pressing challenges (e.g. health, equity, etc.). Physical constraints on how quickly durable assets (including cars) can be replaced in high-demand systems (e.g. car-dependent transport systems), along with uncertainties about the capacity to scale up several technologies in the future (e.g. hydrogen, or advance biofuels, as well as for carbon dioxide removal) (Buckle et al., 2020[2]) may well mean that climate targets are missed. Research carried out by the Intergovernmental Panel on Climate Change suggests that rapid growth in energy and materials demand – including as a result of transport systems through increased vehicle use – reduces the chances of achieving stringent mitigation targets (IPCC, 2018[3]). In addition, such an approach may exacerbate other environmental and social challenges (e.g. creating large impacts from mining for batteries and increasingly reducing travel options).

A strong focus of climate action therefore needs to be on **redesigning systems so that – in their functioning – they require less energy and materials, and produce less emissions[1] while improving wider well-being goals** (Buckle et al., 2020[2]; OECD, 2021[4]). In other words, climate action, and pathways towards net-zero, should aim for transformational change in the systems themselves (see Box 1.1). While also requiring significant technological innovation, development and deployment, this transformative approach to achieving net-zero systems can help countries to achieve more stringent mitigation action in the short term while also reducing the risks and trade-offs implicit in an approach dominated by supply-side technological developments. By embedding equity and other well-being considerations (e.g. health) in the efforts to redesign systems, transformational pathways can make politically difficult policies (e.g. carbon pricing due to equity concerns) more feasible (Buckle et al., 2020[2]), while ensuring that both climate and wider well-being outcomes (e.g. Sustainable Development Goals) are delivered by design.

Unfortunately, in addition to focusing on parts, using the wrong proxies for progress has often led to leaving unquestioned the desirability of high (and growing) demand systems. Moreover, the underpinning demand-side changes involved in transformational approaches, including in behaviour, are often not well represented in dominant approaches to energy modelling, which tend to further reinforce the idea that a growing demand (be it of mobility or consumption more broadly) is inevitable and exogenous from the systems' design. As this report highlights, there are also measurement biases that reinforce approaches that are over-optimistic concerning what technological change can achieve and at what pace. This may have led to an under appreciation of the potential and benefits of so-called low-demand scenarios (Grubler et al., 2018[5]).

This report builds on previous work (see Box 1.2) and applies the OECD Well-being Lens[2], a process to support countries in triggering transformational climate action, to the surface passenger transport sector (excluding water transport). The objective is to identify policies for the transport sector that can ultimately contribute to transformational pathways leading to net-zero societies by design.

The report focuses on urban settings (accounting for approximately 40% of total passenger transport emissions),[3] and emphasises the need to include whole cities and their commuting zones[4] in policy considerations. Policies related to inter-city and international travel, as well as the relationship between transport solutions for interconnected urban and rural areas, are beyond the scope of this report. The reduction of car dependencies in urban areas discussed in this report, however, is fundamental to promoting sustainable modes for inter-city travel, and numerous potential synergies can be made between policies and infrastructure for urban and non-urban trips.[5] The improvement of metropolitan governance and strategic planning at the functional urban area scale (see Chapter 4), and the use of concepts such as Place Making and Complete Streets in rural territories are also key and discussed throughout the report.

Box 1.1. Distinguishing incremental from transformational pathways

The International Panel for Climate Change analysed four stylised pathways for achieving a 1.5°C goal. A pathway relying on transforming systems in a way that reduces energy and materials demand (P1 in Figure 1.1) increases the chances of achieving stringent mitigation targets (IPCC, 2018[3]) compared to pathways with high energy and materials demand growth. Pathways with high energy and materials demand growth delay mitigation action and rely more heavily on technologically focused approaches to reducing emissions. For this very stringent goal, these pathways also have to deploy potentially controversial and unproven technologies at a large scale to remove carbon dioxide from the atmosphere (P2-P4 in Figure 1.1).

Figure 1.1. Pathways to limit global warming to 1.5°C by 2100

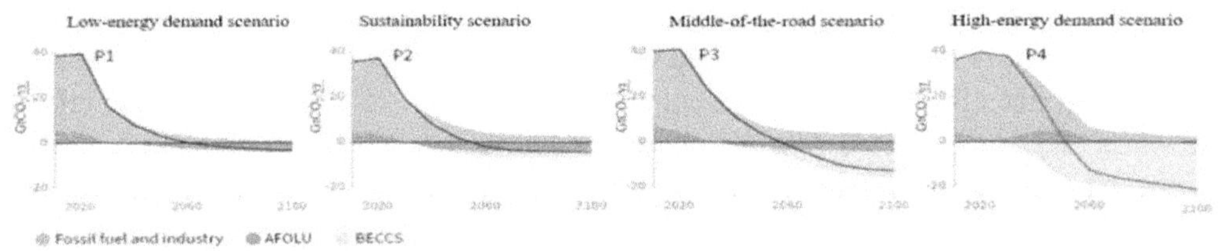

Note: AFOLU and BECCS stand for Agriculture, Forestry and Other Land-Use and Bio-energy with carbon capture and storage respectively. P1 is a scenario with low energy demand (LED) (Grubler et al., 2018[16]) and reflects recent literature with a stronger focus on demand-side measures; P2 is a sustainability oriented scenario (based on SSP1) developed with the AIM model (Fujimori et al., 2017[17]); P3 is a middle-of-the-road scenario (based on SSP2) developed with the MESSAGEGLOBIOM model (Fricko et al., 2017[18]) and P4 is a fossil-fuel intensive and high energy demand scenario (based on SSP5) developed with the REMIND-MAgPIE model (Kriegler et al., 2017[19]). In short, the three SSPs referred to here include scenarios following a sustainability path (SSP1), a middle-of-the-road development pattern (SSP2), further and a fossil-fuel based economic development (SSP5). A description of the different SSP scenario narratives can be found in (O'Neill et al., 2017[20]).
Source: IPCC Special report on 1.5°C (IPCC, 2018[14]).

Note: AFOLU: agriculture, forestry and other land use. BECCS: bioenergy with carbon capture and storage.
Source: IPCC (2018[3]).

The type of policies being prioritised largely determines the nature of change (incremental or transformational, see below) and of pathways, which ultimately determines the type of system and results achieved. Since evidence suggests that transformational pathways increase the chances of meeting climate goals, identifying which policies can trigger transformational change and pathways (P1-like), and thus lead to net-zero systems by design (i.e. low energy and material demand), is fundamental.

The Well-Being Lens process, further described in Chapter 2, has been designed to help countries identify and prioritise policies that have the potential to transform systems and to increase the effectiveness of climate action. To do so, this report distinguishes policies with the potential to bring about incremental and transformational change.

Most climate action in the transport sector prioritises policies to improve vehicle emissions, which leads to pathways like P4 in Figure 1.1. In these pathways, less emission-intensive vehicles (i.e. an incremental change to the system) are expected to offset the emissions of an increasing vehicle fleet.[1]. For the contrary, if policies to reverse car dependency are prioritised in climate strategies, this can lead to transformational change (as the functioning of the system will have changed), contributing to transformational pathways and net-zero systems by design (as car independent[6]).

Incremental change refers to change to the properties of the parts or elements in a system change that do not affect the way the system functions. For example, most transport and urban systems lead to more traffic, which in turn increases emissions. Climate strategies that prioritise policies to improve vehicle emissions but that are not coupled with policies targeting the dynamics underlying increased vehicle use are an example of climate strategies, which lead to incremental change and P2-P4-like pathways. Since the system dynamics or functioning remains intact, so do the system's results. As put by Systems Innovation (2021[6]):

> *"[T]he unfortunate reality is a traffic jam of autonomous electric cars is still a traffic jam".*

Transformational change refers to a change in the way a system is organised. The "rules of the game" change and the system can thus achieve – by design – different results than those of the previous system. For example, policies aimed at reallocating urban space (see Chapter 3) can change the system's functioning and lead to disappearing traffic, which is significantly different from the increase in traffic and vehicle use observed in today's systems. The "rules of the game" are, in this example, the way in which public space is allocated (e.g. roads for car use vs. space for other uses), which can change the attractiveness and competitiveness of private vehicles *vis-à-vis* other transport modes, and thus influence people's choices.

> *"Do we want to spend our time fighting against car usage or do we want to develop a system that truly works better than the car paradigm? A change in parts [incremental change] will do the former, only a change in systems [transformational change] will do the latter. (Systems Innovation, 2021[6])*

1. Such policy prioritisation is often informed by misleading indicators on the emissions reduction potential of technologies (see Chapter 6).

Box 1.2. Recent OECD work on transformational policies for achieving net-zero goals

Climate change, and many of the challenges underpinning our current and future well-being, are fundamentally complex in nature (Hynes, Lees and Müller, 2020[7]). Climate change is a systemic problem, generated by the structure of the system, rather than from one or more specific component parts that can be replaced or optimised. Such challenges require innovative thinking and transformational policies.

Accelerating Climate Action (OECD, 2019[8]) set out an approach for integrating well-being and climate mitigation action[1] to help accelerate the pace of greenhouse gas emissions reduction while also advancing other crucial agendas (e.g. inequality, health, jobs and environmental quality). The report highlighted the need to rethink what is meant by progress beyond just gross domestic product (GDP) growth and to set criteria to help design, implement and monitor policy in terms of well-being objectives (climate stability included).[2] By making the synergies and trade-offs between mitigation and wider well-being goals more visible, it was argued that climate policies could become "more acceptable, feasible and effective" (OECD, 2019[8]).

Buckle et al. (2020[2]) highlighted risks that countries' actions to recover from the COVID-19 pandemic that might run counter to their longer term climate goals. They analysed countries' actions in two sectors in the context of three stylised recovery pathways (see below). They concluded that a "well-being" approach would help quantify and make more visible the synergies and trade-offs between different goals, encouraging greater co-ordination and policy coherence. This was seen as crucial at a time when governments need to deliver both climate action and important near-term improvements in well-being (e.g. health, environmental health and reduced inequalities). In the case of surface transport, the report argued for shifting the focus from mobility (physical movement) towards delivering accessibility (the possibility to access places with ease), and shed light on the potential of such a shift to reduce emissions in the short term, and to align the climate and wider well-being agendas (OECD, 2019[8]).

The report discussed three stylised recovery pathways ("rebound", "decoupling" and "wider well-being") [3] different in the extent to which they reflected climate mitigation and well-being goals. Wider well-being described a recovery pathway that could yield early emissions reductions, enhance the chances of meeting the Paris Agreement's temperature goal and address key well-being priorities (e.g. jobs, income and health). As discussed in the paper, this pathway could reduce the risks of not getting to net-zero in time, since it would avoid reliance on unproven carbon dioxide (CO_2) removal technologies, which could also exacerbate competition for land. A wider well-being pathway could therefore substantially reduce trade-offs with other important Sustainable Development Goals, including biodiversity and food security, compared to alternative recovery pathways (decoupling and rebound pathways). The report also mapped in detail the consistency of COVID-19 recovery measures already announced for the transport and residential sectors with the three stylised pathways, thus advancing the sectoral policy work.

This approach was applied (and developed further) in a project with Israel to support the development of its long-term low, emissions strategy and its medium-term mitigation goals. This work validated the importance of using a well-being lens and resulted in two outputs: 1) a working paper on "Long-term low-emission development strategies: Cross-country experience" (Aguilar Jaber et al., 2020[9]); and 2) a report on Accelerating Climate Action in Israel: Refocusing Mitigation Policies for the Electricity, Residential and Transport Sectors (OECD, 2020[10]).

Building on the work described above, the current report applies the latest version of the Well-being Lens process to the surface transport sector.

1. The terms climate strategies, climate action and climate policies are used interchangeably throughout this report.

2. Some countries already guide their policy decisions by well-being objectives (e.g. New Zealand) and this has gained momentum during the recovery from COVID-19 (e.g. in Germany and the Netherlands) (Buckle et al., 2020[2]).
3. Rebound would prioritise a rapid re-establishment of economic growth and macroeconomic stability. It would not prioritise CO_2 emissions reductions nor progress on wider social or environmental objectives. Like rebound, decoupling is also assumed to be focused on the conventional metric of economic success, i.e. GDP growth. Decoupling, however, represents a significant step towards placing climate change mitigation at the heart of the recovery strategy. Decoupling would restore economic growth and macroeconomic stability and aim for an absolute decoupling of CO_2 emissions, i.e. emissions would be flat or falling with positive GDP growth. It would incentivise (incremental) improvements in energy efficiency and a rapid scaling up of low-carbon energy. Wider well-being would integrate economic recovery, CO_2 emissions reductions and well-being outcomes. This pathway would prioritise improvements in current well-being (e.g. income, jobs, health, etc.) rather than focusing simply on aggregate GDP growth (as indeed, positive well-being outcomes may not always correlate with GDP) and would take into account the resources needed to maintain well-being over time (e.g. human, physical, natural and social capital). The synergies and trade-offs between these diverse goals are complex and context-dependent, so wider well-being would encompass approaches that help decision makers to identify, quantify and exploit economically efficient synergies and to manage trade-offs between them.

This report is structured as follows. Chapter 2 defines the outcomes that a sustainable system should achieve, and the importance for policy makers to shift from a mobility-oriented to an accessibility-oriented perspective to transition to "sustainable-by-design" systems. It also provides a brief explanation of the transport and urban system dynamics leading to car dependency and high emissions, and gives a summary of the policy changes needed to reverse such dynamics. Chapters 3-5 describe these dynamics in greater detail and, based on examples from international practices, illustrate how different policy tools can contribute to changing these dynamics. Chapter 6 discusses the role of improved vehicle technology and pricing mechanisms in transformative climate strategies. Chapter 7 reviews the measures implemented by governments and the rapid changes that resulted from those measures as a response to the COVID-19 crisis. Chapter 8 concludes.

References

Aguilar Jaber, A. et al. (2020), "Long-term low emissions development strategies: Cross-country experience", *OECD Environment Working Papers*, No. 160, OECD Publishing, Paris, https://doi.org/10.1787/1c1d8005-en. [9]

Buckle, S. et al. (2020), "Addressing the COVID-19 and climate crises: Potential economic recovery pathways and their implications for climate change mitigation, NDCs and broader socio-economic goals", *OECD/IEA Climate Change Expert Group Papers*, No. 2020/04, OECD Publishing, Paris, https://dx.doi.org/10.1787/50abd39c-en. [2]

Grubler, A. et al. (2018), "A low energy demand scenario for meeting the 1.5 °C target and sustainable development goals without negative emission technologies", *Nature Energy*, Vol. 3/6, pp. 515-527, http://dx.doi.org/10.1038/s41560-018-0172-6. [5]

Hynes, W., M. Lees and J. Müller (eds.) (2020), *Systemic Thinking for Policy Making: The Potential of Systems Analysis for Addressing Global Policy Challenges in the 21st Century*, New Approaches to Economic Challenges, OECD Publishing, Paris, https://doi.org/10.1787/879c4f7a-en. [7]

IPCC (2018), *Global Warming of 1.5°C*, Intergovernmental Panel on Climate Change, Geneva, https://www.ipcc.ch/sr15 (accessed on 16 May 2021). [3]

OECD (2021), "Circular economy – waste and materials", in *Environment at a Glance Indicators*, OECD Publishing, Paris, https://dx.doi.org/10.1787/f5670a8d-en. [4]

OECD (2020), *Accelerating Climate Action in Israel: Refocusing Mitigation Policies for the Electricity, Residential and Transport Sectors*, OECD Publishing, Paris, https://doi.org/10.1787/fb32aabd-en. [10]

OECD (2019), *Accelerating Climate Action: Refocusing Policies through a Well-being Lens*, OECD Publishing, Paris, https://dx.doi.org/10.1787/2f4c8c9a-en. [8]

Purba, A. et al. (2017), "A current review of high speed railways experiences in Asia and Europe", http://dx.doi.org/10.1063/1.5011558. [12]

Systems Innovation (2021), *Mobility Systems Innovation*, Systems Innovation, https://www.systemsinnovation.io/post/mobility-systems-innovation (accessed on 13 August 2021). [6]

UK Department of Transport (2020), *Decarbonising Transport: Setting the Challenge*, UK Department of Transport, London, https://assets.publishing.service.gov.uk/government/uploads/system/uploads/attachment_data/file/932122/decarbonising-transport-setting-the-challenge.pdf. [1]

United Nations Department of Economic and Social Affairs (2017), *World Urbanization Prospects*, United Nations, New York, NY, https://population.un.org/wup (accessed on 20 July 2021). [11]

Notes

[1] Also reducing reliance on CO_2 removal technologies. As discussed in Buckle et al (2020[2]), "relying on carbon dioxide removal to offset any overshoot in CO_2 emissions is at best a risky strategy, as these technologies are currently not commercially available at scale, may involve difficult trade-offs with other goals and may not be publicly acceptable".

[2] By building on systems thinking, the Well-Being Lens allows policy makers to identify policies with the potential to reverse key system dynamics behind high emissions and other undesirable outcomes (e.g. growing inequality, poor health, etc.).

[3] The United Nations Department of Economic and Social Affairs estimates that 55% of the population lived in urban settings in 2017, and that two-thirds will live in urban settings by 2050 (United Nations Department of Economic and Social Affairs, 2017[11]).

[4] According to the EU-OECD definition of functional urban areas, cities incorporate an urban centre, defined as "a set of contiguous, high-density (1 500 residents per square kilometre) grid cells with a population of 50 000 in the contiguous cells", and any contiguous local unit (e.g. municipality, district) that has at least 50% of its population inside the identified urban centre. This scale is thus much larger than inner cities, and includes suburban areas. A city's commuting zone includes "a set of contiguous local units that have at least 15% of their employed residents working in the city." Together, a city and its commuting area are defined as a functional urban area.

[5] For example, (Purba et al., 2017[12])find that having high population density near rail stations and good public transport connectivity to the rail station are key to the success of high-speed rail services in Europe and Asia.

[6] Car independent systems are those in which a bulk of daily activities can be done without a car or a motorcycle. People only move from less emitting and space intensive modes (e.g. active, then micro-mobility and public transport/ micro-transit) to the more emitting and space intensive ones (e.g. cars or motorcycles), as they make less frequent trips. Car and motorcycle use is reserved for those trips that can create more value than the costs they impose to society (i.e. reserved for specific purposes or circumstances); but they are not systematically the most convenient, nor the only, available option in most places.

2 Transport strategies for net-zero systems by design: changing priorities

This chapter provides a summary of the results obtained from applying the three steps of the Well-Being Lens process to the surface transport sector. The first step – envision – defines the outcomes that a well-functioning system should achieve. The second step – understand – provides a snapshot of the key dynamics leading to unsustainable-by-design transport and urban systems. The chapter explains how mobility-oriented mental models and policies lead to unsustainable results and limit the scope and effectiveness of climate strategies. It also provides a snapshot of what climate strategies embedded in a system redesing logic will look like for the sector.

Achieving the Paris Agreement goals will require transformational change. The OECD Well-being Lens process aims to help policy makers identify policy packages with the potential to achieve such change. It triggers two mind-set shifts, that this report argues are needed to meet net-zero targets on time: i) from means (e.g. GDP) to ends (well-being); and ii) from parts to systems functioning. The first shift allows *envisioning* an increase in well-being (health, equity, etc.) through low-demand systems (rather than considering high demand as a condition for high life quality). For policy-making, this means that managing or reducing demand becomes a policy lever. The second shift sheds light on the importance of *understanding* the systems' dynamics driving unsustainable results. For policy-making, this means focusing climate action on reversing such dynamics and redesigning systems.

This report applies the three steps of the Well-being Lens process to the passenger surface transport sector,[1] with a focus on urban areas and their hinterlands. The first step of the process, envision, is about defining the outcomes that a sustainable system should achieve.

The second step, understand, is about identifying: i) key dynamics in the system's structure that are leading to unsustainable results (i.e. the vicious cycles); ii) relevant actors in the system; and iii) barriers to systemic change (e.g. mindsets, policies in place, governance, budget allocation, monitoring frameworks, power dynamics). This report focuses on an analysis of the key systems dynamics[2] underlying car dependency (sub-step i), and discusses how a mobility-oriented perspective, monitoring frameworks and governance arrangements – and the policies that result from these – lead to such results (elements of sub-step iii). Further analysis of the relevant actors, institutional arrangements and power dynamics (which may explain, for example, why a mobility-oriented perspective has prevailed) are interesting areas for future research.[3]

The third step, redesign, is about identifying the policies with the potential to reverse the undesired dynamics discussed in Step 2, and the way forward for ensuring their implementation. It is about identifying actions that would accelerate the transition towards urban and transport systems that – by design – produce desirable and sustainable results.

Section 2.1 focuses on the first step of the Well-being Lens process: envision. It defines the outcomes that a well-functioning[4] system should achieve. Section 2.2 focuses on the second step: understand. It provides a snapshot of the key dynamics leading to unsustainable-by-design (i.e. car-dependent) transport and urban systems (analysed in more detail in sections 3,4, and 5). It also discusses how mobility-oriented mental models and policies lead to such unsustainable dynamics, and limit the scope and effectiveness of climate strategies.Section 2.3 provides a summary of the type of policies and actions that can help urban and transport systems shift away from unsustainable dynamics, and in this way help accelerate the tansition towards net-zero, while also improving well-being.

2.1. Envision sustainable-by-design transport systems

A first step to transitioning towards sustainable systems is to define the type of results a well-functioning system should provide, as to then understand how current systems should be (re)organised/designed to achieve those results. By sustainable systems, we refer to systems with the possibility to continue a specific behaviour over long periods of time (e.g. without hitting limits that hinder such functioning). This depends on **environmental, social and economic sustainability, which are intrinsically interrelated. The notion of sustainability also embeds the notion of resilience throughout this report, as the ability to cope with crises and shocks is a necessary characteristic of systems that last.**

This report defines **the sustainable delivery of accessibility** as the key desirable outcome of sustainable transport systems.[5] This is based on two ideas. First, as discussed in (OECD, 2019[1]), people's well-being does not ultimately depend on how much and how far they can travel, but on the possibility to easily access opportunities and meet their needs (e.g. consumption, leisure, work, health services, etc.) with ease (accessibility), including by not having to travel long distances, or not having to travel at all. Second, access needs to be created sustainably, i.e. by enabling the conditions for most trips to be done safely and conveniently through active and/or shared modes (including public transport). These modes are less space-intensive than private vehicles,[6] allowing for a better balance between proximity and mobility[7] (see Section 2.2). They are also less emission- (and pollution-) intensive.

Current transport and urban systems perform poorly in the sustainable delivery of accessibility. Accessibility is limited, in particular for low-income households, and the most space- and emission-intensive transport modes are privileged.

Figure 2.1 shows what the transition from "unhealthy" to "healthy" transport systems could look like. The left panel illustrates the most frequently used transport means in (current) unsustainable transport and urban systems. The right panel illustrates the most frequently used transport means in sustainable systems, as described above. The figure uses the food pyramid analogy. The healthiness of a food diet can be assessed by positioning the foods we eat in a pyramid, according to their frequency and amount. If sugar and fat are the bottom of the pyramid (i.e. eaten often), our diets are unhealthy, and will likely lead to undesirable results such as diabetes or obesity.

Figure 2.1. From unhealthy to healthy transport systems

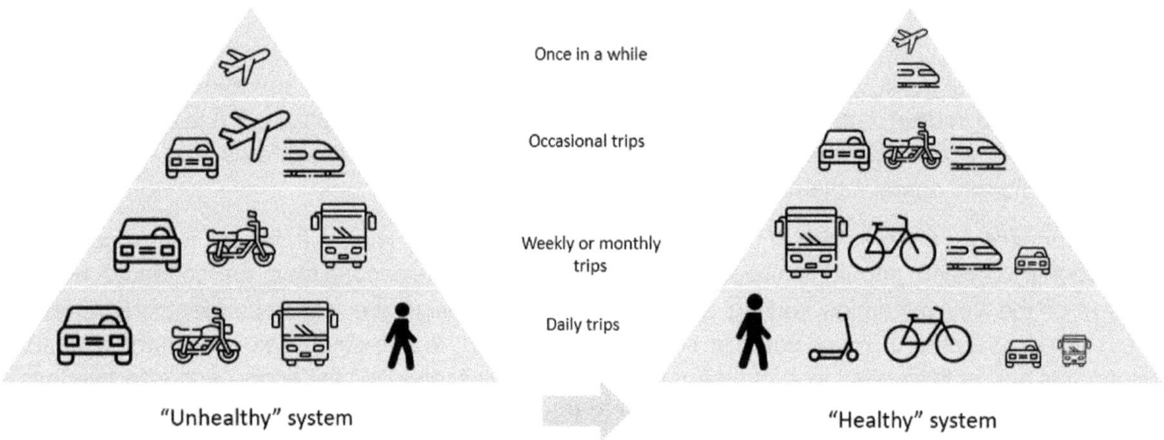

Notes: The icons illustrate the most frequent means of transportation used per type of trip. As modal shares vary widely across territories, this figure is thus to be understood as an illustration rather than a precise representation of average modal shares.

Applying this analogy, "unhealthy" transport (and urban) systems are those in which people use motorised, and in particular private, vehicles (the sugar and the fat) for the majority of their trips (represented at the bottom of the pyramid, in the left panel). This is the case in most territories today, where distances to places are long, and where private motorised vehicles (cars, motorbikes) are the safest and quickest (and sometimes only) transport means available. Importantly, even when often less convenient and safe than cars, public transport is also used by many, often "captive users", to cover the bulk of their daily trips, due to average long distances to their places of interest. Thus, also adding emissions that could be avoided if high shares of those trips were shorter and made by active modes; as well as if public transport was invested in and made better and cleaner.

The outcome of such a system is high traffic volumes (mobility), with several negative impacts, such as high emissions, air pollution, poor road safety, and disease (e.g. caused by air pollution as well as a lack of physical activity). Long distances and restricted travel options also result in poor and unequal accessibility. As will be explained in detail in Section 2.2, the choice to drive a car or a motorbike is not solely a result of people's individual preferences (as is often argued). It is, to a large extent, the result of transport and urban systems shaped by mobility-oriented policies, i.e. policies focused on allowing people to move as fast and as far as possible. Such systems ignore the mismatch between increased travel and access to services and opportunities (Ferreira, Beukers and Brömmelstroet, 2012[2]) and the importance of creating proximity (see Section 2.2).

"Healthy", or sustainable-by-design, transport and urban systems are those in which people walk, cycle and use micro-mobility for the majority of their trips (represented at the bottom of the pyramid, in the right panel). People use more emitting and space-intensive modes for less frequent trips (towards the top of the right-hand pyramid). This is possible in systems in which distances between people and places are short (there is proximity), and where the public space is organised in such a way that active and shared modes (including public transport) are the fastest and safest modes for most people (including children) to get to places. This implies that, by design, these systems will yield lower mobility and emissions while at the same time result in healthier lifestyles, and higher quality and more equitable access to opportunities.

Section 2.2 explains why current transport and urban systems are "unhealthy", and what can be done to transition towards "healthy" systems.

2.2. Understand why current transport and urban systems are unsustainable

Transport and urban systems are social systems created and shaped by people through a more or less co-ordinated series of decisions and actions. These decisions and actions are, in turn, the result of what we measure and consider success, which ultimately depends on the mental models that shape what we see.

Mental models can be thought of as the lens through which humans observe reality.[8] They are the unquestioned, and often implicit or unconscious, assumptions through which we understand the world. The type of systems in which we operate are shaped, and reinforced, by these implicit assumptions, which are, in turn, shaped by the stories that we have been exposed to (Figure 2.2; see also Box 2.2).

Figure 2.2. Systems, actions and mental models

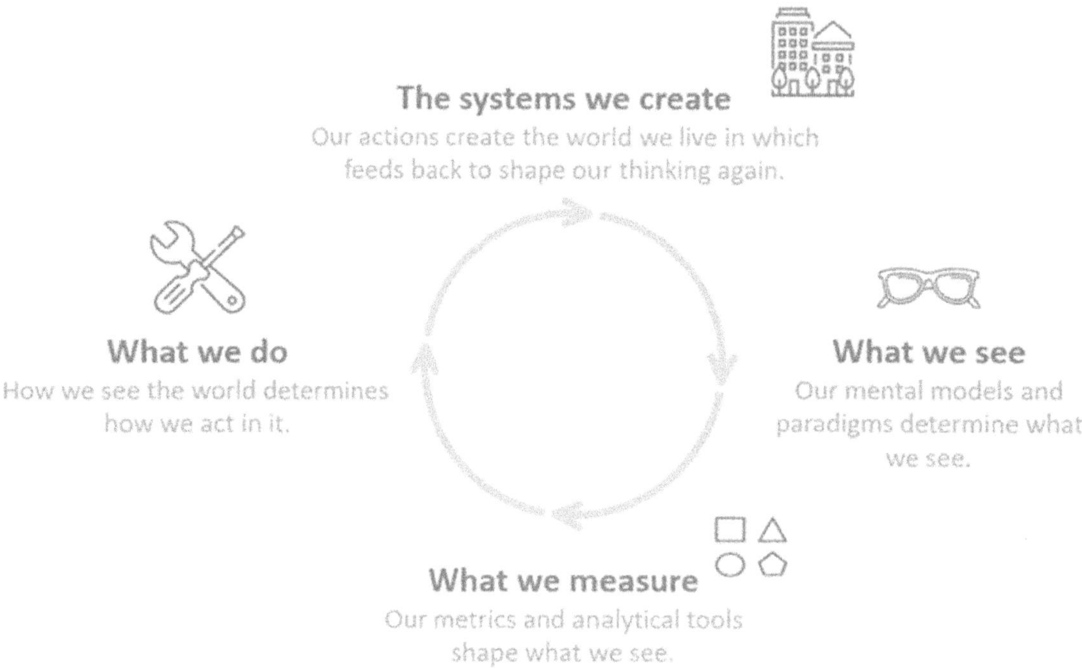

Source: Adapted from Systems Innovation (2021[3]).

This section focuses on understanding why current transport and urban systems are "unhealthy", or unsustainable-by-design. It is an invitation to question some of the implicit assumptions through which transport and urban systems have been shaped in the past.

The first sub-section provides a snapshot of the functioning of most transport and urban systems ("the system we create" in Figure 2.2). This functioning, as will be explained, leads to car-dependency and increased traffic volumes, making systems "unhealthy" by design. The following sub-section analyses how mobility-oriented policy decisions ("what we do" in Figure 2.2) and the mental models and measurement frameworks underlying them ("what we see" and "what we measure" in Figure 2.2) have locked (and continue locking) transport and urban systems into "unhealthy" dynamics. It also explains why mobility-oriented and analytical (rather than systemic) decision making limits the scope and effectiveness of climate strategies, leaving countries ill equipped to achieve net-zero goals on time.

2.2.1. The system we create

Figure 2.3 illustrates the dynamics often observed in transport and urban systems. Understanding these dynamics (or functioning) can help policy makers identify what drives the behaviours/results they are trying to influence), and what needs to change in the system structure (or design) to achieve different results. This report uses system dynamics: an approach to understanding the cause-effect relationships that lead systems to behave as they do, and thus produce the results that we observe (e.g. unsustainable levels of emissions, increased traffic volumes, etc.).[9]

One of the key insights policy makers can get from system dynamics analysis is that the results observed in a system (e.g. people using a car for the bulk of their trips) are not entirely a result of people's independent choices, but that these choices are conditioned by the structure of the system in which these choices are made. If the choices people are making are unsustainable, and if those choices depend on the system's design, redesigning systems to incentivise different choices is a crucial policy lever to achieve more sustainable results.

Based on Sterman (2000[4]), this report finds that three dynamics lead to car dependency, and are at the heart of why people use cars for the bulk of their trips. These dynamics are **induced demand**, **urban sprawl**, and the **erosion of shared and active modes of transport.**

Induced demand refers to the phenomenon by which investments in road expansion to reduce congestion end up having the opposite effect. Congestion increases because the more roads there are, the more attractive the car becomes and the more people choose to drive (see Section 3.1). Urban sprawl is the phenomenon by which people move further away from cities – which tend to concentrate the places of interest– when they can to them within a reasonable time budget, e.g. 30 minutes by car. The more roads expand, the more this is possible. Daily distances increase (as the new catchment area[10] grows), density decreases, and single-use development[11] is fostered. Both these dynamics erode active and shared modes (the third dynamic), either because they are not safe and/or because they are less convenient than, for example, driving a car. As distances increase active modes such as walking, cycling or micro-mobility are no longer an option. Also, as density decreases and single-use development expands, public transport is also less of an option, as it is difficult to get good service. Note that active and shared modes are often referred to as "alternative" modes, shedding light on how central cars (and private motorised vehicles more broadly) are in current mental models (see Box 2.2).

Figure 2.3. Key system dynamics leading to unsustainable transport systems

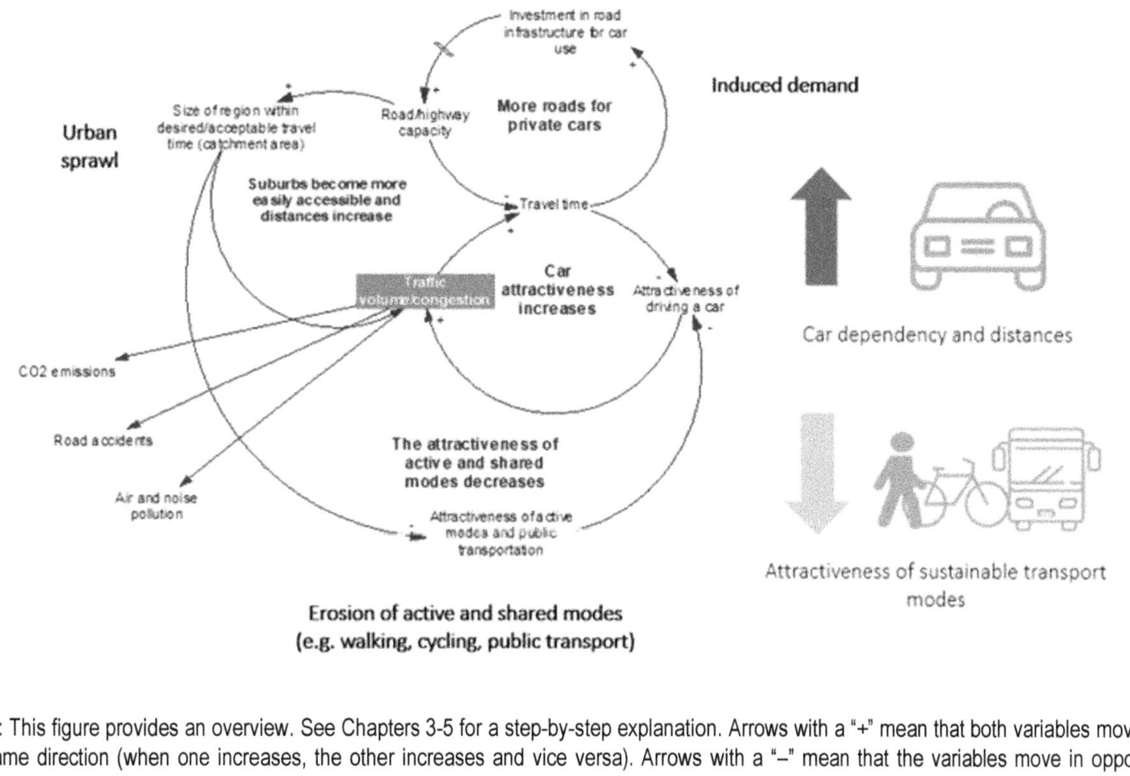

Notes: This figure provides an overview. See Chapters 3-5 for a step-by-step explanation. Arrows with a "+" mean that both variables move in the same direction (when one increases, the other increases and vice versa). Arrows with a "–" mean that the variables move in opposite directions (when one increases, the other decreases and vice versa). The two small lines on a specific arrow denote a delay.
Source: Authors, based on Sterman (2000[4]).

The dynamics illustrated in Figure 2.3 underlie the observed sustained increase in car use, travel distances and traffic volumes, which are the source of high emissions and a number of negative impacts on people's well-being. Among these are air and noise pollution, congestion, road injuries and fatalities, and reduced travel options, which lead to unequal access to opportunities. According to the ITF (2021[5]), private vehicle travel[12] is responsible for three-quarters of all emissions from urban passenger transport, and this is the result of the continued growth in private vehicle ownership as well as the increasing average size of vehicles. Based on data from the International Energy Agency, the ITF report also highlights that under the current conditions, private vehicle ownership will grow by around 30% over the next ten years.

One of the key messages of this report is that **the increased use of cars and related traffic volumes is not a fatality to which transport and climate policies need to adapt to, but the result of unsustainable system dynamics, which can be redesigned**. As shown by Litman (2021[6]), people would choose to drive less, use active and shared modes more often if incentives and policy decisions did not favour automobiles over other modes of transport.

Furthermore, decarbonising a system that "encourages" more vehicles is a very difficult, if not impossible, task. Regardless of its feasibility, it is certainly not the most efficient or effective way to reduce emissions at the pace and scale needed (nor solve other key challenges, such as health or equity) (see section 2.2.2).

Reversing the dynamics described above should be at the core of transport and climate strategies. Most transport and climate strategies, however, either leave the dynamics intact or reinforce them. Section 2.2.2 dives deep into why this is the case.

2.2.2. Mobility-oriented transport policies

As illustrated in Figure 2.2, "the systems we create" are a result of "what we do". What has been done in terms of transport policy, as explained by Chapman (2019[7]), has historically been to support mobility for economic growth, with other outcomes – including health and climate stability – seen as second-order priorities (Chapman, 2019[7]). Most transport policies are mobility-oriented: for decades, the priority of transport policies has been improving mobility via travel speed (Chapman, 2019[7]).

Such policy decisions are guided by analytical tools and measurement frameworks, which determine "what we see" (and what we don't). Mobility-related metrics, such as vehicle-kilometres, passenger-kilometres (passenger), tonne-kilometres (freight) or number of trips, have historically been the gauges of "success" (bottom of Figure 2.4). Increasing mobility is, in turn, often used as a proxy for increased well-being and a prosperous territory, similar to how gross domestic product (GDP) growth is used as a proxy of progress or higher well-being at the economy level (see OECD (2019[1]); Hickel et al. (2021[8])).

Figure 2.4. Systems, actions and mental models: Application to the transport sector

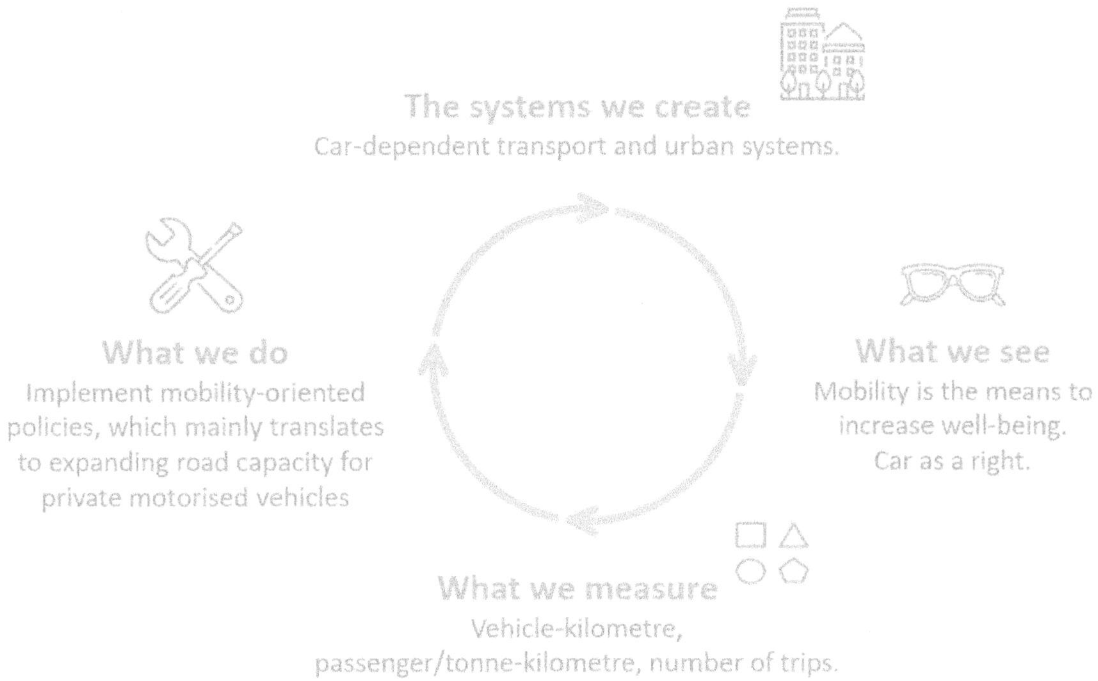

Source: Adapted from Systems Innovation (2021[3]).

The use of mobility as a proxy for "well-being" is linked to the deeply engrained mental model that the way to improve people's well-being is by allowing them to travel as far and as fast as possible (i.e. increased mobility), with as much flexibility as possible. This and other related (also deeply engrained) ideas shape current policy decisions and citizens' expectations, constituting a crucial barrier to systemic or transformational change. Some of these related ideas include:

- The role of policy makers is to adapt to people's choices, that are exogenous to (or independent from) the system in which they are embedded. In the transport sector, policy makers need to adapt to the inevitable growing use of cars as the city develops (Jones et al., 2018[9]) and income increases.[13] This is based on the idea that people should be free to choose what is best for them, and that they tend to consider that driving a car is better than other transport options, unconditioned by the context. This leads to the association that car use is a "right" (ITF, 2021[5]).[14]
- The "free" use of public space and road infrastructure (e.g. streets, parking slots) by cars, and the spread of the cost of such infrastructure across society is considered "normal" to ensure the "right" described above.[15]
- Travel time is seen as the key "disutility" to be minimised. Air pollution, noise and road fatalities are seen as inevitable consequences of living in dense cities (e.g. the idea that if a person wants silence, they should move to the countryside or to lower density suburbs).
- Cities and urban design are "fixed" (i.e. cannot be changed) and as cities grow, distances increase, and the only way to facilitate access to places is by allowing more, and faster, mobility. The street and territory redesign needed to make active (e.g. walking, cycling) and shared modes attractive can help in some cases, but it is only possible in already dense inner-city areas.

Lamb et al. (2020[10]) also identify deeply engrained ideas at the source of discourses of climate delay (Figure 2.5), which can be applied to the transport sector. When these ideas are coupled with the mobility-oriented mental models described above and the analytical paradigm described in Box 2.1, they lead to the decoupling focus (see more below) of current climate strategies and are a fundamental barrier to transformational climate action. "Technical optimism" is likely the most widespread discourse when it comes to reducing emissions in the transport sector.[16] Technological optimism refers to the idea that technological improvements will allow countries to reduce emissions at the pace and scale needed. It sees technology as a way to increase vehicle performance (in terms of speed, fuel consumption, emissions, etc.), rather than improving the way systems are organised, where technological potential is mostly untapped and could lead to enormous emission reductions (see Chapter 6). The focus on technology applied to improving parts can be traced to a widespread analytical, rather than systemic, mindset (Box 2.1). "Appeal to well-being" is often also used to explain why reducing the number of cars to reduce emissions is not an option (as mobility is conflated with well-being, as explained above), and thus climate strategies are constrained to lowering vehicles' emissions (i.e. decoupling growing mobility from emissions).

More broadly, Hickle et al. (2021[8]) identify a growth-oriented paradigm as a key barrier to net-zero systems. The authors argue that "Growth is an unquestioned norm", and that this is problematic since decarbonisation is more challenging in systems driving increases in energy demand.

Figure 2.5. Mental models underlying discourses of climate delay

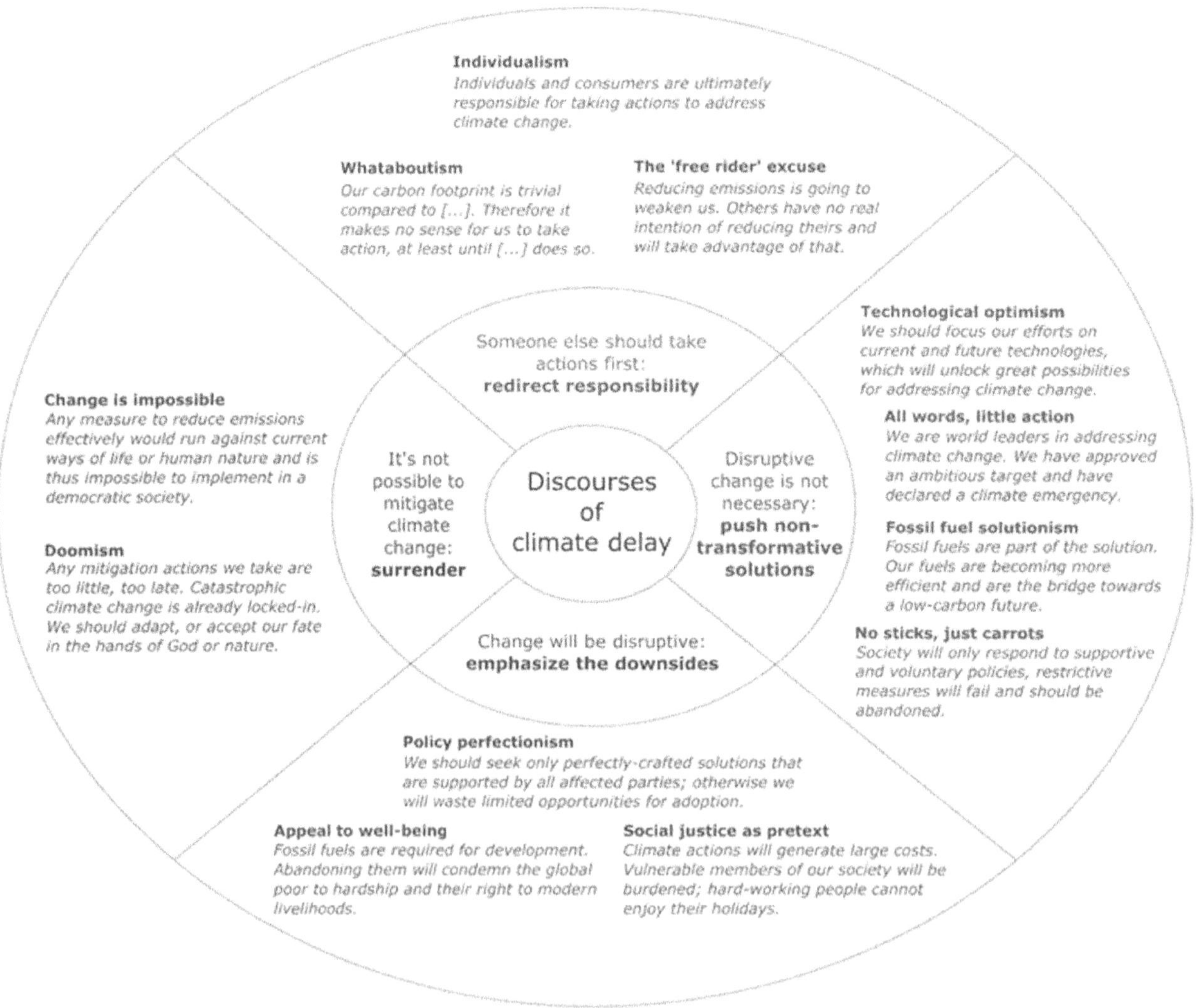

Source: Extracted from Lamb et al. (2020[10]).

Box 2.1. Differences between an analytical and systems thinking, and why this is important for achieving net-zero goals

There are two fundamentally different, and complementary, ways of thinking and understanding the systems[1] around us: analytical thinking and systems thinking. Like tools in a toolbox, these ways of thinking are complementary, and using one or the other depends on the task.

Currently, however, there is a tendency to use analytical thinking to solve complex problems such as climate change or growing inequalities, for which systems thinking could be a better tool. This box explains the differences between analytical and systems thinking and why thinking in systems can unlock opportunities for achieving net-zero goals.

The analytical thinker breaks wholes into parts and focuses on optimising or replacing individual parts. The world is like a machine, and thus when trying to "repair the machine", the analytical thinker tries to find the "piece" that is causing the problem, as to repair or replace it. An implicit assumption of this way of proceeding is that the whole is equal to the sum of its parts. This translates into the idea that the way parts are organised is not important: interactions between the parts do not affect the results or behaviour of the system (i.e. synergies[2] do not exist), the properties of the parts do. Isolating, dividing and improving parts (e.g. vehicle emissions) is, thus, the logical way to solve problems.

The assumption that the whole is the sum of its parts does not hold for every system. Complexity science shows that, in complex systems,[3] the whole can be more or less than the sum of its parts, depending on the way these parts are arranged (i.e. depending on positive or negative synergies).

> "You think that because you understand 'one' that you must therefore understand 'two' because one and one make two. But you forget that you must also understand 'and'." *(Meadows, 2008[11])*

One of the key insights of complexity science is that the results observed from complex systems emerge from the systems' structure, from the interactions among the parts rather than from the properties of the parts in themselves. If results depend on the system's structure or design, there are opportunities for changing the results by redesigning the system's interactions, which is what systems thinking allows one to do.

To solve problems, the system thinker focuses their attention on systems as wholes, on how parts could be reorganised to achieve better results. This is why this report recommends placing policies such as street redesign at the centre of climate strategies.

Figure 2.6. Analytical and systems thinking

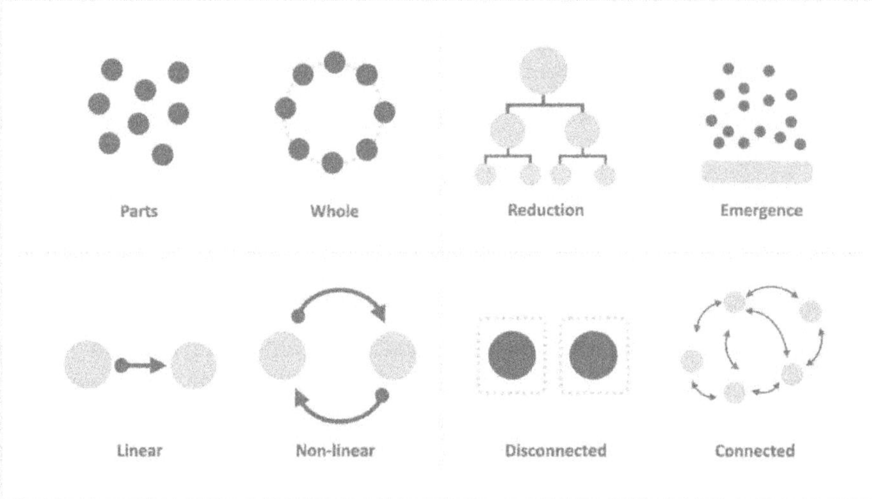

Note: The figure compares the focus of analytical thinking (on the left of each quadrant) to the focus of systems thinking (on the right of each quadrant).
Source: Systems Innovation (2021[12]).

The Well-Being Lens process applied in this report is a guide for applying systems thinking to policy making. It provides a set of tools, such as the causal loop diagrams in Sections 3.1, 4.1 and 5.1, that can help policy makers observe the system's functioning at the source of emissions, and focus climate strategies on achieving **better functioning systems for better lives**.

1. A system is a set of elements whose interconnections determine its structure and behaviour. Elements are things, people, factories, bikes. Interconnections are the way the elements are organised: rules, incentives, sanctions, information.
2. A synergy is a particular type of interaction between parts; it is a non-linear interaction where the specific way the parts interact creates an effect greater or less than the simple sum of their effects in isolation.
3. A complex system is a system composed of many interdependent parts or components. The economy, the financial market, cities, transport systems, the food system, etc. are all complex systems.
Sources: Meadows (2008[11]); Systems Innovation (2020[13]).

The ideas and mental models are not independent from the stories that people have been exposed to. In the case of the transport sector, it is important to recognise that the mobility- and automobile-centric mind-set that we have today is a construction, as illustrated in Box 2.2. As such, constructing a "different story", one of "automobile independence", is possible; and this could importantly support the implementation of the type of policies put forward in this report (Box 2.3). Incorporating communication efforts as a core element of climate strategies, and linking these actions to well-being outcomes, could also significantly increase policy acceptability. A number of authorities (e.g. Brussels, see below) are taking key steps in this direction.

Box 2.2. Stories matter: shaping car-dependent cities

Stories, and narratives more broadly, shape reality. Narratives are sets of stories, which include and exclude certain things. Reality, and what people find acceptable or unthinkable, greatly depend on which narratives dominate. This box provides an example of communication efforts that have contributed to a dominant car-centric narrative. The significant resources invested in advertisement reinforce this narrative.[1] Efforts to counter the car-centric narrative, although less funded, are also numerous. Examples of such efforts are provided in the next box.

A communication campaign for car-centric cities

> *"A hundred years ago, if you were a pedestrian, crossing the street was simple: You walked across it. Today, if there is traffic in the area and you want to follow the law, you need to find a crosswalk. And if there's a traffic light, you need to wait for it to change to green… To most people, this seems part of the basic nature of roads. But it's actually the result of an aggressive, forgotten 1920s campaign led by auto groups and manufacturers that redefined who owned the city streets." (Stromberg, 2015[14])*

Mental models are highly dependent on the stories people have been exposed to (Saltmarshe, 2018[15]), which are, in turn, subject to, to a great extent, political economy factors and power dynamics within systems. The in-depth analysis of these factors (e.g. the influence of the automobile industry in shaping the transport system) is beyond the scope of this report, but is an interesting area for future research.[2]

The mass introduction of cars to cities was a disruptive change for which advertisement played a significant role (Freund and Martin, 1993[16]; Stromberg, 2015[14]). Cars were, not always widely accepted by the public. Before the mass introduction of cars, streets functioned like parks or malls, in which people could move carelessly (Dukes, 2013[17]). As Norton (2011[18]) explains, the public considered it to be the driver's responsibility to pay attention, not the pedestrian's, and the public response to the skyrocketing number of road fatalities after the introduction of cars was outrage. Cars were considered to be violent intruders.

This idea has changed radically, towards the idea that streets are for cars. Pedestrians became the intruders and the ones that need to pay attention (or get blamed if they are hit by a car). This idea persists today. Indeed, if a child is hit by a car, the first thing that likely comes to mind is that the parents are irresponsible. There is also a general perception that pedestrian deaths caused by vehicles, while tragic, are inevitable. For example, in the United States, 17 pedestrians – mainly from low-income, black and Latino neighbourhoods - were killed every day in 2018. That is one person having chosen to walk on a street killed every 90 minutes (Moran, 2021[19]). Unfortunately, these deaths do not receive the same media coverage, or congressional attention, as other tragedies like mass shootings.

Since the 1920s, the automobile industry has been dedicating significant resources to communication campaigns to increase the public's acceptability and desirability of cars, which has, as Norton (2011[18]) demonstrates, reshaped cities and mainstreamed a number of deeply engrained ideas in society. Through such communication efforts to individuals and governments alike, the auto industry has been able to convey the message that vehicles are essential to improving well-being (Freund and Martin, 1993[16]) The car has become a symbol of freedom, social status and power, and opposition to the car is perceived as a direct threat to basic needs such as freedom and safety (Gössling, 2020[20]).

Norton (2011[18]) identifies the "jaywalking" campaign as a turning point. The campaign managed to redefine "what streets are for" and to normalise the idea that pedestrians did not have the right to walk freely on streets. This campaign is an interesting example of how framing and communication efforts can change people's perception of reality, to accept – and even fiercely support – what previously was unacceptable or unthinkable. The term "jaywalker" was a pejorative word used to define people not knowing how to conduct themselves in a city (Norton, 2007[21]). The term aimed to ridicule people not crossing on the recently installed pedestrian crossings and helped redefine who the street belonged to, as well as who is to blame in the case of a road fatality (e.g. jaywalkers were pictured as threatening public safety).

> *"The ridicule of their fellow citizens is far more effective than any other means which might be adopted". (Norton, 2007[21])*

This quote, from one of the heads of the pro-automobile coalition Motordom, highlights the importance given to communication – and in particular to the technique of shaming – to switch the public's perception on what streets were for, and whether it was the vehicle's or the pedestrian's "recklessness" to blame in case of a road fatality. .Before the 1920s, people considered cars to be intruders. By the 1930s, they considered pedestrians ("jaywalkers") as being in the way of cars (Norton, 2007[21]); and since then, streets have belonged to cars.

Changing mental models and mainstreaming the idea that streets are for cars significantly influenced the shape of transport and urban systems (see first 3 panels in Figure 2.7).

Figure 2.7. A short history of traffic engineering

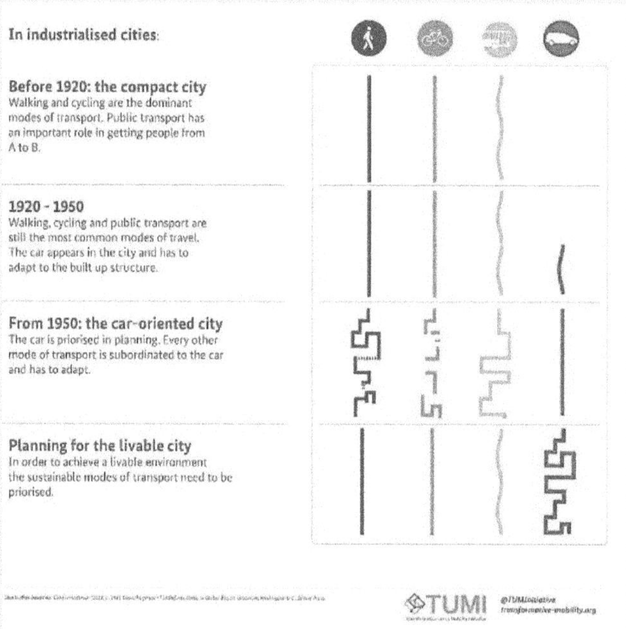

Source: Adapted by Daniel Ernesto Moser based on Colville-Andersen (2018[22]).

1. Zenith Media (2019[23]) estimates advertising expenditure by the automotive industry at USD 35.5 billion in 14 key markets in 2018, with the United States accounting for half of such expenditure (USD 18 billion).

2. For an overview of the key political-economic factors underlying car dependence, see Mattioli et al. (2020[24]).

Box 2.3. Stories matter: towards car independency

> *"Our cities do not need driver-less cars. Instead, they desperately need more car-less drivers!"*
>
> *Marco Te Brömmelstroet*

Communication efforts towards car-independent territories have the potential to change the narrative again, towards one more conducive to delivering sustainable transport systems. Examples of such efforts are multiple, from governments to non-governmental organisations and civil society movements.

Bruxelles Mobilité, for example, launched a communication campaign around walking (Bruxelles Mobilité, 2021[25]). The campaign uses humour and ridicule to convey the practicality of walking by presenting it as a high-tech technology (making reference to the "technological solutionism" discourse explained above). Similarly, Bike is Best conveys the message that bikes are the best tools for short journeys, by making an analogy with overdimensioned tools for other uses (BikeIsBest, 2021[26]). Possible, a UK charity, compiles stories of traffic reduction measures and allow users to "explore a world of Car Free Cities" for change towards people-friendly, clean air cities (Possible, 2021[27]) (Possible, 2021[28]).

The global campaign "Vision Zero" is another example of an effort for changing the narrative, in this case from seeing traffic fatalities as inevitable externalities of transport systems towards the idea that "no one should be killed or seriously injured from using the road network" (Towards Zero Foundation, n.d.[29]). This leads to the idea of "The Safe System", a design approach viewing human life and health as "the first and foremost consideration when designing a road network". In 2015, Mexico City committed to Vision Zero and reduced traffic fatalities by 18% in the first two years. The narrative change around traffic fatalities that the campaign fostered was identified as key to its success (Ballesteros, 2018[30]; Vision Zero Network, n.d.[31]). The case of Superblocks (see Section 3.2.2) is another example of how important these communications efforts are for policy acceptability and implementation.

The *Journée sans voiture* (day without cars) organised once a year in Paris is a way for people to experiment using the space allocated to roads for different uses (Ville de Paris, 2021[32]). Such events, in particular if organised more frequently (e.g. once a month), could increase the acceptability of policies towards car-independent systems. La Rue est à Nous and Parking Day are examples of citizen-led campaigns aiming to build a collective imaginary of cities with less cars. These campaigns shed light on how urban space could be used differently, and, in the case of La Rue est à Nous, on the health benefits arising from improved air quality and physical activity from active modes, in particular for children (La Rue est à Nous, 2021[33]; Parking Day, n.d.[34]). Scholars such as Marco Te Brömmelstroet, from Utretch and Amsterdam Universities, and artists such as Jan Kamensky, are also making active communication efforts on social media (e.g. LinkedIn), via online courses, creative videos, video repositories and talks, to overcome the car-centric story for cities. See, for example, Te Brömmelstroet (2020[35]; 2020[36]) and (Kamensky, 2021[37]).

A mobility-centred mental model, and the mobility-centred policies resulting from it, is problematic for many reasons. First, it disregards the importance of creating proximity for ensuring access (this is referred to as the "proximity blind spot" in the remainder of this report). Many of the decisions leading to the three dynamics behind car dependency would not have been an option if policies were not "proximity blind". Second, it reduces the scope and effectiveness of climate strategies in the sector. The rest of this section is dedicated to discussing these two consequences in detail.

Proximity-blind policies

As mentioned above, a mindset focused on mobility leads to proximity-blind policies. Mobility is seen as the means to contribute to well-being, disregarding the importance of proximity. Mobility is, however, a bad proxy (or performance indicator) for the contribution of transport systems to well-being (Silva and Larson, 2018[38]; ITF, 2019[39]) (Box 2.4). As explained in Section 2.1, people's well-being does not ultimately depend on how much and how far they can travel (i.e. increased mobility). Rather, it depends on the possibility to access places with ease, including by not having to travel long distances (or to travel at all).

Box 2.4. Mobility is a misleading proxy for well-being

Mobility is a misleading proxy for the transport system's contribution to well-being. Fist, increasing mobility may be a symptom of deteriorating accessibility (ITF, 2019[39]). Total mobility can grow when people and places of interest (e.g. schools, shops, hospitals, gardens, etc.) are poorly connected, and when connections by active and shared transport modes are limited. For example, mobility increases if children cannot go to school by foot or bike due to safety concerns, and have to be driven. Mobility also increases when proximity to shops decreases (e.g. local shops close) and people need to drive to meet their basic needs. Second, growing mobility may hide a widening accessibility gap between population groups. As motorised private vehicles become the most attractive or only way to get to places (as explained in Chapter 3), access to opportunities may be reduced for less affluent households,* increasing inequality and reducing their well-being.

A number of indicators are used to measure mobility or physical movement, reflecting either the movement of vehicles or of people. As the ITF highlights (2017[40]) "[b]y narrowing down the problem to maximising physical movement, both [types of indicators] fail to provide accurate information about changes in access to goods, services, activities and destinations. Consequently, the importance of non-motorised modes, land-use decisions, mobility substitutes (e.g. home office, delivery services), etc. are overlooked". For example, when vehicle-kilometres or other indicators focused on traffic are measured, the value of public transport is reduced, as these indicators do not account for public transport's high load factors (passengers per kilometre travelled), which indicators such as passenger-kilometres could capture. The passenger-kilometres indicator, however, poorly reflects the value of active modes and many shared services (e.g. micro-mobility and e-bikes), as these are not high-occupancy services. Measuring the number of trips could better reflect, to a certain extent, the value of non-motorised modes; however, measuring the number of trips still falls into the trap that "more [mobility] is better", hiding, for instance, the fact that people could be better off if they could meet several needs in one single trip.

As explained in Section 2.1, accessibility, or "the opportunity of individuals to participate in activities" (ITF, 2017[40]), is a better proxy for assessing the transport system's contribution to people's well-being. Measuring accessibility directly would therefore better inform decisions. Accessibility is more complex to measure than mobility because it depends on both mobility and proximity, and on various factors such as land use and transport availability. A number of indicators exist though. The most common (and simplest forms) are contour-based accessibility measures. Contour-based indicators measure the number of opportunities/services/facilities (e.g. jobs, green spaces, transport stations) which can be reached within a given travel time, distance or cost; or the time/cost (average) required to gain access to a fixed number of opportunities/services/facilities from different locations (ITF, 2017[40]). Because accessibility needs to be delivered sustainably and equitably, this type of indicator should ideally be calculated for different modes of transport and for different locations and population groups.

For further information on accessibility indicators (contour and others) and their use for improving planning and appraisal, see ITF (2019[39]).

* While less affluent households may travel less due to affordability issues, those who can afford to use a private vehicle drive more often and longer distances. Overall mobility can therefore increase.

Transport systems, thus, contribute to people's well-being when they enhance accessibility. Accessibility is the interaction of mobility and proximity (Silva and Larson, 2018[38]) (Figure 2.8). Because trade-offs exist between space used for mobility and space used for other purposes (e.g. commercial or leisure areas, or housing), delivering accessibility sustainably requires striking a balance between facilitating mobility and creating proximity.

Figure 2.8. Accessibility, mobility and proximity

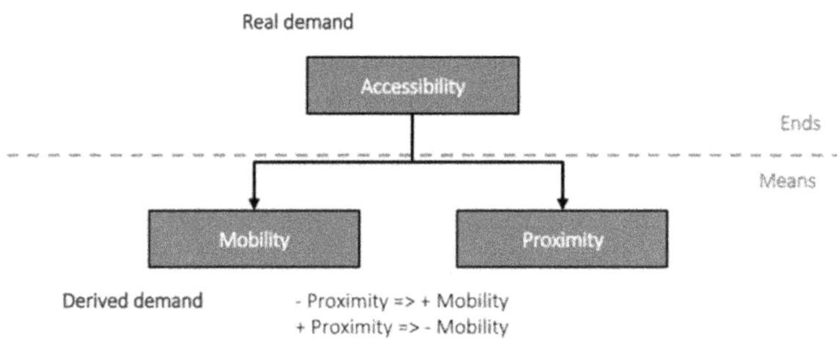

Source: Silva and Larson (2018[38]).

Policies focused on mobility rather than accessibility ignore the trade-off between mobility and proximity. This "proximity blind spot" explains, to a great extent, why policies have allocated a high – arguably excessive (Crozet, 2019[41]) – share of public space to fast, yet space-intensive,[17] means of transport, such as private cars. This comes at the expense of dedicated space for sustainable, cost[18]- and space-efficient modes, and for creating proximity. For example, inner space in cities that has been prioritised for roads has often contributed to pushing other uses (e.g. housing) to the fringes, promoting urban sprawl (see Section 4.1 for a detailed description of the dynamic).

Overall, proximity-blind policies lead to systems in which people need to travel further distances to meet their needs. In such systems, the car is often the most convenient or only available option, thus people "choose" to drive for the bulk of their trips (left panel of Figure 2.1).

Proximity-blind policies compensate for the lack of proximity with yet more mobility, locking systems into a vicious cycle of car dependency, high emissions, and low and unequal accessibility.

Decoupling emissions from mobility

Another important consequence of mobility-oriented policy and mind-sets is that climate strategies have focused on decoupling emissions from growing mobility, which is assumed to be independent from the system and unquestionably linked to well-being, prosperity and freedom. In other words, climate action has concentrated on decarbonising the existing high-mobility and car-dependent (but low-proximity and limited accessibility) system.

A focus on decoupling strategies has also been reinforced by approaching policy-making through an analytical, rather than a systemic logic. When taking an analytical approach, the analyst identifies the part in the system causing the undesired result, and looks for a solution to such cause. Since most emissions come from combustion motorised vehicles, these are, from an analytical point of view, identified as the part or element in the system to be optimised or improved (i.e. as the problem); while ignoring the systems' functioning that leads, in the case of transport, to an increase in the number of vehicles and traffic (see more on the difference between analytic and systemic mind-sets in section 2.2.2).

A focus on decoupling high/growing mobility from emissions has resulted in an overriding emphasis on improving or replacing combustion engine (especially private) vehicles which is considered to be the main challenge for attaining low emissions. Decoupling strategies, thus, improve vehicle energy efficiency and push for the switch to engines powered by lower carbon energy sources (e.g. EVs), leading to pathways highly dependent on technological change to optimise an element in the system. Meanwhile, efforts to reduce the number of vehicles, distances travelled, car use and more generally growing mobility are perceived as going against people's freedom and well-being. If undertaken, such efforts are kept at the margin of climate action. They are often considered to be something that can help, but only an option for very specific places (e.g. city centres of large metropoles) and/or for very specific people (e.g. those who already like to cycle), rather than as core actions to redesign the system and reverse the dynamics behind car-dependency.

Decoupling strategies are unfit to achieve net-zero targets on time. By focusing on decoupling growing/high mobility from emissions, decoupling strategies miss the opportunity to reduce emissions by avoiding unnecessary trips and long distances, and by enabling the conditions for triggering a significant modal shift from more to less sustainable modes. By keeping car dependency intact, traffic volumes continue to increase, and it is therefore not surprising to see that emissions reductions from decoupling efforts, e.g. from vehicle electrification, have been ineffective in most countries. As Lamb et al. observe, "while the electrification of road transport holds much promise, its impact has been hardly visible in the period up to 2018, and looking forward it is in danger of being offset by growing levels of travel activity and countervailing trends such as increasing vehicle size and weight" (Lamb et al., 2021[42]). This is similar to decoupling efforts at the economy level being offset by economic growth" [19] (Lamb et al., 2021[42]). ODYSSEE-MURE (2020[43]) estimates the main drivers of energy consumption (used here as a proxy for emissions) in the European Union (EU) and its member states. They find that the increase of energy consumption in the EU's transport sector was mainly driven by an increase of activity (+80.3 million tonnes of oil equivalent [Mtoe]). While energy savings simultaneously reduced energy consumption (-50.4 Mtoe), these reductions could not keep up with the increases driven by the increased activity. Thus, climate strategies focused on a decoupling logic "swim against the current"; and in fact, there are also important rebound effects from improvements in vehicle performance (see Chapter 6) that are hardly ever reflected in appraisal or policy prioritisation exercises. As a result estimated reductions from vehicle technology improvements are often overstated, while the role of policies with the potential to redesign the system (which can limit rebound effects) is underestimated.

Modelling of future scenarios also suggests that the level of emissions reductions that decoupling strategies can achieve is, overall, insufficient to reach net-zero goals at the pace needed (Buckle et al., 2020[44]). For instance, the new NZE2050 case developed by the International Energy Agency[20] confirms that triggering behavioural change (including for the transport sector) will be indispensable for meeting stringent mitigation targets. The NZE2050 sets out further measures (in addition to decoupling measures) that would be required to reach carbon neutrality by 2050 instead of 2070 (which the previous Sustainable Development Scenario [SDS] was in line with). It concludes that "behaviour changes are… essential to achieve the pace and scale of emissions reductions in the NZE2050, and they account for around 30% of the difference in emissions between the SDS and NZE2050 in 2030".

Fulton, Mason and Meroux (2017[45]) and Fulton (2018[46])[21] develop world urban transport scenarios and find that emissions can be reduced by about 44% (in 2050, relative to 2015) in a scenario focused on improving vehicle technology (i.e. decoupling strategies). This contrasts with a reduction of 76% in a scenario where technological improvements are embedded in a wider policy package promoting the use of active modes and shared/high-occupancy vehicles, including important changes in urban planning (i.e. systems redesign) (Figure 2.9). Importantly, the scenario focused on technological improvements (2R) is a high mobility scenario since high private vehicle use remains. Private vehicle use and passenger-kilometres even increase by 8% (both) compared to the business-as-usual (BAU) scenario, as the assumed accelerated shift towards automated vehicles exacerbates the overuse of private vehicles. In contrast, the scenario that depicts a shift away from car dependency would yield almost 50% less vehicle kilometres and 8% less passenger kilometres than the BAU scenario by 2050[22] via the increase in shared vehicle trips and greater public transport and non-motorised travel (as well as changes in land use). This would allow achieving much greater reductions in energy use and emissions, from both petroleum use and electricity; as modelling does not assume a complete decarbonisation of electricity; and despite the increased uptake of electrification assumed in both scenarios, the share of internal combustion engine vehicles continues to be important during the studied period. The latter is important, as even if the decarbonisation of electricity is achieved, lower demand will still do the “heavy lifting” early on (Brand et al., 2020[47]), as the complete electrification of the fleet is unlikely to take place in the first half of this century (even if the pace picks up) (Fulton, Mason and Meroux, 2017[45]). Interestingly, the cost of the scenario that results in the most emissions reductions (3R) is less than the cost of the scenario focused on improvements in vehicle technology (2R). Cost savings emerge mainly after 2030 and arise from reduced costs of vehicle purchase (as fewer vehicles are purchased), energy savings, and reduced road and parking infrastructure costs. Costs are reduced by 40% compared to the BAU scenario, leading to over USD 5 trillion in savings per year. When comparing the costs of the 2R to the BAU scenario, the authors find that induced demand and more costly vehicles (e.g. bigger vehicles) mostly offset the cost savings from lower cost EVs and autonomous vehicles. Both cost savings and emissions reductions (see Lamb et al. (2021[42])) can be offset by dynamics such as induced demand, shedding light on the importance of designing climate strategies with the potential to reverse such dynamics.

Figure 2.9. World urban transport scenario: Results for decoupling and systems redesign policies

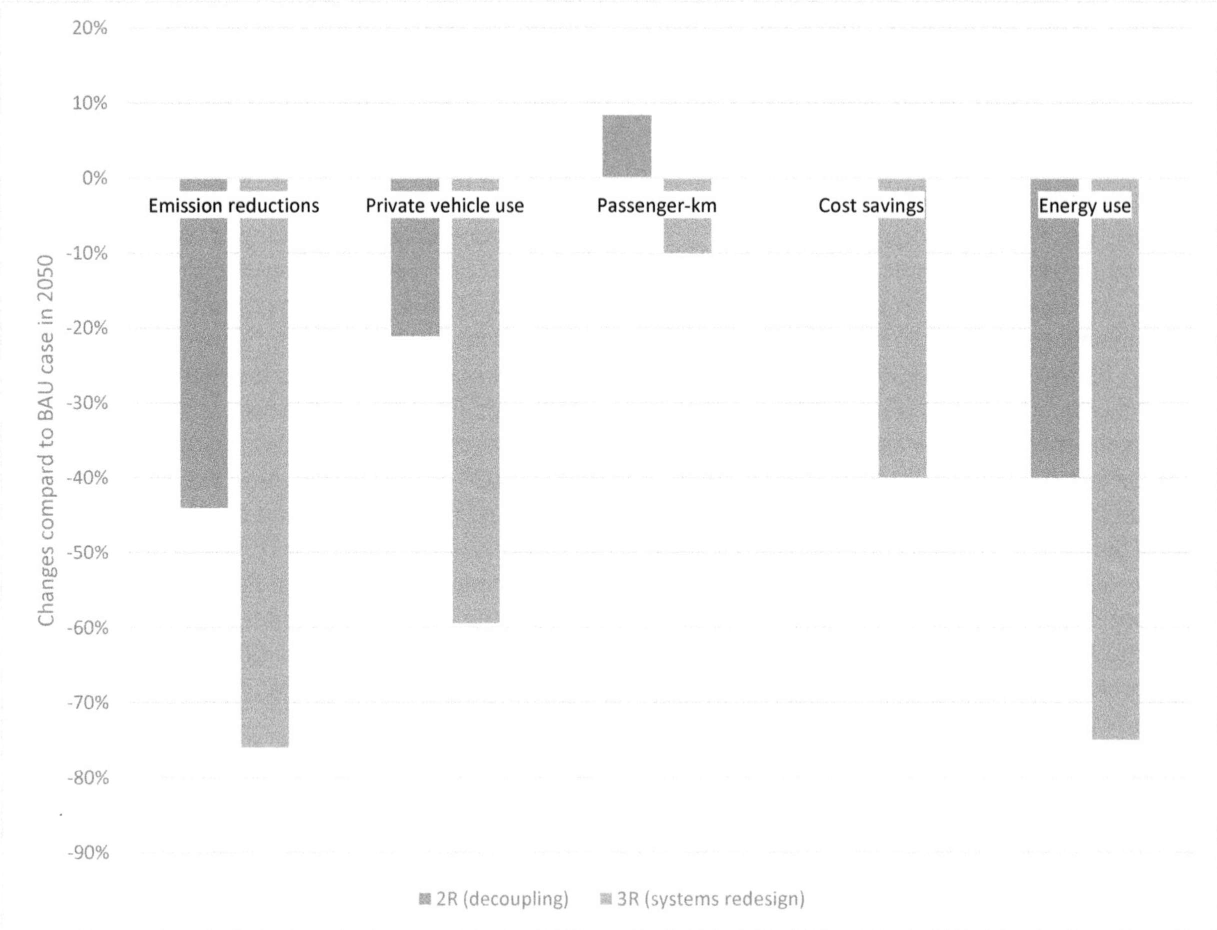

Notes: BAU: business as usual. Results from the 2R and 3R scenarios, compared to the business-as-usual case in 2050. 2R: scenario focused on improvements in vehicle technology (i.e. decoupling strategies). 3R: scenario where improvements in vehicle technology are part of policy packages aiming to create the conditions for higher use of active modes and shared/high-occupancy vehicles, including important changes in urban planning (i.e. systems redesign).
Source: Authors, based on Fulton, Mason and Meroux (2017[45]).

The ITF (2021[5]) reaches similar conclusions, showing two scenarios yielding an 87% and a 73% reduction in worldwide urban and non-urban passenger transport emissions by 2050 (relative to 2015 levels). It shows that this could be possible if technological change is embedded into the aim of "reshaping" transport systems[23] (bringing -73% reduction). Building on the recovery to accelerate transformational change (Reshape + scenario) could further reduce emissions in the short run (achieving -87% reduction in 2050). The Reshape+ scenario also yields much lower total travel demand (passenger-kilometres) than the BAU scenario, and this is key to drastically cutting down emissions. This reduction of total travel demand, in line with the claims made in this report, is not at the expense of well-being, as accessibility by both car and public transport, and the relative competitiveness of public transport *vis-à-vis* the car are improved in this scenario (ITF, 2021[5]).

Decoupling strategies also leave potential synergies untapped, and create significant (and evitable) trade-offs between climate mitigation, other environmental goals and wider well-being outcomes. This leads to missed opportunities to increase the cost-effectiveness and public acceptability of climate policies.

Synergies between climate action and other challenges that need to be solved within the same time frame (e.g. the Sustainable Development Goals, the 2030 Agenda, etc.) can increase the cost-efficiency, cost-effectiveness and acceptability of policies. Increasing policy acceptability is fundamental for achieving net-zero goals: while potentially cost-efficient and effective in theory, unimplemented policies – or policies whose ambition needs to be lowered due to public resistance – are ineffective. Examples of untapped synergies are multiple. For instance, the replacement of combustion cars with EVs improves air quality, and thus health. But it fails to unleash the (mental and physical) health benefits that can come from the use of active modes such as walking and cycling (modes which would also improve air quality). Decoupling strategies also fail to align the climate, road safety, equity, gender equality[24] and social inclusion agendas. By isolating climate and other problems caused by car-dependent systems, decoupling strategies are part of policy frameworks that lead to sub-optimal solutions and create continuous trade-offs. For instance policies aiming to reduce road fatalities in car-dependent systems often use the promotion of pedestrian overbridges or subways to address what is considered to be an externality of (inevitable) car-dependent systems. Such infrastructure can increase safety to a certain extent, but it importantly reduces the attractiveness of walking and cycling, as going up and down stairs increases the time and effort for people choosing such means. It thus contributes to the erosion of sustainable modes (a dynamic discussed in detail in Chapter 5), reducing the scope for modal shift, while also importantly limiting accessibility for non-car users (Anciaes and Jones, 2018[48]). Furthermore, it has been observed that the increased time and effort for pedestrians to go up and down stairs results in them crossing at other (highly unsafe) places rather than using the overbridges (Bhagat, Manoj Patel and Palak Shah, 2014[49]).

As shown by the examples above, by locking in car-dependent lifestyles, decoupling strategies can also perpetuate inequalities (Powell et al., 2021[50]): car dependency creates a vicious cycle where the gap between the possibility and ease to access opportunities (i.e. accessibility gap) between car and non-car owners increases. As higher shares of the population "opt" for a car, businesses locate in areas with good car access and poor public transport access, and authorities focus their efforts on accommodating new car use (Mattioli, 2013[51]). ITF (2021[5]) shows that policies focused on ensuring access to car use, which climate policies focused on decoupling do, can cause forced car ownership, in particular for lower income households living in areas with fewer alternative transport options.[25] In these cases, private vehicles, and their associated costs, become the only way to satisfy people's needs, locking them into car dependency and transport-related costs.

According to the ITF (2021[5]), equity issues are better served by policies ensuring "[a] right to carry out daily activities without needing a car". Given the car-dependent nature of current systems, allowing for such a right requires redesigning transport and urban systems, and embedding efforts for improving vehicle technologies into wider, systemic, policy packages (see section 2.3 and chapters 3-5). Focusing climate action on redesigning systems to shift them away from car dependency opens the door to policies (such as street redesign) that can simultaneously reduce emissions, increase safety, encourage the use of active modes (which can improve health via better air quality and physical activity), and address equity and social exclusion (e.g. through the promotion of human interactions).[26]

Decoupling strategies, which importantly rely on the shift towards EVs also imply the replacement of a big (and growing) private vehicle fleet, and thus increasing the already unsustainable level of materials consumption (OECD, 2019[52]). As highlighted by Xu et al. (2020[53]), "[t]he success of the transition to electric vehicles will depend partly on whether the material supply can keep up with the growth of the sector in a sustainable way and without damaging the reputation of EV". For example, the IEA estimates that total mineral consumption would need to quadruple over the next 20 years to meet net-zero goals by 2070 (IEA, 2021[54]). EVs and battery storage account for approximately half of such consumption (IEA, 2021[54]), which would need to be further accelerated if net-zero goals are to be met by 2050. In a recent study, Xu et al. (2020[53]) estimate the material demand that would be required to sustain light-duty EVs if their development was aligned with the IEA Stated Policy (STEP) and the SDS scenarios.[27] They find that the increase in EVs in line with these scenarios would require a radical expansion of the global production capacity for lithium, cobalt and nickel; and most probably the discovery of new resources.[28] Even if new resources were discovered in time, the environmental impacts associated with their extraction would necessarily increase (Swaminathen, 2020[55]; Katwala, 2018[56]). Environmental impacts from mineral extraction include land-use change, water use and waste generation (IEA, 2021[54]). Land-use change directly affects ecosystems and people and can cause habitat loss for endangered species as well as the displacement of communities (Katwala, 2018[56]). Mining requires large volumes of water, which can cause water contamination from acid mine drainage, the disposal of tailings and wastewater discharge from the mining process (IEA, 2021[54]). Alongside these three major environmental challenges, the mining development process can result in air pollution, gaseous emissions and noise pollution, and may also have a number of social impacts (health and safety, human rights, etc.) (IEA, 2021[54]).

The replacement of increasing private vehicle fleets could also put pressure on the power sector. Global electricity demand from EVs is expected to increase from less than 100 terawatt hours (TWh) in 2019 to almost 1 000 TWh in 2030 (approximately 4% of global electricity consumption in 2019) according to the IEA's SDS (IEA, 2020[57]). This requires additional power system infrastructure (plants, networks), which can have trade-offs with land-use and biodiversity (Gasparatos et al., 2017[58]). While EVs can be a great source of flexibility that can provide a broad range of services to the power system, facilitating the integration of variable renewable energy sources such as solar and wind, they can also increase total and peak demand (Gschwendtner, 2021[59]) and exacerbate stress on the power grid if charging from multiple users is not well co-ordinated (e.g. simultaneous charging in the evening after coming home from work). In this respect, having a higher share of shared fleets (which are not incentivised by decoupling strategies) would most likely be conducive for grid integration, because these could support the early deployment of vehicle-to-grid (V2G) technologies[29] by enabling more centralised infrastructure to serve many cars and thus installation and maintenance costs (Gschwendtner, 2021[59]). As discussed in chapter 6, even efforts to implement circular batteries will be very limited in a growing fleet scenario, and transitioning towards a system that can deliver better access with a smaller fleet would be needed for efforts to electrify vehicles to be more feasible, effective and truly sustainable.

Finally, by not dealing with car dependency, decoupling strategies fail to enable the conditions for other relevant policies, such as carbon prices, to also be more acceptable and effective. Pricing carbon is fundamental for steering sustainable choices. In car-dependent systems, these options are, however, not always available, or may not be safe or convenient enough to trigger people's behavioural change. The effectiveness of pricing and other market-based mechanisms depends on the availability and attractiveness of sustainable options. For example, price elasticities are much lower when dense networks of public transport are not available (see Chapter 6). Carbon pricing acceptability will likely be low in a context in which low-income households are car dependent, for whom transport costs are already high and alternative modes of transport may not be available (Mattioli et al., 2020[24]; Handy, 2020[60]; OECD, 2019[61]). The Yellow Vests (Gilets Jaunes) movement in France is a concrete example of low policy acceptability, and thus low policy effectiveness, due (to an important extent) to the absence of enabling conditions.

Climate and transport strategies need to change radically, from a focus on decarbonising the current unsustainable-by-design system (left panel of Figure 2.1) towards enabling the conditions for sustainable-by-design systems (right panel of Figure 2.2). While there is an increasing willingness to reverse car dependency (ITF, 2021[5]), mobility- and decoupling-focused transport and climate strategies stand in the way of the transition towards sustainable transport and urban systems in most countries.

"Cleaner", but still car-dependent, systems are not enough to achieve net-zero goals and simultaneously improve well-being. As argued by Systems Innovation (2021[62]), electric and autonomous vehicles "are tools, they are not a solution to systems-level dysfunctionalities".

Achieving net-zero carbon goals will require moving beyond mobility and analytical mind-sets and decoupling-oriented climate strategies. A first step towards this shift is to envision the outcomes that sustainable-by-design systems should achieve, as described at the beginning of this section. The second step is to understand why current systems lead to unsustainable results, and identify what mental models or implicit assumptions shaped such systems, so as to question and revise them as needed. Once assumptions are in line with the observed systems' functioning, and policy goals are informed by such understanding and set based on the vision defined in the first step, policy packages can be re-designed to accelerate the transition towards better systems for better lives.

The next section dives deep into what such policy packages could look like concretely; chapters 3-6 provide more detail.

2.3. Redesign systems by changing policy priorities

Climate strategies prioritising accessibility via the policies put forward in this report would be radically different from today's strategies. The difference arises from the way the problem is defined.

As discussed before, by taking an analytical (or linear) approach, the analyst looks for a direct cause of emissions, and for a solution to that cause. In the surface transport sector, most emissions come from combustion motorised vehicles, which increase is seen as exogenous, and its cause, thus, is not analysed (see Section 3.1). From a mobility-centred perspective, the increase of traffic volume is also seen as the inevitable consequence of "progress" (see section 2.2.2). If the increase in the number of vehicles does not depend on the system's functioning (i.e. is exogenous) and is inevitable (i.e. as a decrease would result in poorer life quality or less "progress"), then the type of vehicles in circulation are the problem, and the solution to reduce emissions is to electrify them or improve their fuel performance.

This is why, an analytical approach, coupled with a mobility-oriented perspective, constrains climate strategies to decoupling emissions from vehicle use. In transport jargon, such an approach and perspective push climate policies to place an overriding focus on "improve" effects.[30] Section 2.2.2 explained why this focus is unfit to achieve net-zero targets.

This report takes a systemic approach and moves towards an accessibility-centred perspective. An accessibility-centred perspective sees the sustainable delivery of accessibility – rather than mobility – as the key desirable outcome of well-functioning transport systems. A systemic approach shows that recurrently high levels of emissions and poor, unequal and unsafe accessibility are the result of a system that is not working properly as a whole. The problem is no longer (just) the emissions performance of the vehicles in circulation, but the system's functioning or dynamics leading to an increase in the number of vehicles and traffic. These dynamics depend, for example, on the way roads (and public space more broadly) are organised. The solution is thus no longer to (just) improve vehicles' performance, but to improve the system's functioning (briefly explained in section 2.2). To continue with the analogy, the focus is on changing the direction of the escalator, so that it helps us go faster, rather than slowing us down.

Because the system's functioning is defined as the main problem to be tackled, and growing mobility is no longer seen as unquestionably linked to progress or well-being, climate strategies are, from a systemic and accessibility-centred perspective, no longer constrained to improving the type of vehicle (i.e. to decoupling emissions from increased vehicle use). Climate strategies can, instead, focus on reversing the dynamics that lead to car dependency and overuse and thus transition towards car independent systems.[31]

Reversing the dynamics that lead to car dependency and overuse can lead to transformational change (see Box 1.1) via systems redesign so that systems deliver high and quality (including safe) accessibility with low emissions. In other words, reversing these dynamics means changing the way the system functions, and thus its results: from induced demand to disappearing traffic (transformational change #1, see Chapter 3); from sprawl to proximity (transformational change #2, see Chapter 4); and from the erosion of active and shared modes to making these modes the fastest, most comfortable and safest modes, so that they become people's first choice (transformational change #3, see Chapter 5).

Modelling suggests that climate strategies aimed at redesigning systems to deliver high accessibility and low emissions have a greater potential to reduce emissions than strategies limited to decoupling emissions from vehicle use (i.e. "improve" effects)[32] (see section 2.2.2). Climate strategies focused on improving the system's functioning so that it delivers accessibility sustainably prioritise policies that set the conditions for avoiding unnecessary trips, by creating proximity, and for a shift towards sustainable transport modes, by reallocating public space, investment and technology to increase the attractiveness of such modes. Emission reductions via decoupling (i.e. improve effects) are also important in accessibility-oriented climate strategies, but they are part of a wider effort to improve systems, rather than embedded in systems that are unsustainable-by-design.

This report calls for a shift towards accessibility-oriented climate strategies centred on redesigning transport and urban systems so that these can, by design, foster accessibility sustainably. As explained in section 2.2, an accessibility-oriented perspective is fundamental because it sheds lights on the importance of achieving a balance between mobility and proximity. Creating proximity is crucial to reducing emissions, as proximity can "avoid" large distances and trips (e.g. through increasign the scope for trip chaining[33]) as well as to increase the attractiveness of sustainable modes such as walking and cycling, which are most competitive for short distance trips. As described above, accessibility-oriented climate strategies can also foster synergies and avoid trade-offs that decoupling strategies tend to exacerbate.

This section presents an overview of the policies with the potential to accelerate the transition towards car independency, further described in Chapters 3-7. This section can also be read as a summary of the results of the third step of the Well-being Lens process: redesign.

2.3.1. Transformational transport policies for net-zero systems by design

Policies focused on street redesign and management, spatial planning, and the development of multi-modal networks should be at the core of climate strategies. These policies can help strike a balance between mobility and proximity, and reverse the dynamics leading to car-dependent and high-emission transport and urban systems. Changes at the level of governance and monitoring frameworks are fundamental to facilitate the implementation of such policies, and innovation and technological change – both at the parts and the systems level – have a major role to play to increase the effectiveness of climate strategies.

Street redesign and policies for better managing public space (roads included) can lead to "**disappearing traffic**", reversing the dynamic of "**induced demand**" (Cairns, Atkins and Goodwin, 2002[63]; Goodwin, Hass-Klau and Cairns, 2015[64]). Street redesign and public space management policies are based on the recognition that public space, currently mostly allocated to roads for cars, should accommodate multiple transport modes and uses beyond transport. A fairer allocation of public space (and in particular of roads) across transport modes and other uses is a condition for creating proximity, and for increasing the attractiveness of active and shared transport modes. Chapter 3 describes Superblocks as an example of radical street redesign, and discusses the potential of parking and road-pricing policies to contribute to ensuring that public space is designed and managed with the aim of enhancing accessibility. In a nutshell:

- Barcelona's Superblocks reorganise the city into polygons of approximately 400 m x 400 m. Inner roads are not closed to motorised vehicles, as these can enter the superblock but they cannot cross it (and have to stay within a speed limit of 10 km/h). Superblocks convert streets from a single function (i.e. dedicated to motorised vehicles) to spaces welcoming active modes and with multiple functions (e.g. recreational) (Ajuntament de Barcelona, 2014[65]). Superblocks are "low-cost urbanism" (López, Ortega and Pardo, 2020[66]) with the potential to transform the urban ecosystem and bring health, safety, social and environmental benefits (e.g. better air quality, emissions reductions) in the short run.
- Parking policies, as used (or not used) today, incentivise car use by subsidising, underpricing or providing an oversupply of parking space. Parking policies could instead be designed to regulate

and discourage car use (Kodransky and Hermann, 2011[67]), by putting a price on space scarcity. Higher parking prices, smart parking meters and zoning are some of the ways in which parking policies could play a regulatory role and help to reduce emissions and air pollution, and enhance well-being.

- Road pricing can contribute to shifting away from a "predict and provide" approach towards an emphasis on better managing the use of existing roads. Road-pricing schemes have often been set with the aim of increasing traffic speeds and reducing delays for motorists, often considered to be congestion's most important disutility (ITF, 2019[68]; van Dender, 2019[69]). Road-pricing schemes will, however, better deliver climate and well-being goals if they are designed with the aim of efficiently using road space.The most efficient road-pricing schemes from international experience are those that are distance-based and with differentiated prices (e.g. peak hours, vehicle's emissions level, load factors). Road pricing can be a powerful tool if combined with street redesign and re-allocation in favour of sustainable modes.

Urban sprawl can be contained – and reversed – via spatial planning aimed at redesigning territories, supported by improved governance frameworks. Chapter 4 focuses on the changes needed in terms of governance and monitoring for effectively integrating transport and land-use planning,[34] which is fundamental for sustainably redesigning territories. In the current situation, decisions on transport and urban planning, land-use management, or housing (all fundamental from an accessibility lens) are not systematically integrated or co-ordinated across territories with metropolitan areas or regions. In a nutshell:

- Metropolitan transport authorities have been found to be excellent institutional configurations for developing strategic planning for metropolitan areas and regions, striking a balance between place-based local planning and ensuring coherence at the metropolitan level. Especially when embedded in larger metropolitan bodies with land-use planning competencies, metropolitan transport authorities can importantly contribute to integrated planning (see Chapter 4)[35], which can facilitate territory redesign.
- Planning, and decision making more broadly, (including by metropolitan transport authorities) needs to be guided by accessibility-oriented monitoring frameworks. Frameworks such as the 15-minute city (see Chapter 4) can steer decisions towards sustainable urban restructuring (e.g. for urban renewal and new development). For example, the 15-minute framework guides decisions towards the creation of proximity by defining three radii accessible by foot and bike within which authorities need to ensure access to a certain number of services (Duany and Steuteville, 2021[70]).
- Parking regulation and transport assessments for new developments, such as residential buildings and offices, have an impact on urban form. Revising regulation to move from minimum towards maximum parking standards and requiring developers to produce multi-modal, rather than traffic-oriented, transport assessments are both key actions to reverse sprawl and encourage compact development. These changes are also key to ensuring shifts towards sustainable modes (e.g. by guiding new developments in areas served by public transport) and facilitate the creation of proximity (e.g. by freeing parking space for other uses).

Redesigning urban space may be perceived as a slow or challenging process, which could only bring benefits in the long term. There are, however, numerous examples of rapid and successful changes (especially in terms of street redesign) that reap benefits in the short term, such as Superblocks and the numerous initiatives implemented during the COVID-19 pandemic (see Chapter 7). Changes in urban and territorial form are deeper and will be longer term changes. Examples in Chapter 4 show, however, that the redesign of large city areas could be achieved within the next 10 years, and that benefits from such redesign would be visible in the short-term (likely earlier than the benefits from widespread vehicle electrification, often perceived as being shorter-term efforts).

Policies fostering the development of multi-modal transport networks are fundamental to reverse the **erosion of active and shared modes of transport**. There are huge opportunities for enlarging the offer of collective, flexible and sustainable modes of transport by integrating new technologies and business models along policy frameworks that are conducive to making shared and active modes central. Necessary actions to accelerate the creation of multi-modal transport networks that can provide sustainable and quality options (see Chapter 5) include:

- Strengthening public transport networks, including by increasing investment and improving the methodologies for determining public transport pricing and planning, e.g. to avoid the public transport low-cost, low-revenue, low-quality trap.
- Integrating and mainstreaming on-demand and shared services such as e-bikes, other micro-mobility options and micro-transit. This can be done via new technologies, "softer regulation" that promotes cooperation between government and service providers, and government subsidies in areas where micro-mobility or on-demand services can bring social and environmental benefits but may not be profitable for the private sector. Support to the development of new vehicles (e.g. innovative micro-mobility) and the expansion of services for multipurpose trips (e.g. cargo e-bikes, shared bikes and e-bikes with baby seats, kids' bikes) could also contribute to making shared mobility more attractive. Mainstreaming on-demand and shared services can help unleash important mitigation potential and reduce strain and crowding on public transport, further increasing its attractiveness.

Importantly, the policies addressing the different dynamics can reinforce each other. The shift towards public space (Chapter 3) and territorial design (Chapter 4) that prioritise walking, cycling, micro-mobility and shared modes, can greatly facilitate the development of multi-modal transport networks, making these modes more attractive (e.g. fast, safe, reliable, comfortable) than private individual vehicles. In turn, systems in which active, shared and high occupancy modes are the norm will require less cars, and can further liberate space (e.g. previously devoted to car parking and use), thus increasing the scope for street and whole-of-territories redesign, allowing for the creation of proximity between people and places (e.g. recreational space, markets, etc.) and for expanding the use of sustainable modes (see Chapter 5).

Policies aiming at systems redesign also have the potential to convert vicious circles into virtuous ones. While the dynamics described in section 2.2.1 reinforce each other resulting in higher traffic volumes and emissions, the dynamics that policies in this report can trigger – i.e. those leading to disappearing traffic, proximity, and a greater attractiveness of active and shared modes – reinforce each other, this time in a desired direction: that of sustainable accessibility. TfL (2018[71]) refers to this as the "virtuous circle of road danger reduction". In Paris, for example, six out of ten people cycling in the city today were not doing so before policies reallocated road space to bike lanes during the COVID-19 pandemic (see Chapter 7). Such reallocation has resulted in an increase in the number of cyclists, which can lead to even more cyclists, since the more cyclists there are, the more people may consider cycling as a safe and convenient option.

Synergies between space reallocation and market-based mechanisms such as carbon pricing, fundamental for the transition towards sustainable systems, are particularly interesting. For example, evidence suggests that the impact of fuel prices on people's choice is low when alternatives to car driving are not available; and that prices' impact on people's choice increases when public transport infrastructure is available (Avner, Rentschler and Hallegatte, 2014[72]), to which space reallocation can contribute to improving. Policies reallocating space away from car use and parking can also contribute to road safety goals, in particular if they build on "safe system" approaches (see Chapter 3). This is very different from a situation in which one problem is solved and another is exacerbated (or its resolution becomes more difficult). For example, as discussed above, pedestrian bridges reduce road fatalities, but they also reduce the attractiveness of active modes, rendering the transition towards low-emission systems more difficult.

2.3.2. *The potential of systems innovation*

Innovation has a major role to play in climate strategies that aim to reverse the dynamics underlying car dependency. **This report calls for climate strategies that foster systems innovation to design sustainable systems.**

Systems innovation is innovation aimed at transforming the systems' functioning. Innovation efforts have, so far, mainly focused on technological change to improve parts, e.g. vehicle emissions. While important, placing an overriding focus on innovation at the vehicle level has been a barrier for innovation (including low-tech innovation) to address car dependency and achieve the transformational change needed to achieve net-zero goals. Innovation can, and given the scale of the challenge should, go beyond technology and parts.

New technologies can open up enormous opportunities for emission reductions if they are embedded in the aim of improving the system's functioning (Systems Innovation, 2021[62]). For example, until a few decades ago, it was unimaginable to share vehicles (bikes, cars, etc.) and combine transport modes as efficiently as can be done today with GPS technologies and apps. This can significantly change transport systems' functioning from one based on private car ownership to one where transport is seen as a service. The potential of such a change, in which transport systems become integrated networks of sustainable modes, has not yet been unlocked, partly as these technologies are not embedded in policy packages to transition towards car-independent systems. Furthermore, policy frameworks surrounding these technologies currently foster private and low occupancy rather than active, shared and high occupancy (e.g. translating into more ride-hailing than ride-sharing). In addition, there is limited financial support to expand the offer of vehicles and business models for shared active and micro-mobility options.

Improving vehicles' performance (i.e. innovation at the parts' level) remains fundamental, and the effectiveness of such efforts can significantly be increased if they are embedded in a wider systemic transformation. For example, in systems fostering shared mobility (e.g. transport as a service), EVs can become more competitive via higher vehicle utilisation, turnover of the vehicle stock and cost-effectiveness of technological change (Taiebat and Xu, 2019[73]; IEA, 2020[57]; Goetz, n.d.[74]). Smaller fleets could also reduce resource use and the EVs' pressure on the power sector in terms of energy demand (Kamiya and Teter, 2019[75]) (see Chapter 6).

While innovation at the parts' level and systems innovation can be complementary, innovation efforts at the parts' level currently tend to jeopardise systems innovation. For example, incentives to purchase EVs or more efficient vehicles reinforce car dependency by reducing the attractiveness of active modes or public transport (e.g. EVs allowed to use bus lanes), or simply by further locking-in space for car use (e.g. exceptions from parking fees), space which becomes unavailable for other uses (e.g. wide and safe bike lanes). To avoid these trade-offs, incentives for the purchase of EVs (including charging infrastructure) should be thought of as complementary to street redesign, spatial planning and policies fostering the development of multi-modal networks (see Section 6.2).

To facilitate policy priorisation towards systems innovation, evaluation methods behind policy comparisons and evaluation need to better reflect the limitations of opting for strategies and pathways that place an overriding focus on technological change to improve parts (e.g. adequately reflecting rebound effects and real-world, rather than laboratory, emissions). These also need to better reflect the multiple benefits of transformational policies (discussed in Chapters 1 and 3-5).

Innovating at the systems level can also increase the effectiveness of carbon pricing. Redesigning systems so that they allow people to avoid trips and choose active and shared modes (because these have become the fastest, safest and most convenient modes) can significantly increase the feasibility and effectiveness of ambitious carbon prices, as well as raise fewer distributional issues. Similar to incentives for cleaner vehicles, carbon pricing should be seen as one policy lever, rather than the policy lever, to achieve net-zero transport systems for better lives (IMF / OECD, 2021[76]) (Rosenbloom et al., 2020[77]).

2.3.3. Policies and dynamics in a nutshell

Table 2.1 summarizes the policies discussed in this report. It identifies policies that target each of the dynamics behind car-dependency (described in more detail in section 2.2 and chapters 3 to 5), and illustrates which of these policies are central in climate strategies following a decoupling (second column from the right) or a redesign (last column) logic. The table highlights that policies currently regarded as supporting (or optional) actions become central in strategies focused on reversing unsustainable systems dynamics. From this perspective, policies currently considered as core climate policies are in reality supporting policies, as, on their own, they do not directly target key dynamics at the source of car dependency and high emissions. Overall, policies in Table 2.1 are complementary: policies that redesign systems shift the direction towards sustainable systems, while market-based instruments and incentives and regulations towards vehicle improvements can accelerate the pace of such transition.

In addition to providing an overview of policies discussed in the report, Table 2.1 could be used as a checklist for governments to assess whether (and the extent to which) climate efforts are focused on redesigning systems or mainly on improving parts (potentially in unsustainable-by-design systems); i.e. whether policies target the key dynamics underlying unsustainable results. A key limitation of most policy assessments is that these describe the type of instruments used (e.g. market vs non-market instruments) without making the distinction between policies with the potential to trigger transformational or incremental change. Understanding this is important because ensuring that sufficient efforts go to redesign actions with the potential to trigger transformational change can significantly increase the likelihood of reaching the Paris Agreement goals while improving people's lives (see Box 1.2).

Table 2.1. Which policies target which dynamics?

	Disappearing traffic (reversing induced demand)	Proximity (reversing urban sprawl)	Active and shared modes become the norm (reversing erosion)	Hierarchisation of policies according to their capacity to trigger transformational change	At the centre of current climate strategies (decoupling strategies)	At the centre of climate strategies focused on redesigning systems
Market-based instruments / Incentives and regulations for vehicle improvement						
Carbon prices[1]		X	X	Supporting	Yes	Yes
Taxes and other incentives to increase the uptake of cleaner vehicles (including electric vehicles)[2]				Supporting	Yes	Yes
Investment and support of charging infrastructure[3]				Supporting	Yes	Yes
Street redesign and improved management of public space[4]						
Street redesign	X			Core	No	Yes
Parking policy	X			Core	No	Yes
Road pricing	X			Core	No	Yes
Spatial planning aimed at increasing proximity[4]						
Parking standards for new developments		X		Core	No	Yes
Mainstreaming accessibility-based planning via governance and monitoring changes (e.g. 15-minute city framework, metropolitan transport authorities)		X		Core	No	Yes
Multi-modal assessments for new developments		X		Core	No	Yes
Minimum (rather than maximum) parking requirements for new developments		X				
Policies for developing multi-modal and sustainable networks[4]						
Investments in public transport and better pricing methodologies			X	Core	No	Yes
Policies increasing the attractiveness of shared bicycles, micro-mobility (through direct support, regulation fostering cooperation and promoting innovation in these sectors)			X	Core	No	Yes
Policies to integrate micro-transit (e.g. on-demand vans) into public transport networks			X	Core	No	Yes

1. If coupled with other policies addressing systems dynamics.
2. Depending on the design, they could reinforce erosion dynamics (e.g. use of bus lanes by electric vehicles could increase bus congestion and reduce their attractiveness).
3. Depending on planning, can exacerbate induced demand (e.g. charging stations mostly for private car use).
4.The policies identified in this report as part of this broad category are not exhaustive
Note: The list of policies presented in this table is not comprehensive.

References

Ajuntament de Barcelona (2014), *Metropolitan Area Urban Mobility Plans (PMU)*. [65]

Anciaes, P. and P. Jones (2018), "Estimating preferences for different types of pedestrian crossing facilities", *Transportation Research Part F: Traffic Psychology and Behaviour*, Vol. 52, pp. 222-237, http://dx.doi.org/10.1016/j.trf.2017.11.025. [48]

Avner, P., J. Rentschler and S. Hallegatte (2014), "Carbon price efficiency: Lock-in and path dependence in urban forms and transport infrastructure", *Policy Research Working Paper*, World Bank, Washington, DC, https://doi.org/10.1596/1813-9450-6941 (accessed on 29 March 2021). [72]

Ballesteros, L. (2018), "Changing culture to save lives: Mexico City's bold commitment to Vision Zero", press release, Vision Zero Network, https://visionzeronetwork.org/mexico-citys-bold-commitment-to-vision-zero (accessed on 10 August 2021). [30]

Bergerot, A., G. Comolet and T. Salez (2021), "Les usagers de la route paient-ils le juste prix de leurs circulations?", No. 283, French Ministry of Economy, Finance and the Recovery, Paris, https://www.tresor.economie.gouv.fr/Articles/2021/04/27/les-usagers-de-la-route-paient-ils-le-juste-prix-de-leurs-circulations (accessed on 26 July 2021). [86]

Bhagat, P., E. Manoj Patel and E. Palak Shah (2014), "Pedestrian priority in urban area and usefulness towards community", *IJRET: International Journal of Research in Engineering and Technology*, Vol. 3/1, pp. 2321-7308, http://dx.doi.org/10.15623/ijret.2014.0301088. [49]

BikeIsBest (2021), "The best tool for the job", https://www.youtube.com/watch?v=V6ChTqlI-Yk (accessed on 21 July 2021). [26]

Brand, C. et al. (2020), "Road to zero or road to nowhere? Disrupting transport and energy in a zero carbon world", *Energy Policy*, Vol. 139, p. 111334, http://dx.doi.org/10.1016/j.enpol.2020.111334. [47]

Bruxelles Mobilité (2021), "Les pieds", https://www.youtube.com/watch?v=EAkm773d7RQ (accessed on 1 July 2021). [25]

Buckle, S. et al. (2020), "Addressing the COVID-19 and climate crises: Potential economic recovery pathways and their implications for climate change mitigation, NDCs and broader socio-economic goals", *OECD/IEA Climate Change Expert Group Papers*, No. 2020/04, OECD Publishing, Paris, https://dx.doi.org/10.1787/50abd39c-en. [44]

Cairns, S., S. Atkins and P. Goodwin (2002), "Disappearing traffic? The story so far", *Municipal Engineer*, Vol. 151/1, pp. 13-22, http://dx.doi.org/10.1680/muen.151.1.13.38856. [63]

Chapman, R. (2019), "Managing environmental and energy transitions for regions and cities", prepared for the Expert Meeting on Managing the Transition to a Climate-Neutral Economy for Regions and Cities", OECD, Paris, https://www.oecd.org/cfe/regionaldevelopment/Chapman-2019-Managing-Transition-Regions-Cities.pdf (accessed on 19 August 2020). [7]

Colville-Andersen, M. (2018), *Copenhagenize: The Definitive Guide to Global Bicycle Urbanism*, Island Press/Center for Resource Economics, http://dx.doi.org/10.5822/978-1-61091-939-5. [22]

Crozet, Y. (2019), "Cars and space consumption: Rethinking the regulation of urban mobility", *International Transport Forum Discussion Papers*, No. 2020/13, OECD Publishing, Paris, https://doi.org/10.1787/8abaa384-en. [41]

Duany, A. and R. Steuteville (2021), "Defining the 15-minute city", *Public Square: A CNU Journal*, https://www.cnu.org/publicsquare/2021/02/08/defining-15-minute-city (accessed on 8 March 2021). [70]

Dukes, J. (2013), "The modern Moloch", *99% Invisible*, https://99percentinvisible.org/episode/episode-76-the-modern-moloch (accessed on 30 June 2021). [17]

Ferreira, A., E. Beukers and M. Brömmelstroet (2012), "Accessibility is gold, mobility is not: A proposal for the improvement of Dutch transport-related cost-benefit analysis", *Environment and Planning B: Planning and Design*, Vol. 39/4, pp. 683-697, http://dx.doi.org/10.1068/b38073. [2]

Freund, P. and G. Martin (1993), *The Ecology of the Automobile*, Black Rose Books, London, https://www.researchgate.net/publication/289117639_The_Ecology_of_the_Automobile (accessed on 24 June 2021). [16]

Fulton, L. (2018), "Three revolutions in urban passenger travel", *Joule*, Vol. 2/4, pp. 575-578, http://dx.doi.org/10.1016/j.joule.2018.03.005. [46]

Fulton, L., J. Mason and D. Meroux (2017), *Three Revolutions in Urban Transportation: How to Achieve the Full Potential of Vehicle Electrification, Automation, and Shared Mobility in Urban Transportation Systems Around the World by 2050*, UC Davis and Institute for Transportation & Development Policy, https://merritt.cdlib.org/d/ark%253A%252F13030%252Fm52c3sbx/1/producer%252FSTEPS-2050.pdf. [45]

Gasparatos, A. et al. (2017), "Renewable energy and biodiversity: Implications for transitioning to a green economy", *Renewable and Sustainable Energy Reviews*, Vol. 70, pp. 161-184, http://dx.doi.org/10.1016/j.rser.2016.08.030. [58]

Goetz, M. (n.d.), "Electric vehicle charging considerations for shared, automated fleets", policy brief, UC Davis, Institute of Transportation Studies, https://3rev.ucdavis.edu/sites/g/files/dgvnsk6431/files/files/page/3R.EVSE_.final_UPDATED_Oct17.pdf. [74]

Goodwin, P., C. Hass-Klau and S. Cairns (2015), "Evidence on the effects of road capacity reduction on traffic levels", *Traffic Engineering & Control*, Vol. 39/6, pp. 348-354. [64]

Gössling, S. (2020), "Why cities need to take road space from cars – and how this could be done", *Journal of Urban Design*, Vol. 25/4, pp. 443-448, http://dx.doi.org/10.1080/13574809.2020.1727318. [20]

Gschwendtner, C. (2021), "Vehicle-to-grid (V2G) and car sharing: Joining forces to decarbonize electricity and transport?", *Energy Blog*, ETHzürich, https://blogs.ethz.ch/energy/v2g-and-car-sharing-joining-forces (accessed on 10 August 2021). [59]

Handy, S. (2020), *What California Gains from Reducing Car Dependence*, National Center for Sustainable Transportation, http://dx.doi.org/10.7922/G25X276H. [60]

Harich, J. (2010), "Change resistance as the crux of the environmental sustainability problem", *System Dynamics Review*, Vol. 26/1, pp. 35-72, http://dx.doi.org/10.1002/sdr.431. [78]

Hickel, J. et al. (2021), "Urgent need for post-growth climate mitigation scenarios", *Nature Energy*, Vol. 6/8, pp. 766-768, http://dx.doi.org/10.1038/s41560-021-00884-9. [8]

Hinton, J. (2021), *Relationship-to-Profit: A Theory of Business, Markets, and Profit for Social Ecological Economics*, Thesis for Degree of Doctor of Philosophy in Sustainability Science and Economics, Stockholm University, http://dx.doi.org/10.13140/RG.2.2.31508.73603 (accessed on 5 July 2021). [84]

IEA (2021), *The Role of Critical Minerals in Clean Energy Transitions*, World Energy Outlook Special Report, International Energy Agency, Paris, https://www.iea.org/reports/the-role-of-critical-minerals-in-clean-energy-transitions. [54]

IEA (2020), *Global EV Outlook 2020: Entering the Decade of Electric Drive*, OECD Publishing, Paris, https://doi.org/10.1787/d394399e-en. [57]

IEA (2020), *World Energy Outlook 2020*, OECD Publishing, Paris, https://dx.doi.org/10.1787/557a761b-en. [82]

IMF / OECD (2021), *Tax Policy and Climate Change: IMF/OECD Report for the G20 Finance Ministers and Central Bank Governors, April 2021, Italy*, http://www.oecd.org/tax/tax-policy/imf-oecd-g20-report-tax-policy-and-climate-change.htm (accessed on 13 September 2021). [76]

IPCC (2014), *AR5 Climate Change 2014: Mitigation of Climate Change*, Intergovernmental Panel on Climate Change, Geneva, https://www.ipcc.ch/report/ar5/wg3 (accessed on 23 June 2021). [81]

ITF (2021), *ITF Transport Outlook 2021*, OECD Publishing, Paris, https://dx.doi.org/10.1787/16826a30-en. [5]

ITF (2021), "Reversing car dependency: Summary and conclusions", *ITF Roundtable Reports*, No. 181, OECD Publishing, Paris, https://doi.org/10.1787/bebe3b6e-en. [85]

ITF (2019), "Improving transport planning and investment through the use of accessibility indicators", *International Transport Forum Policy Papers*, No. 66, OECD Publishing, Paris, https://doi.org/10.1787/46ddbcae-en. [39]

ITF (2019), "The social impacts of road pricing: Summary and conclusions", *ITF Roundtable Reports*, No. 170, OECD Publishing, Paris, https://doi.org/10.1787/d6d56d2d-en. [68]

ITF (2019), *Transport Connectivity: A Gender Perspective*, International Transport Forum, Paris, https://www.itf-oecd.org/transport-connectivity-gender-perspective (accessed on 27 August 2021). [89]

ITF (2017), *Income Inequality, Social Inclusion and Mobility*, ITF Roundtable Reports, No. 164, OECD Publishing, Paris, https://doi.org/10.1787/g2g7ae77-en. [40]

ITF (2015), *ITF Transport Outlook 2015*, OECD Publishing, Paris, https://dx.doi.org/10.1787/9789282107782-en. [80]

Jones, P. et al. (2018), *Urban Mobility: Preparing for the Future, Learning from the Past*, CREATE, https://www.researchgate.net/publication/329168103_Urban_Mobility_Preparing_for_the_Future_Learning_from_the_Past (accessed on 16 March 2021). [9]

Kamensky, J. (2021), *Jan Kamensky website*, http://www.jan-kamensky.de/ (accessed on 20 September 2021). [37]

Kamiya, G. and J. Teter (2019), "Shared, automated… and electric?", International Energy Agency, Paris, https://www.iea.org/commentaries/shared-automated-and-electric (accessed on 17 March 2021). [75]

Katwala, A. (2018), "The spiralling environmental cost of our lithium battery addiction", WIRED, https://www.wired.co.uk/article/lithium-batteries-environment-impact (accessed on 16 March 2021). [56]

Kodransky, M. and G. Hermann (2011), *Europe's Parking U-Turn: From Accommodation to Regulation*, Institute for Transportation & Development Policy, New York, NY, https://itdpdotorg.wpengine.com/wp-content/uploads/2014/07/Europes_Parking_U-Turn_ITDP.pdf. [67]

La Rue est à Nous (2021), "La rue est à nous", website, https://larueestanous.fr (accessed on 1 July 2021). [33]

Lamb, W. et al. (2020), "Discourses of climate delay", *Global Sustainability*, Vol. 3, http://dx.doi.org/10.1017/SUS.2020.13. [10]

Lamb, W. et al. (2021), "A review of trends and drivers of greenhouse gas emissions by sector from 1990 to 2018", *Environmental Research Letters*, Vol. 16/7, p. 073005, http://dx.doi.org/10.1088/1748-9326/abee4e. [42]

Litman, T. (2021), *Socially Optimal Transport Prices and Markets Principles, Strategies and Impacts*, Victoria Transport Policy Institute, Victoria, British Columbia, https://www.vtpi.org/sotpm.pdf. [6]

López, I., J. Ortega and M. Pardo (2020), "Mobility infrastructures in cities and climate change: An analysis through the superblocks in Barcelona", *Atmosphere*, Vol. 11/4, p. 410, http://dx.doi.org/10.3390/ATMOS11040410. [66]

Mattioli, G. (2013), "Car dependence, sustainability and the transport policy stalemate: The potential trade-offs between intra- and inter-generational equity", *The International Journal of Sustainability Policy and Practice*, Vol. 8/1, pp. 45-57, http://dx.doi.org/10.18848/2325-1166/cgp/v08i01/55416. [51]

Mattioli, G. et al. (2020), "The political economy of car dependence: A systems of provision approach", *Energy Research & Social Science* 66, p. 101486, http://dx.doi.org/10.1016/j.erss.2020.101486. [24]

Meadows, D. (1999), *Leverage Points: Places to Intervene in a System*, The Sustainability Institute, Hartland, VT, https://donellameadows.org/wp-content/userfiles/Leverage_Points.pdf (accessed on 16 June 2021). [79]

Moran, M. (2021), "Right of way: Race, class, and the silent epidemic of pedestrian deaths in America", *Journal of the American Planning Association*, Vol. 87/2, pp. 302-303, http://dx.doi.org/10.1080/01944363.2021.1885273. [19]

National Institute on Aging (2019), "Social isolation, loneliness in older people pose health risks", web page, https://www.nia.nih.gov/news/social-isolation-loneliness-older-people-pose-health-risks (accessed on 6 July 2021). [83]

Norton, P. (2011), *Fighting Traffic: The Dawn of the Motor Age in the American City*, The MIT Press, https://mitpress.mit.edu/books/fighting-traffic (accessed on 19 March 2021). [18]

Norton, P. (2007), "Street rivals: Jaywalking and the invention of the motor age street", *Technology and Culture*, Vol. 48/2, pp. 331-359, http://dx.doi.org/10.1353/tech.2007.0085. [21]

ODYSSEE-MURE (2020), *European Union Energy Profile: Energy Efficiency Trends and Policies*, European Union, https://www.odyssee-mure.eu/publications/efficiency-trends-policies-profiles/european-union.html (accessed on 17 March 2021). [43]

OECD (2019), *Accelerating Climate Action: Refocusing Policies through a Well-being Lens – Highlights*, OECD Publishing, Paris, https://www.oecd.org/environment/accelerating-climate-action-2f4c8c9a-en.htm (accessed on 19 April 2020). [61]

OECD (2019), *Accelerating Climate Action: Refocusing Policies through a Well-being Lens*, OECD Publishing, Paris, https://dx.doi.org/10.1787/2f4c8c9a-en. [1]

OECD (2019), *Global Material Resources Outlook to 2060: Economic Drivers and Environmental Consequences*, OECD Publishing, Paris, https://dx.doi.org/10.1787/9789264307452-en. [52]

Parking Day (n.d.), "Parking Day", website, http://www.parkingday.fr (accessed on 29 July 2021). [34]

Possible (2021), *Car Free Stories: The irresistible rise of people-friendly, clean air cities*, http://www.newweather.org (accessed on 22 September 2021). [28]

Possible (2021), *Explore a world of Car Free Cities*, https://wearepossible.github.io/carfreestories/ (accessed on 22 September 2021). [27]

Powell, S. et al. (2021), *Net Zero Transport: The Role of Spatial Planning and Place-based Solutions*, Royal Town Planning Institute, https://www.rtpi.org.uk/media/7600/rtpi-net-zero-transport-january-2021.pdf. [50]

Rosenbloom, D. et al. (2020), "Opinion: Why carbon pricing is not sufficient to mitigate climate change – and how "sustainability transition policy" can help", *Proceedings of the National Academy of Sciences*, Vol. 117/16, pp. 8664-8668, http://dx.doi.org/10.1073/pnas.2004093117. [77]

Saltmarshe, E. (2018), "Using story to change systems", *Stanford Social Innovation Review*, https://ssir.org/articles/entry/using_story_to_change_systems (accessed on 19 March 2021). [15]

Silva, C. and A. Larson (2018), "Challenges for accessibility planning and research in the context of sustainable mobility", *International Transport Forum Discussion Papers*, No. 2018/07, OECD Publishing, Paris, https://doi.org/10.1787/8e37f587-en. [38]

Sterman, J. (2000), *Business Dynamics: Systems Thinking and Modeling for a Complex World*, Irwin/McGraw-Hill, http://jsterman.scripts.mit.edu/Business_Dynamics.html (accessed on 8 March 2021). [4]

Stromberg, J. (2015), "The forgotten history of how automakers invented the crime of "jaywalking"", Vox, https://www.vox.com/2015/1/15/7551873/jaywalking-history (accessed on 10 March 2021). [14]

Swaminathen, A. (2020), "The massive environmental cost of batteries", ONiO, https://www.onio.com/article/environmental-cost-of-batteries.html (accessed on 16 March 2021). [55]

Systems Innovation (2021), *Mobility Systems Innovation*, Systems Innovation, https://www.systemsinnovation.io/post/mobility-systems-innovation (accessed on 13 August 2021). [62]

Systems Innovation (2021), *Reflexive Thinking Canvas*, Systems Innovation, https://www.systemsinnovation.io/post/reflexive-thinking-canvas (accessed on 25 March 2021). [3]

Systems Innovation (2021), *Systems Innovation Platform*, website, https://www.systemsinnovation.io (accessed on 26 August 2021). [12]

Systems Innovation (2020), *Complexity Theory: A Field Guide to Complex Systems*, Systems Innovation, https://drive.google.com/file/d/1KV9z_ZrS33dD4gLAAplWrVdzzqBRppPP/view (accessed on 26 August 2021). [13]

Taiebat, M. and M. Xu (2019), "Synergies of four emerging technologies for accelerated adoption of electric vehicles: Shared mobility, wireless charging, vehicle-to-grid, and vehicle automation", *Journal of Cleaner Production*, Vol. 230, pp. 794-797, http://dx.doi.org/10.1016/j.jclepro.2019.05.142. [73]

Te Brömmelstroet, M. (2020), "Library of cycling documentaries", *Urban Cycling Institute Blog*, https://urbancyclinginstitute.com/library-of-cycling-documentaries (accessed on 3 August 2021). [36]

Te Brömmelstroet, M. (2020), "Library of cycling marketing", *Urban Cycling Institute Blog*, https://urbancyclinginstitute.com/library-of-cycling-marketing (accessed on 3 August 2021). [35]

TfL (2018), *Vision Zero Action Plan: Taking Forward the Mayor's Transport Strategy*, Transport for London, London, http://content.tfl.gov.uk/vision-zero-action-plan.pdf. [71]

Towards Zero Foundation (n.d.), "The Safe System", web page, http://www.towardszerofoundation.org/thesafesystem (accessed on 10 August 2021). [29]

UK Department for Transport (2014), *Value for Money Assessment for Cycling Grants*, Department for Transport, London, https://assets.publishing.service.gov.uk/government/uploads/system/uploads/attachment_data/file/348943/vfm-assessment-of-cycling-grants.pdf (accessed on 25 August 2021). [87]

van Dender, K. (2019), "Taxing vehicles, fuels, and road use: Opportunities for improving transport tax practice", *OECD Taxation Working Papers*, No. 44, OECD Publishing, Paris, https://dx.doi.org/10.1787/e7f1d771-en. [69]

Ville de Paris (2021), *Retour en images sur une journée sans voiture*, https://www.paris.fr/pages/journee-sans-voiture-10107 (accessed on 22 September 2021). [32]

Vision Zero Network (n.d.), "What is the Vision Zero Network?", web page, https://visionzeronetwork.org/about/vision-zero-network (accessed on 10 August 2021). [31]

World Economic Forum (2015), *Top Ten Urban Innovations*, prepared by the Global Agenda Council on the Future of Cities, World Economic Forum, Geneva, http://www3.weforum.org/docs/Top_10_Emerging_Urban_Innovations_report_2010_20.10.pdf. [88]

Wright, D. (ed.) (2008), *Thinking in Systems*, Chelsea Green Publishing, https://www.chelseagreen.com/product/thinking-in-systems. [11]

Xu, C. et al. (2020), "Future material demand for automotive lithium-based batteries", *Communications Materials*, Vol. 1/1, pp. 1-10, http://dx.doi.org/10.1038/s43246-020-00095-x. [53]

Zenith Media (2019), *Global Intelligence: Automotive Adspend Forecasts*, Zenith Media, https://www.zenithmedia.com/wp-content/uploads/2019/03/Automotive-adspend-forecasts-2019-executive-summary.pdf (accessed on 13 August 2021). [23]

Notes

[1] Excluding water transport.

[2] The report uses system dynamics, an approach for understanding the structure and dynamics of the system being analysed, and identifies high leverage points for fostering change. Leverage points are places to intervene in a system's structure (Meadows, 1999[79]), and are based on the idea that "different types of solutions have different amounts of leverage to change the system" (Hinton, 2021[84]). Low leverage points refer to places where an action generates little change in the system's behaviour and results. High leverage points are places where an action triggers important changes in the system's behaviour and results. The closer to the root causes of a problem, the higher the leverage. For more, see Meadows (1999[79]).

[3] Tools such as the Systems Improvement Process developed by Harich (2010[78]), which combines system dynamics and root cause analysis, could be particularly useful moving forward.

[4] **The terms well-functioning, sustainable and "healthy" systems are used interchangeably throughout this report.**

[5] Even when based on evidence, defining a well-functioning system and its desirable results are, to a great extent, normative choices, as what is "rational" or "right" is socially constructed (Hinton, 2021[84]).

[6] The terms "private vehicles" and "private motorised vehicles" are used intercheangeably throughout this report. The term "cars" is often used as a shortcut for "private motorised vehicles" (i.e. including motorcycles and sport utility vehicles [SUVs]).

[7] Accessibility being the interaction between mobility and proximity (see Annex A).

[8] The "Well-being Lens" process is called as such since a first step towards better results is a decision-making process based on a well-being – rather than a GDP-focused – lens. For the transport sector, this translates into a decision-making process based on accessibility, rather than mobility (see Section 2.2.2 for a discussion).

[9] The results that a system produces depend on its cause-effect relationships, and in particular on its feedback loops (i.e. non-linear cause-effect relationships). Cause-effect relationships are often non-linear in complex systems (such as transport and urban systems), pointing to the need for a systemic approach, allowing the analyst to apprehend non-linear dynamics (Sterman, 2000[4]).

[10] "A catchment area is the area from which a city, service or institution attracts a population that uses its services" (https://en.wikipedia.org/wiki/Catchment_area).

[11] Single-use development (and logic) refers to a type of urban development in which each area focuses on a specific land use, e.g. suburbs tend to be residential neighbourhoods, places of interest are often concentrated in city centres or in specific areas (e.g. shopping malls), and offices are clustered in working districts.

[12] In 2015, private vehicles accounted for half of total passenger-kilometres in cities, or 2.6 times more than by public transport (ITF, 2021[5]). Importantly, private vehicles have much lower load factors than public transport and thus passenger-kilometres travelled by private vehicles translate into a great amount of vehicle-kilometres.

[13] Evidence from world cities shows that the intensity with which incomes translate into car ownership vary greatly, and that policies and infrastructure play an important role in changing the extent to which these are correlated (Jones et al., 2018[9]; ITF, 2015[80]).

[14] Which in turn greatly influences what is considered to be acceptable or "fair" in terms of policy decisions. The ITF (2021[85]) argues that *how to provide an equal access to car use* often dominates the policy-making discourse.

[15] For example, a report by the French Treasury finds that in very dense urban areas, car drivers pay only 8% of the full cost of driving. If less dense and urban areas are considered, they cover on average one-third of the costs (Bergerot, Comolet and Salez, 2021[86]).

[16] Supported by measurement biases when evaluating policy options. See Chapter 6.

[17] For example, on the space of a typical lane width (9-9.5 feet, 2.7-2.9 metres), an automobile can move approximately 2 000 people per hour, compared to 25 000 for heavy rail transport (Systems Innovation, 2021[62]).

[18] The UK Department for Transport (2014[87]) finds that small investments encouraging safe environments for cyclists (e.g. separate bike lanes, bike-sharing schemes, etc.) can have payouts as large as 35:1. Improved safety significantly increases cycling adoption, which can lead to better health, air quality and faster commutes (cycling is, on average, 40% faster than private motorised transport during peak hours) (World Economic Forum, 2015[88]).

[19] Figure 5.7 in IPCC (2014[81]) decomposes the evolution of fossil energy CO_2 between 1970 and 2010 as follows: changes in population (+87%), per capita GDP adjusted with purchasing power parity (PPP) (+103%), energy intensity in GDP (-35%) and CO_2 intensity of energy (-15%). The figure shows that emissions have grown in absolute terms, since the emissions reductions achieved through energy efficiency and decarbonisation efforts (decoupling strategies) have largely been offset by the continuous growth of global population and GDP. As highlighted in (OECD, 2019[1]) GDP is also a bad proxy for well-being.

[20] The *World Energy Outlook 2020* models a NZE2050 case that would reach net-zero CO_2 emissions by 2050 (IEA, 2020[82]).

[21] The studies compare three global urban transport scenarios: 1) a BAU scenario; 2) 2Revolution (assuming automation and electrification), in which the policy focus is on improving technologies, with "shift" and "avoid" efforts being second-order priorities; and 3) 3Revolution (assuming automation, electrification and shared mobility), which puts an emphasis on "avoid" and "shift" effects, through urban planning policies for higher use of active modes and shared/high-occupancy vehicles, in addition to accelerated electrification of the fleet.

[22] In this scenario, rapid automation of vehicles is also assumed, but these are mainly used as part of shared services.

[23] The Reshape+ scenario builds on the recovery to accelerate the implementation of an array of "avoid", "shift" with urban development and street redesign as central elements, while also incentivising technological change.

[24] Women depend heavily on public transport, and utilise it more than men, often resulting in longer and more numerous trips (ITF, 2019[89]).

[25] This was reflected in the decoupling-focused scenario discussed above, in which vehicle use and passenger-kilometres increase compared to the BAU scenario (Fulton, Mason and Meroux, 2017[45]).

[26] Human interactions have been found to have a significant impact on people's health. They contribute to longer lives, a higher sense of purpose and improved mood, with some research pointing to potentially improved cognitive function. It has been shown, especially among older people (who find themselves alone due to lack of transportation and mobility, retirement, or loss or separation from friends and family), that loneliness is linked to a higher risk of obesity, heart disease, anxiety, depression and Alzheimer's disease, to name a few (National Institute on Aging, 2019[83]).

[27] With the higher EV deployment featured in the Sustainable Development Scenario leading to 1.7-2 times higher material demand than in the STEP scenario.

[28] This holds even without considering the potential demand from heavy duty vehicles and other sectors in the economy (Xu et al., 2020[53]).

[29] V2G technology enables bidirectional power flows between EVs and the electricity grid (Gschwendtner, 2021[59]).

[30] Climate policies in the transport sector have often been categorised into policies that: avoid unnecessary trips and long distances; shift trips from less to more sustainable modes; and improve the fuels and technologies of vehicles used for travel.

[31] Car indepent systems are those in which a bulk of daily activities can be done without a car or a motorcycle. People only move from less emitting and space intensive modes (e.g. active, then micro-

mobiliy and public transport/ micro-transit) to the more emitting and space intensive ones (e.g. cars or motorcycles), as they make less frequent trips. Car and motorcycle use is reserved for those those trips that can create more value than the costs they impose to society (i.e. reserved for specific purposes or circumstances); but they are not systematically the most convenient, nor the only, available option in most places.

[32] The analysis could go further. Analysts may wish to explore what the political economy factors are, or which role the "rules of the game" (i.e. structure) of the economic system in which transport and urban systems are embedded play in defining such dynamics. While it is beyond the scope of this report, this is an area of interesting research for the future. The Systems Improvement Process developed by Harich (2010[78]), combining system dynamics with root cause analysis, is an interesting tool to explore the root causes of the dynamics described in this report. Likely, some of the root causes underlying the transport and urban system dynamics would also apply to other systems, such as electricity, housing or food systems, which would allow emissions to be addressed by multiple sectors simultaneously. The closer the analyst gets to the root cause of the problem, the higher the leverage point, and thus the effectiveness of the policy intervention. The closer the analyst gets to the root cause, however, the more the system's resistance to change is likely to increase.

[33] Trip chaining means grouping errands or activities into a single trip instead of returning home (or to a departure point) in between each one.

[34] In addition to better co-ordination, it is fundamental to consult and co-ordinate with businesses and people living in the areas to be redesigned.

3 Transformational change #1: From induced demand towards disappearing traffic

This chapter describes induced demand, which is identified as one of the three key dynamics underlying car dependency and high-emission transport systems. It also presents policies with the potential to reverse this dynamic, and contribute to the transition towards "disappearing" rather than growing traffic.

3.1. Traffic growth is not an inevitable result of transport systems

Most traffic growth leads to congestion.[1] Congestion, a result of an imbalance between car traffic volume and road infrastructure capacity, has been a major problem in urban settings for decades. The mobility-oriented solution to it has been to expand road capacity, by building roads, adding lanes, or modifying the flow or direction of traffic (Sterman, 2000[1]). The expansion of road capacity also includes the space allocated to parking, since roads only account for a fraction of the land devoted to cars.[2]

Road capacity expansion, illustrated in Figure 3.1, leads to a balancing feedback loop[3] and can be described as follows: when traffic volume increases, travel time increases, due to congestion. When the same trips take longer than the desired or accepted travel time, there is pressure from the population (usually private vehicle owners) to reduce congestion, so that the travel time comes closer to the desired or accepted travel time.

In Figure 3.1, traffic volume is presented as a given, an exogenous variable. This reflects the widely accepted idea that people choose to drive a car independently of the system dynamics, and that the government's role is to respond to the increased demand by increasing road capacity. Policies follow then a "predict and provide" logic: future traffic volumes, seen as exogenous, are predicted, and the policy maker's role is to "provide" a solution to the increased volumes. The solution is often expanding road infrastructure.

Figure 3.1. Road capacity expansion under a "predict and provide" mind-set

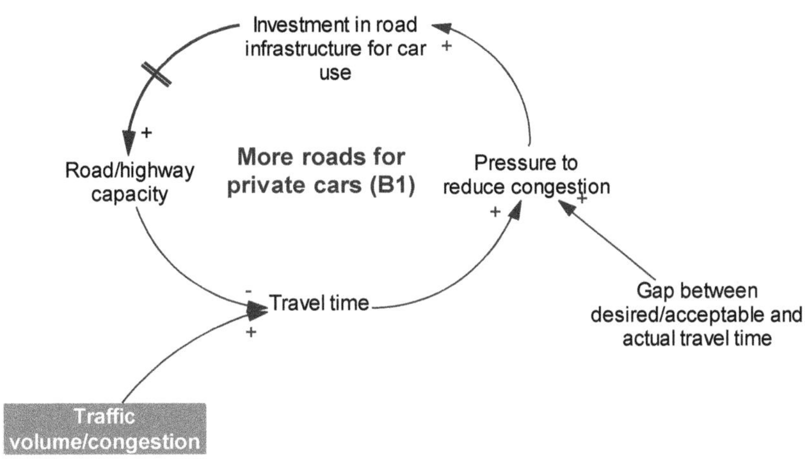

Notes: Arrows with a "+" mean that both variables move in the same direction (when one increases, the other increases and vice versa). Arrows with a "–" mean that the variables move in opposite directions (when one increases, the other decreases and vice versa). The two lines on the arrow denote a delay. The figure can be read as follows: as traffic volume/congestion increases, travel time also increases. As travel time increases, the pressure (e.g. from the population) to reduce congestion increases, which may lead to higher investments in road infrastructure for car use. Such higher investments result in higher road/highway capacity (e.g. more lanes, more roads), which in turn decreases travel time. As travel time decreases and the gap between desirable/acceptable and actual travel time closes, the pressure to reduce congestion also decreases, etc.
Source: Adapted from Sterman (2000[1]).

Traffic volume (and mobility in general) is, however, not exogenous (Sterman, 2000[1]). People's preference to drive a car is not solely the result of individual choices, but instead shaped by the type of system within which such choices are made. Urban systems[4] are currently structured in a way that makes the car the most attractive, and sometimes the only, option available. Among other factors (e.g. low-density and single-use development, explained later Chapter 5), road expansion and prioritisation of road space for car use have played, and continue to play, a key role in shaping urban and transport systems.

Figure 3.1 provides a partial view of the dynamics at play in these systems. In reality, the increase in traffic volume is endogenously incentivised, as illustrated in Figure 3.2. As road/highway capacity increases, there is less congestion and travel time decreases (the "+" in the diagram means the variables move in the "same direction", thus when congestion decreases, travel time decreases, and vice versa). Being able to travel faster increases the attractiveness of driving, incentivising more trips per day and longer distances (average trip distance), which increases traffic volume. Traffic volume increases travel time and congestion again. Evidence suggests that the dynamics described in the B2 and B3 loops (see Figure 3.2) increase traffic volume and congestion faster than the B1 loop "road capacity expansion" can reduce it (Sterman, 2000[1]). This explains why, despite the rapid expansion of road infrastructure, the average time spent in traffic has steadily increased, which can increase emissions and pollution, but also negatively affect people's well-being. Figure 3.2 sheds light on this phenomenon by which road expansion increases car traffic, and which is known as induced demand (WSP and RAND Europe, 2018[2]).

Figure 3.2. Induced demand

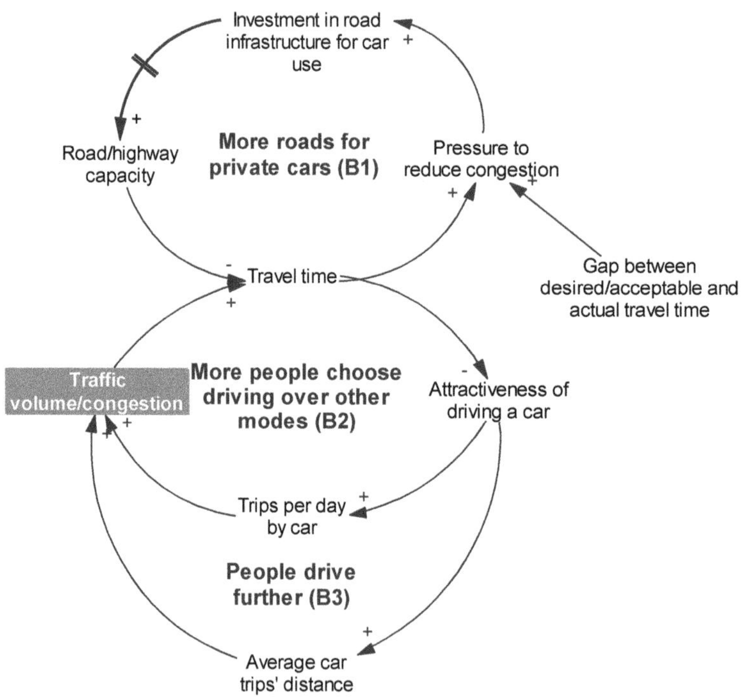

Notes: Arrows with a "+" mean that both variables move in the same direction (when one increases, the other increases and vice versa). Arrows with a "–" mean that the variables move in opposite directions (when one increases, the other decreases and vice versa). The two lines on the arrow denote a delay. The lower loops of this figure can be read as follows (see Figure 3.1 for the upper loop): as traffic volume/congestion increases, travel time decreases, which increases the attractiveness of driving a car. This in turn may increase the number of trips per day by car, and encourage people to drive longer distances. Both more frequent and longer trips contribute to the increase in traffic volume/congestion, which increases travel time. As travel time increases, the attractiveness of driving a car decreases, etc.
Source: Adapted from Sterman (2000[1]).

As explained in detail in Section 2.2.2, the increase in traffic volume and its negative impacts are not a fatality; they are the consequence of urban and transport systems shaped and structured around a mobility-oriented logic. Induced demand has been a well-known dynamic in transport analysis since the 1990s (SACTRA, 1994[3]), and a number of studies have quantified the phenomenon since then. For instance, using data from 2000 to 2016, Iracheta Carroll (2020[4]) found that in the Mexico City Metropolitan Area,[5] around 2 000 additional vehicles enter the fleet for every USD 11.3 million (MXN 100 million PPP) spent on road-related infrastructure. In 2016, investment in road-related infrastructure reached USD 981 million, which would have induced an increase in the vehicle fleet of 165 000-185 000 additional vehicles, or about one-third of the additional vehicles that entered the vehicle fleet that year.

While the evidence from transport analysis on the phenomenon of induced demand (illustrated in the three dynamics in Figure 3.3) is strong, most countries have not re-examined their mobility-oriented logic when it comes to transport policy and investment decisions (ITF, 2019[5]). For example, appraisal and planning frameworks in most countries are still focused on mobility and travel time savings[6] (ITF, 2019[5]). This biases policy decisions towards privileging road infrastructure (ITF, 2019[5]). This bias is also reinforced by the "proximity blind spot" (see Section 2.2.2), which implies that investment decisions pay little or no attention to the creation of proximity , which is fundamental for "healthy"[7] transport systems, as explained in Section 2.1. In addition, road capacity expansion implies that a higher share of public space, and investment, is allocated to car driving and parking to the detriment of other modes and uses of public space beyond transport, further limiting the possibility of creating proximity, and also reducing the attractiveness of active and shared modes. The creation of proximity is also physically made difficult by road capacity expansion, as this causes community severance[8] (Anciaes, Jones and Mindell, 2015[6]).

The increase in traffic volume described above is not without consequences. Some of the negative impacts of such an increase include carbon dioxide (CO_2) emissions, air pollution and road accidents, among others (ITF, 2020[7]; Jones et al., 2018[8]) (Figure 3.3).

Figure 3.3. The impacts of induced demand

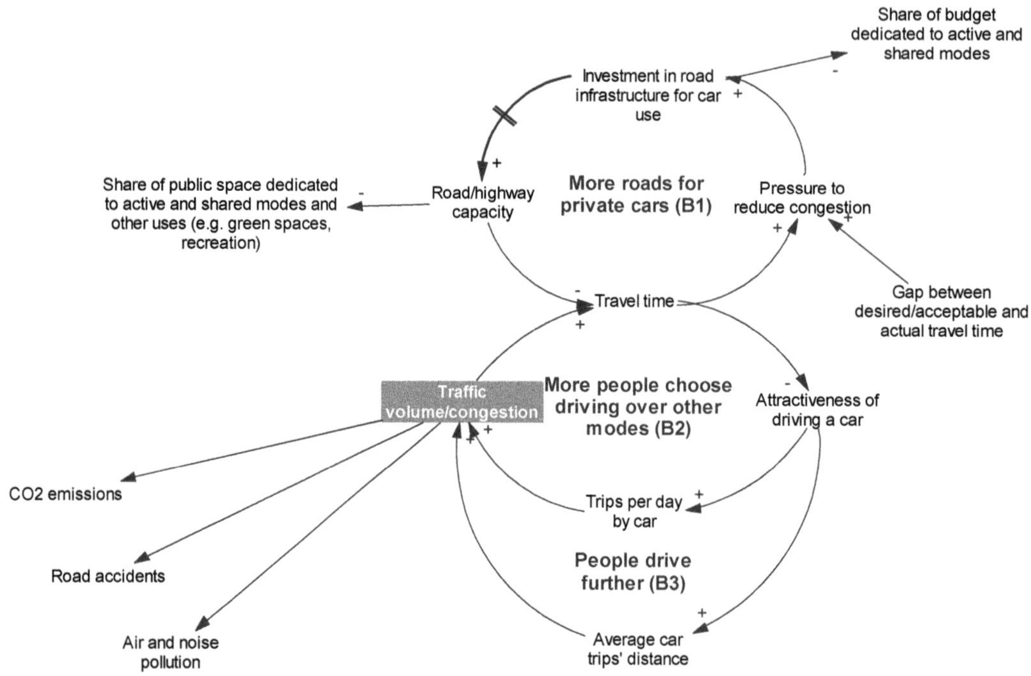

Notes: Arrows with a "+" mean that both variables move in the same direction (when one increases, the other increases and vice versa). Arrows with a "–" mean that the variables move in opposite directions (when one increases, the other decreases and vice versa). The two lines on the arrow denote a delay. This figure describes some of the results from the dynamics triggered by high investment in road infrastructure for car use. These include: a low share of public space dedicated to active and shared modes and other uses, a low share of budget dedicated to active and shared modes, high levels of CO_2 emissions, road accidents, and air and noise pollution.
Source: Adapted from Sterman (2000[1]).

As will be explained in more detail in Chapters 4 and 5, induced demand triggers, and is at the same time reinforced by, a number of other vicious cycles (i.e. feedback loops that generate undesirable outcomes). As a result, car dependency increases, which also limits the policy options available to mitigate transport emissions and the negative consequences related to an increase in traffic (see, for example, Chapter 6 for a discussion on how car dependency affects the feasibility, and thus effectiveness, of carbon prices).

The next section presents policy tools with the potential to reverse this dynamic and contribute to the transition towards transport systems that result in "disappearing", rather than growing, traffic.

3.2. Putting street redesign and improved management of public space at the core of climate strategies

As explained in Section 2.1, the current structure of transport (and urban) systems, which can be thought of as the way in which territories are organised, performs poorly in terms of the sustainable delivery of accessibility and, thus, of well-being. How public space is designed and used is a crucial element of this. This report calls for climate strategies for the transport sector that, at their core, focus on the reallocation and redesign of public space, as well as on improving the way in which public space is managed. This is central for reverting induced demand, and for territories to ensure sustainable accessibility (i.e. easy access to places and opportunities via sustainable transport modes).

Section 3.2.1 introduces the concepts of Complete Streets and Place-making, which reflect a shift in mind-set and can be seen as guidelines for policies focused on redesigning public space and improving the management of public space. Section 3.2.2 introduces good practice examples, including by using radical street redesign, parking policy and road pricing. It also discusses implementation challenges. Chapter 4 discusses the wider organisation of territories, going beyond public space.

3.2.1. A mind-set shift: Making public space about people and places

Today, most public space is allocated to roads for cars. It is estimated that 50% of public space in European cities is dedicated to roads (EIT Urban Mobility, n.d.[9]). This is the case, for example, in Paris, despite private cars accounting for 15% of trips[9] (ITF, 2021[10]) and significant efforts to reallocate public space. This sheds light on how unequal the "starting point" is in terms of the allocation of public space. Creutzig et al. (2020[11]) analyse public space allocation in Berlin (see Figure 3.4). Figure 3.4 compares the public space dedicated to different transport modes (excluding public transport)[10] to the share of people using such a mode. Note that public space is disproportionately allocated to cars, even when Berlin is not among the countries with the highest motorisation rate (342 cars per 1 000 residents).

Figure 3.4. Berlin's allocation of public space in comparison to the city's modal shares

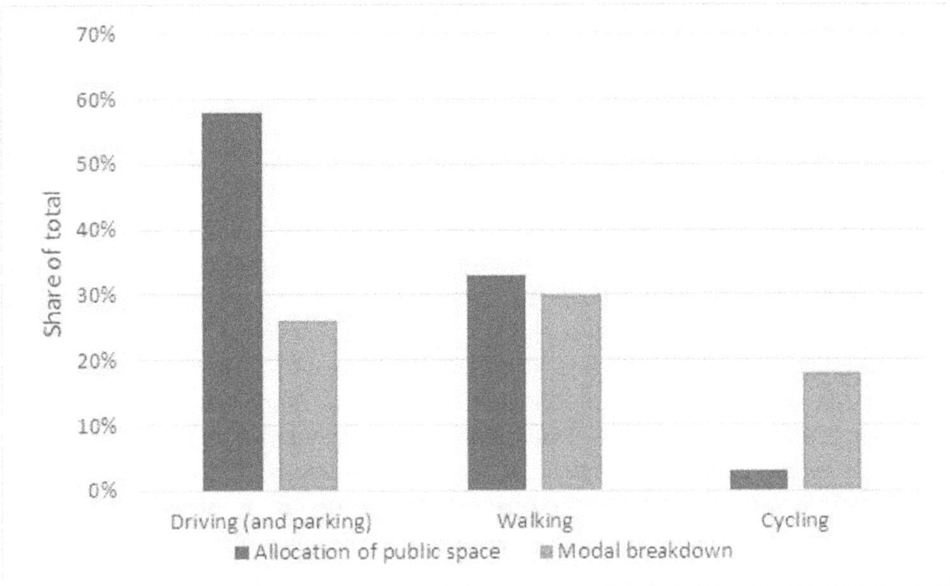

Notes: Data are not given for the allocation of street space for public transportation.
Sources: Authors, based on Creutzig et al. (2020[11]); Berlin.de (n.d.[12]).

The privilege given to cars increases their attractiveness, leading people to "choose" driving over other means of transportation (see Chapter 5 for a discussion on the resulting performance gap between public transport and cars). Colville-Andersen (2018[13]) coined the term "arrogance of space" to highlight the mismatch between the share of public space allocated to the different means of transportation and the modal split. While there have been improvements in terms of biking infrastructure in a number of cities, the space allocated to bike lanes is still marginal compared to that dedicated to cars and motorcycles. For example, in Amsterdam, 51% of the public space is allocated to cars and motorcycles, against 7% for bike lanes (while the modal share for bicycles is 27%) and 40% for pedestrian infrastructure (Nello-Deakin,

2019[14]). On average, car users have 3.5 times more space available on a street than non-car users (Creutzig et al., 2020[11]). Also, according to UN-Habitat (2016[15]), the area accessible within walking distance from an arterial road declined by 10% on average (with significant variabilities across regions) between 1990 and 2015. Intersection density,[11] an indicator of the ease with which a person can shorten travel distances by walking or cycling, also declined across the globe over the same time period (UN-Habitat, 2016[15]). Blocks have also dramatically increased in size – from 3.8 to 5.2 hectares on average (1990-2015) – even though evidence suggests that large blocks reduce walkability and foster traffic congestion (UN-Habitat, 2016[15]). The report concludes that "the global trend toward large blocks with limited intersections significantly compromises walking and biking, making cities less pedestrian and bicycle friendly."

Significant street redesign and reallocation towards more sustainable transport modes, as well as towards uses beyond transport, is a necessary condition to transition towards "healthier" transport systems. In terms of the reallocation of space, prioritising walking, cycling, micro-mobility and public transport (along with investment in more and better infrastructure for these modes) is key to changing their relative competitiveness *vis-à-vis* the car. This is important for having safer and more convenient active and shared modes and for people to choose them, which can lead to significant CO_2 emissions reductions as well as greater well-being improvements, such as better health and safety. In addition, the reallocation of public space (and in particular of roads) towards other uses can facilitate the creation of proximity. For example, public space previously allocated to roads can become parks or recreational areas, increasing accessibility to green spaces, often limited in urban settings. In sum, rethinking the allocation, design and use of public space is key to restoring the balance between mobility and proximity, making the sustainable delivery of accessibility possible. Moreover, as will be discussed in Chapter 4, urban renewal and new development strategies can importantly build on Complete Streets and Place-making approaches (see below) to redesign and reshape cities, even beyond public space.

Projects with street redesign elements such as bus rapid transit,[12] bicycle lanes and pedestrian streets have been growing in number. These projects are, however, often *ad hoc* interventions rather than part of a wider reflection of what streets should look like or could be used for.

The concepts of Complete Streets and Place-making are key to guide the shift in mind-set needed for more systemic street redesign and management. Complete Streets is an approach aiming to safely balance space between different transport modes (walking, cycling, public transport, private vehicles, commercial activities and residential areas) (Box 3.1) (Welle et al., 2018[16]). Complete Streets principles have been associated to greenhouse gas reductions and air quality improvements, as they entail the renovation of street corridors in ways that encourage a modal shift from cars to more sustainable modes (Perk et al., 2015[17]) (see Section 3.2.2 for the example of Barcelona's Superblocks). They have also been associated to economic benefits, such as the increase in sales by local shops.[13] As expressed by Yusuf et al. (2016[18]), "[T]he turn to Complete Streets is a major change in urban street design, as it fundamentally redefines what a street is intended to do, what goals a transportation agency is going to meet, and how the community will spend its transportation funds".

Box 3.1. Complete Streets

While there is no singular design prescription, the main elements of the Complete Street approach include prioritising space for pedestrians (i.e. sidewalks, crosswalks), implementing traffic calming measures,* accommodating bicycles (i.e. protected or dedicated bicycle lanes) and dedicating space for public transport (i.e. bus rapid transit, transit signal priority, bus shelters) (Litman, 2015[19]). The planning of freight and delivery services as part of Complete Streets approaches has also been identified as key to avoid unintended negative consequences (see Box 3.6).

Welle et al. (2018[16]) summarise the main principles behind the Complete Streets approach:

- Accessibility needs to come first. Streets need to focus on providing accessibility before vehicle flow and capacity, aiming at universal accessibility.
- Inclusive design. Streets need to aim at fair and democratic design by favouring the most vulnerable users.
- Safety principles. Street design needs to care for the comfort and well-being of its users.
- Effective for all citizens. Streets need to take into account impacts, benefits, and costs for all users of the city.
- Urban integration. Street design needs to integrate multi-functionality, compatibility and diversity of use.
- Continuity. Streets are envisioned not only in a plan or street section, but consistent in space and time along their corridor.

While still marginal, the adoption of the Complete Streets approach has progressively expanded. In the United States, for instance, already in 2014, 30 states had policies encouraging their adoption, either through issuing laws or executive-level policies (Yusuf et al., 2016[18]). The adoption of the Complete Streets approach has also permeated practice in cities in developing countries, where 90% of road fatalities occur. Cities like São Paulo and Fortaleza in Brazil, Mumbai in India, Bogotá in Colombia, and Shanghai in the People's Republic of China, have all, for instance, participated in a global initiative supported by Bloomberg which aims at redesigning some of these cities' main avenues and neighbourhoods. In Mexico, the Ministry of Territorial, Agrarian and Urban Development developed a manual on the Complete Streets approach to support cities in adopting the approach in 2019. In September 2020, it also launched a new national strategy (4S) on healthy, safe, sustainable and inclusive mobility that aligns with such principles (Ministry of Territorial, Agrarian and Urban Development, 2020[20]). Whether this will be accompanied by the reallocation of funds, however, remains to be seen.

Despite this, the adoption of Complete Streets is not always linked nor seen as central to climate action Moreover, practice tends to be confined to "pilot-" type projects rather than seen as wide-scale action. Superblocks in Barcelona are a concrete counterexample of the implementation of Complete Streets-like approaches as a centrepiece of climate action, which is planned to guide a wide-scale transformation (see Section 3.2.2).

* "Traffic calming consists of physical design and other measures put in place on existing roads to reduce vehicle speeds and improve safety for pedestrians and cyclists. For example, vertical deflections (speed humps, speed tables and raised intersections), horizontal shifts and roadway narrowing are intended to reduce speed and enhance the street environment for non-motorists. Closures that obstruct traffic movements in one or more directions, such as median barriers, are intended to reduce cut-through traffic. Traffic calming measures can be implemented at an intersection, street, neighbourhood or area-wide level" (US Department of Transportation, n.a.[21]).

Closely linked to the Complete Streets approach is the concept of "Place-making", i.e. the notion that streets have a "place" function, in addition to a "connection" or "link" function. The Place-making concept complements the notion of Complete Streets by highlighting that streets and public space need to accommodate uses beyond transport: streets need to allow people to access places, but also have other functions, such as allowing commercial exchanges, leisure and fostering community interactions (Savills, 2016[22]). As highlighted by (Jones, 2009[23]), different streets might have a different balance between their "link" and "place" function. This might also lead to choosing what transport modes might be more suitable to perform the "link" function in one area or another (see, for instance, the case of Superblocks in Section 3.2.2, where most traffic is channelled to the streets surrounding the new blocks). Planning according to the two notions is also synergetic, as prioritising space for more sustainable, and space-efficient modes (in accordance with the Complete Streets notion), can also leave more space available for Place-making.

Other concepts, such as Healthy Streets (Healthy Streets, 2021[24]), Liveable Streets (Tower Hamlets Council, n.d.[25]), Happy Cities (Happy City, n.d.[26]) or people-based planning (Jones, Marshall and Boujenko, 2008[27]) designate similar ideas and combine Complete Streets and Pace-making notions to different degrees. These also highlight the potential synergies between climate and wider well-being benefits (e.g. health, quality of life) that can be made when rethinking the design and allocation of public space. In this respect, Place-making and Complete Streets approaches can also bring synergies between climate and road safety improvements if taking a "safe system approach" when designing Complete Streets. A safe system approach is based on a comprehensive and systemic view of the underlying causes of serious road injuries and deaths (also helping to question the assumption that road fatalities are inevitable externalities; see Chapter 2). Rather than strongly focusing on adherence to the "rules of the road" and assigning most of the responsibility to road users, a safe system approach starts from the principle that human errors are inevitable, but if the road system is adequately designed, then serious injuries and deaths can be avoided (WRI, 2018[28]). A safe system approach argues for action in a number of areas that affect street design (e.g. speed management, intersection design that prioritises safe crossings, road design that is adapted to human error). It is therefore a complementary approach to Complete Streets; ensuring in this way that street reconfiguration also paves the way towards ambitious road safety goals (e.g. Vision Zero, see Box 2.2).

Importantly, Complete Streets and Place-making approaches are not only relevant for large urban areas Space reallocation to multiple uses in the municipality of Groningen provides a concrete example of the potential of the mind-set shifts described above applied to a smaller city (233 218 inhabitants). Freiburg (231 195 population), and Pontevedra (83 000 population) (see Chapter 4) and numerous other (small and big) cities are also moving in this direction and applying these principles both for street redesign as well as for spatial planning. In the case of Pontevedra, a number of measures to radically change street allocation and redesign, as well as parking policy have been coupled with a shift in mind-set for spatial planning (see next Chapter). Moreover, as highlighted in (Box 3.2) the shift in mind-set can also be useful and is actually necessary in rural areas.

Box 3.2. The relevance of Complete Streets for rural areas

The Illinois Department of Public Health developed an implementation guide for adapting the Complete Streets approach to rural areas. The guide highlights work done in certain areas (e.g. Momence, population of 3 300, and Grand Park, population of 1 243) (Dolin et al., 2014[29]). The document highlights a number of reasons why the approach is relevant in a rural[1] environment. As the guidelines discuss, rural areas have a disproportionate share of cyclist and pedestrian fatalities[2] and relatively high shares of obesity. Even when other factors can play a role (e.g. lower incomes, poor quality diets), a Complete Streets approach could contribute to solving both problems by helping promote safer physical activity within these areas (Dolin et al., 2014[29]). In addition, it could also help better connect people to grocery stores and other relevant services that are often located where access by foot, bike or public transport is unsafe or difficult (e.g. the outskirts of the town). It would also facilitate access by more affordable modes, providing relief to some poor communities that allocate large shares of their income to car ownership and operation. Finally, the report identifies as a key challenge the fact that rural roads are often completely managed by state-level authorities, which reflects a focus on facilitating car and truck movement through the towns (Dolin et al., 2014[29]). It argues that a more balanced approach, looking at the needs of the local community and involving different levels of government, could build in the Complete Streets principles to strike a better balance.

1. Defined as "small towns, individual communities, and clusters of communities that are not considered part of a metropolitan area".
2. While rural areas in the United States concentrate less than 20% of the population, but they concentrate 26% of pedestrian fatalities and 31% of cyclist fatalities.

Despite numerous initiatives and the multiple benefits associated to these approaches, public space today is still, in most places, mainly designed with a focus on increasing speeds (OECD, 2015[30]). The priority of infrastructure provision, planning and design is often given to longer, rather than shorter, trips and the transport modes associated to longer trips (e.g. space allocated to cars rather than to cycling or walking). Litman (2008[31]) identifies appraisal and planning methods as key barriers for the redesign of streets following Complete Streets approaches for instance. Because methodologies are focused on estimating and monetising the direct costs of projects, as well as impacts on travel time and vehicle operating savings, they leave policy makers ill-equipped to value the multiple benefits arising from a Complete Street approach. For example, while collision and emissions rates may be captured in measurement frameworks, these frameworks often do not account for: impacts on the accessibility of non-drivers; reducing sprawl, to which Complete Streets can provide some help by creating more attractive places in more central areas; travel choice; comfort; physical activity and related health; or aspects such as energy use, noise, equity, and aesthetic and community aspects of the urban environment (Litman, 2008[31]). In addition, impacts of the individual components of Complete Streets are often modest, but the effects of the different elements put together in a Complete Streets retrofit project are cumulative and synergistic (Litman, 2021[32]). This is, however, challenging to measure with current methodologies.

Appraisal and planning frameworks need therefore to evolve to facilitate the type of street redesign that can unleash emissions reductions and improve well-being[14]. In the United Kingdom, Transport for London (TfL) has developed a Healthy Streets policy, which aims at placing people, and their health, at the centre of street design. The policy is guided by ten elements that are used as indicators to judge whether a street is healthy. Green infrastructure is considered a major component of this policy: in addition to human health, a healthy street needs to enhance biodiversity and aim at ecological resilience (TfL, n.d.[33]). According to TfL, green infrastructure provides "a wide range of benefits, [and] it is one of the most cost-effective ways for TfL and others to meet the environmental and social requirements of the London Plan" (TfL, n.d.[33]). To facilitate the implementation and monitoring of the Healthy Streets policy, TfL has developed a number of guiding documents and tools. Box 3.3 summarises the ten guiding indicators used by TfL to determine how healthy a street is and two innovative tools that are used to implement the Healthy Streets policy.

Box 3.3. Transport for London's tools to support the implementation and monitoring of the Healthy Streets policy

Ten guiding indicators to determine if a street is healthy:

1. They are welcoming places for everyone to walk, spend time in and engage in community life.
2. People choose to walk, cycle and use public transport.
3. There is clean air.
4. People feel safe.
5. The street is not too noisy.
6. It is easy to cross, in order to encourage more walking and to enable connections between communities.
7. It has places that allow people to stop and rest.
8. It has facilities that provide shade and shelter.
9. Its features make people feel relaxed (e.g. through pavement and cycle paths that are not overcrowded, in poor condition or dirty).
10. There are "things to see and do", i.e. streets also provide interesting things, such as street art or attractive views.

Healthy Street Check for designers

The Healthy Street Check is a spreadsheet that allows designers to check the consistency of a certain scheme against the policy's ten indicators. It also supports them in communicating the potential improvements to the public. Projects are assessed at various times. The tool is first used to assess the state of the street before the intervention, guiding the choices between different design options. It is also used in later stages to help further develop the chosen design in detail. The tool assigns a score to the scheme, which can only increase if projects improve safety and prioritise walking, cycling and access to public transport. Projects that are expected to improve walking, cycling and access to public transport are required to be tested against the tool.

Healthy Streets Mystery Shopper Survey

The Healthy Streets Mystery Shopper Survey is a system of dedicated surveys realised in a 100-metre stretch of streets where the surveyor assesses the street against approximately 100 metrics that correspond to the different indicators of the Healthy Street policy. Responses are entered into the system in real time using an app. The information allows the auditor to measure the performance of the street in nine out of the ten indicators based on a score (all except air quality). The system is used to monitor changes in terms of healthy street performance across the city and time. "Before" and "after" surveys are also used to monitor changes after improvement projects. A core sample of 1 520 sites in the city street network (around 1%) is assessed each year, providing a continuous flow of information on the network's conditions. City-wide scores are communicated in addition to the assessment of specific sites.

The Healthy Street Check for Designers and the Healthy Streets Mystery Shopper Survey are seen as complementary tools to provide a fuller picture of street design and appraisal. On the one hand, the Healthy Streets Check can provide "objective" elements that schemes would need to incorporate. On the other, the Mystery Shopper Survey generates data on users' experience when in a certain street.

Source: TfL (2017[34]).

The UCL Centre for Transport Studies and the Bartlett School of Planning developed a methodology that helps classify streets depending on their functions for all street users (UCL, 2014[35]). The methodology is called "link and place" and is based on the idea that streets are not only for connecting or linking places, but are also "places". It situates roads in a matrix, according to their place (as a destination) and link (significance for movement) status. The different combinations of place and link status lead to classifying streets into different categories. This allows identifying the design requirements that are needed to adequately fulfil the specific combined function of a given street (Jones, 2009[36]).

Australia, Ireland, New Zealand and the United Kingdom are a few countries that have used the link and place methodology. The government of South Australia used it to upgrade its street network, while Ireland included the methodology in the *Design Manual for Urban Roads and Streets* (UCL, 2014[35]). The UK Department for Transport and the Department for Communities and Local Government have incorporated link and place principles[15] into their national guidelines. The Mayor of London's Roads Task Force and TfL require boroughs to use the link and place methodology as classification for roads in their bids for funding. The principles also guided the award of a GBP 650 Private Finance Initiative (PFI) project to the London Borough of Hounslow to upgrade and maintain its street network over a 25-year period. Birmingham has also based the analysis of its streets network on the link and place methodology for taking decisions on street design and allocation. In New Zealand, the link and place methodology was used with the aim of better integrating land use and transport by cities such as Auckland, Tauranga and Christchurch. It was then used as a basis for a national-level framework (the One Network Framework) to classify the entire road network and guide planning and investment decisions differently by giving more weight to factors such as the strategic significance of roads and its adjacent land use. The One Network Framework has brought together key stakeholders: urban planners, traffic engineers, transport planners and urban designers (Waka Kotahi NZ Transport Agency, 2021[37]).

The Institute for Transportation and Development Policy also provides some guidelines to facilitate street redesign (and in particular the Complete Streets notion). The institute establishes the following hierarchy of users to whom priority should be given: 1) pedestrian access; 2) non-motorised vehicle movement and parking; 3) public transport; 4) non-motorised goods carriers; 5) freight movement; 6) taxi services/car-pooling/car-sharing; 7) private motor vehicle movement; and 8) private motor vehicle parking (ITDP, 2016[38]).

In sum, as explained at the beginning of this section, reducing emissions at the pace and scale needed while improving people's well-being requires the reallocation and redesign of streets (and public space), as well as improved space management. The concepts of Complete Streets and Place-making, as well as the different frameworks introduced in this section, can guide such a process. While this process may sometimes seem to be an "impossible" endeavour, efforts in this direction made during the COVID-19 pandemic and lockdown periods have shown that these changes can be rapid, and can trigger important effects in the short term (see Chapter 7).

This does not imply that street redesign is an easy process. Section 3.2.2, for example, describes the multiple challenges encountered by Superblocks in Barcelona, a reference example of radical street redesign. The reader is urged, however, not to minimise the limitations that opting for strategies that avoid engaging in systemic redesign will bring. For example, focusing on electrification might be seen as a relatively easy option compared to street redesign in terms of political economy. However, reducing emissions at the pace and scale needed via vehicle electrification in systems or territories with growing traffic volumes is (as mentioned above) very challenging and can compromise the attainment of a number of other goals. The evitable trade-offs and the potential untapped synergies that arise from decoupling-type policies (see Chapter 2) should therefore be taken into consideration when comparing and prioritising policies.

The next subsection presents concrete policy examples of street redesign and the improved management of public space based on a Complete Streets and Place-making logic.

3.2.2. Unleashing emissions reduction opportunities via street redesign and improved management of public space

Policies to redesign streets and better manage public space should have a central role in climate strategies moving forward, but instead these policies are today marginal in climate strategies. Policies to redesign streets and better manage public space can not only stop, but revert, the induced demand dynamic described in Section 3.1. In other words they can result in "disappearing traffic" (Box 3.4), and make sustainable modes central to how people move daily.

In the Netherlands, for instance, improving the conditions for safe biking has been a priority at all levels of government for decades, which has translated into the country having exceptional levels of bicycle ownership and use (there are 17 million inhabitants and 22.8 million bicycles in the country (Netherlans, 2021[39])).The "Tour de Force" programme for example brings together government, private players, research institutions and platforms to empower cycling (see (Tour de Force, 2021[40])). Their target is to increase the total cycling kilometres by 20% from 2017 to 2027, which would make the Netherlands even more unrivalled in the use of bicycles than it already is in the present. In 2018, bicycle use covered 27% of all journeys in the country, which scored much higher than the next biggest cycling nations, Denmark (around 18%) and Germany (10%) (KiM, 2018[41]).

Street design efforts and the provision of adequate and sufficient infrastructure are at the centre of how the Netherlands has succeeded in making cycling one of the most viable transport modes. In Amsterdam the Long-Term Bicycle Plan puts cycling into the heart of urban development and aims to offer seamless biking infrastructure, easier parking facilities and better biking behaviour (City of Amsterdam, 2021[42]). The plan includes guidelines to make cycling routes car-free or separate paths of at least 2.5 metres in width, reflecting a mind-set that effectively favours cycling in terms of street space allocation. Nation-wide, 35000 kilometres of bicycle tracks and 25 cycle superhighways in use or under construction enable bikers to get from origin to destination without major disturbances ((Netherlans, 2021[39]), (Netherlands, 2021[43])). For example, the "RijnWaalpad" highway of 15.8 kilometres (or 18 km when considering the connections to the respective city centre) connects the Arnhem and Nijmegen train stations with tunnels and bridges to make the trip enjoyable and seamless ((n.a.), n.d.[44]). To improve the multimodal use of bikes and trains, train stations in the Netherlands provide large bike parking facilities. An impressive example is the world's largest bike parking facility in the Utrecht Central Station with three storeys and room for 12500 bicycles. The bike-train combination has been proven to work as around half of all train travellers reach the station by bike (BiTiBi, 2017[45]). The national Tour de Force programme aims to build on technology to make cycling even easier by, for example, programming traffic lights to turn green when cyclists approach or creating a system that indicates free spaces in bicycle parking facilities (Tour de Force, 2021[40]).

This section introduces other examples of policies to redesign streets and better manage public space. The next subsection introduces Barcelona's Superblocks, which are an example of street redesign guided by a combination of Complete Streets and place-making ideas. It explains what Superblocks are, what impacts have been observed and which challenges were encountered for their implementation. It then discusses the role that parking policies and road prices could play in street redesign, improved management of road and public space, and related emissions reductions. This section also addresses key implementation challenges for the different policies put forward.

Box 3.4. Evidence of disappearing traffic

The reallocation of road space to favour active (walking and cycling), micro-mobility or public transport modes has often raised claims that traffic is simply displaced to surrounding areas. Nonetheless, case studies investigating this issue show that such impacts are, in general, temporary and smaller in scale than predicted, and thus much of the traffic "disappears" over time. For instance, based on work and evidence from European cities, the European Commission (2009[46]) concludes that "traffic problems following the implementation of a scheme are usually far less serious than predicted; after an initial period of adjustment, some of the traffic that was previously found in the vicinity of the scheme 'disappears' or 'evaporates', due to drivers changing their travel behaviour; as a result, the urban environment becomes more liveable in many respects".

This is also confirmed by Cairns, Atkins and Goodwin (2002[47]), who examine more than 70 case studies of road reallocation in 11 different countries. They judge predictions of traffic problems caused by road space reallocation as "unnecessarily alarmist" and argue that rather "significant reductions in overall traffic levels can occur" if the right conditions are sought. They find an average traffic reduction across the 70 case studies of 21.9%. The median value was 10.6%, meaning that in half of the cases studied, 10.6% or more of the vehicles previously travelling through the area of intervention or the surrounding areas were not found to have rerouted after the space reallocation.

The ITF (2021[10]) brings additional evidence from recent interventions. For instance, in Oslo, interventions on three main roads, which reduced road capacity for car use, resulted in a reduction of car use for commuting of between 16% and 21%, without severe consequences in terms of delays or congestion (ITF, 2021[10]). Another example is Copenhagen, where space designated for car use on a thoroughfare bridge was reduced to increase space for walking, cycling and public transport.

Nonetheless, the literature also points to the importance of undertaking communication and consultation, and careful design, implementation and monitoring. As discussed in Cairns, Atkins and Goodwin (2002[47]), the way schemes are perceived by the public and reported in the media is key. Discussions later in this section provide information on some lessons learnt in this respect.

Sources: Based on European Commission (2009[46]); Cairns, Atkins and Goodwin (2002[47]); ITF (2021[10]).

Radical street redesign holds enormous opportunities: Barcelona's Superblocks

Among the most iconic examples that bring together Complete Streets and Place-making and where climate has been a central focus is that of Superblocks in Barcelona. The development of superblocks is part of the city's response to numerous challenges. Among them are the lack of green space and heat island effects, high noise and pollution, and high transport CO_2 emissions (accounting for 36% of total city CO2 emissions) (Ajuntamient de Barcelona and BCNecología, 2020[48]). The implementation of Superblocks constitutes an exceptional example where transformational action, based on redesigning the urban and transport system, has been put at the centre of climate (both mitigation and adaptation) and other (e.g. green infrastructure, biodiversity) plans and targets (Zografos et al., 2020[49]). To date, six Superblocks have been implemented, which has meant the reconfiguration of 143 hectares in the city, and three more are already being planned (López, Ortega and Pardo, 2020[50]). When fully implemented, the superblocks project will imply a significant reconfiguration of the entire city (in total 503 superblocks are planned and these will cover the entire Barcelona municipality).

The model of mobility and public space based on Superblocks establishes a network that integrates in its perimeter the circulation of all modes of transport. The network of Superblocks reorganises the city into polygons of approximately 400 m x 400 m and around 5 000-6 000 resident population. Inner roads are not closed to motorised vehicles, as these can enter the superblock but they cannot cross it (and have to stay within a speed limit of 10 km/h). The loop system (see Figure 3.5) allows the car to enter the superblock and have access to houses/services in every block, but it forces it to exit through the same side it entered it, since it is not possible to cross the superblock. Sometimes the passage of motorised vehicles inside the superblocks is reserved only for residents, services and urban distribution. Pedestrians and bicycles can cross the superblocks in both directions. Superblocks support in this way converting streets from a single function (basically right-of-ways for vehicles) to spaces with multiple functions (including those as a place) and uses (Ajuntament de Barcelona, 2014[51]) (Rueda, 2019[52]).

Figure 3.5. Road hierarchy in the Superblock model

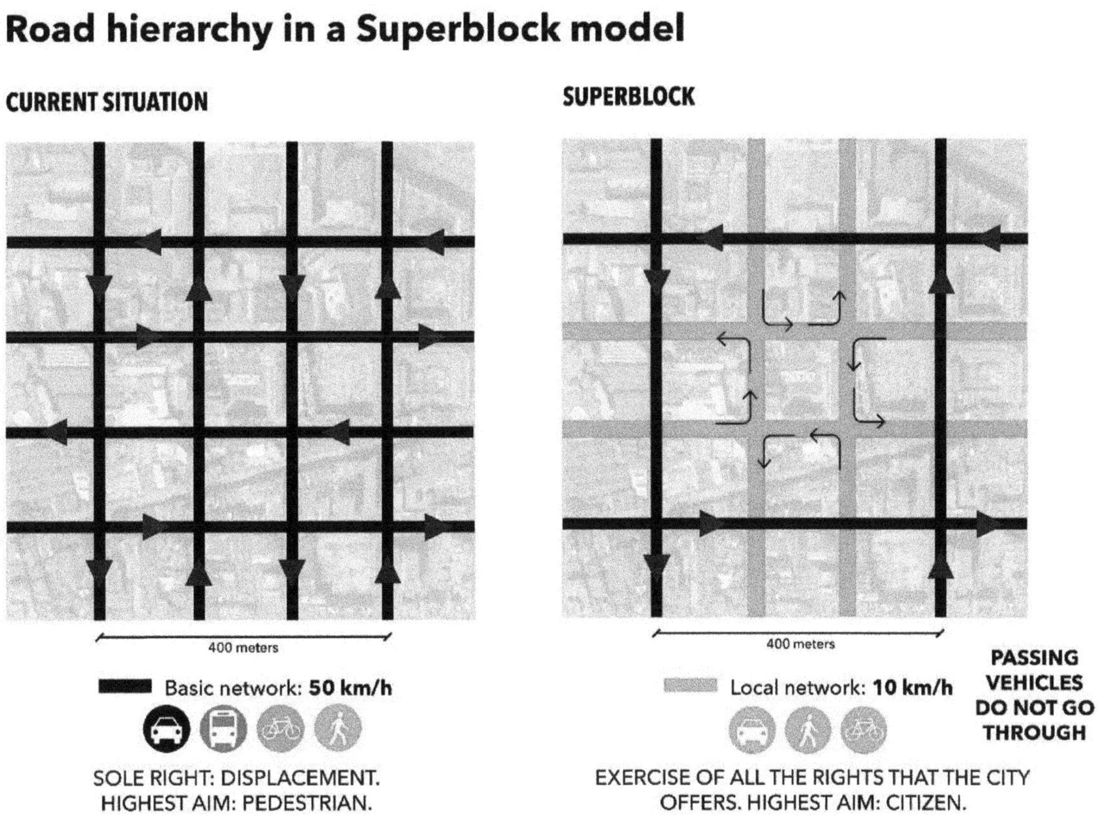

Source: Authors.

The Superblocks model seeks, first of all, to liberate the maximum surface of public space dedicated to traffic, while at the same time ensuring the functionality of the system. By adopting the Superblocks model 70% of space dedicated to traffic could be liberated while only reducing total car travel by 15% (a percentage similar to the traffic reduction in Barcelona due to the 2008 economic crisis), and also maintaining current traffic speeds. Secondly, the model seeks to minimize the dysfunctions generated by the current mobility model (Rueda, 2020[53]).

The mobility plan (PMUS 2018-2024), aims however to go beyond and reduce traffic by 21% by 2024 (Rueda, 2019[54]), while having 79% of all trips made by walking, cycling or public transport (Rueda, 2019[52]); (Postaria, 2021[55]). This, together with the technological changes of the engines expected for a certain percentage of vehicles, will allow reducing CO_2 emissions by 36% (Rueda, 2019[54]) (see.Table 3.1). In addition, this will allow reducing air pollution to values below 40 micrograms / m3 for 96% of the population (today only 56%) (Rueda, 2019[54]),and cutting NO2 emissions in line with European Union standards (Rueda, 2019[52]); (Mueller et al., 2020[56]; López, Ortega and Pardo, 2020[50]). It will also permit reducing noise below 65 dBA for 73.5% of the population (compared to 54%), and drastically reducing serious or fatal traffic accidents (the speed of the perimeter roads of the superblocks is limited to 30 km / h and the interiors to 10 km / h). At the same it will reverse the excessive occupation of land by motorised mobility (6,200,000 m2 of public space will be freed) (Rueda, 2019[54]).

Table 3.1. GHG emissions in Barcelona from motorized transport in thousands of tons for various scenarios

Year	2005	2015	2018	2024	2030
Emissions of GHG (x1000)	1102	1001	897		
% of reduction respect to 2005	0%	9%	19%		
Data source	Energy Agency of Barcelona	Energy Agency of Barcelona	Energy Agency of Barcelona	BCNecologia	BCNecologia
GHG emissions (x1000) resulting from the scenarios PMUS				707	608
% reduction compared to 2005				36%	45%

Source: Barcelona Energy Agency and BCNecologia.

In 2023, there could be 31 superblocks in total, while as said before the long-term plan is to transform the entire municipality of Barcelona (to implement 503 superblocks). The complete reconfiguration would imply a 61% reduction of the public space dedicated to the road network utilised by cars (from 912 km to 355 km), which currently occupy 60% of the total public space in the city (Rueda, 2019[52]). This will allow increasing the average space dedicated to pedestrians from 15, 8% to 67% while increasing the comfort and safety features of streets and sidewalks (Rueda, 2019[52]). Liberated space is also being converted into other uses besides transport, such as playgrounds and picnic areas, which have been chosen in consultation with the local neighbourhoods over time (Roberts, 2019[57]).

Superblocks and the health and environmental benefits they can generate can also importantly contribute to economic improvements. Mueller et al. (2020[56]) estimate that, if all of the planned Superblocks are implemented in Barcelona, 667 premature deaths (estimated to cost EUR 1.6 billion) could be prevented every year. This is due to lower exposure to pollution (NO2 emissions are accounted for in the study), noise and heat (accounting for 291, 163 and 117 preventable deaths respectively) as well as to increased physical activity generated by a modal shift from cars and motorcycles to walking and cycling (accounting for 36 preventable deaths) and increased access to green space (accounting for 60 preventable deaths).

Figure 3.6. Annual premature death that the "Superblocks" Model could avoid

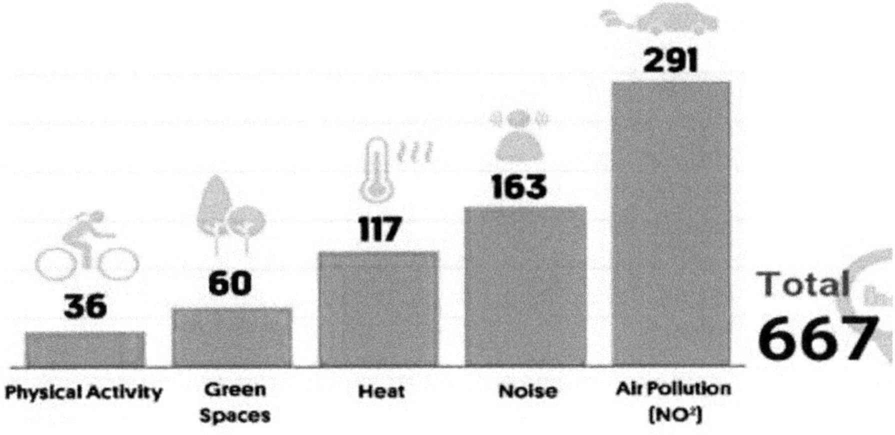

Source: (Mueller et al., 2020[56]).

The implementation of the superblock model is not a problem, but rather a solution, from a traffic point of view and it is not a problem from an economic point of view either. The development of superblocks does not involve investment in hard infrastructure. Rather, it is about transforming the urban environment by changing the use of existing infrastructure. As described in López, Ortega and Pardo (2020[50]), it is "very low-tech and low-cost urbanism", yet it has the potential to completely transform the urban ecosystem. The implementation of the 503 superblocks, based on tactical urbanism (see below) can be carried out with an investment of around 300 million euros. The budget of the City Council of Barcelona was, for the year 2021, equivalent to 3,400 million euros. In the event that the 503 superblocks were implemented in a period of 4 years, the accumulated budget of the City Council for this period would be EU 13.6 billion. This would represent only 2% of the accumulated budget (Rueda, 2020[58]).

Importantly, while the implementation of superblocks has been anchored in the urban mobility plans for the city,[16] it also implies a radical change in land-use policy (Zografos et al., 2020[49]). The reallocation and redesign of road space is a central feature of Superblocks, and thus these interventions have huge potential for addressing and reversing induced demand. Furthermore, the comprehensive planning and thinking behind such projects also bring together a number of actions that can allow addressing other dynamics behind car dependency, creating a number of synergies to transform urban and transport systems. On the one hand, the integration of bicycle lanes and the reorganisation of bus services as part of these interventions (see below) is key to address the erosion of alternative modes. On the other, reconfiguring neighbourhoods and liberating space from car use is an important step in changing the urban landscape. This brings important opportunities for increasing proximity to amenities and services, reducing longer distance trips, and making developed areas more attractive, all of which can contribute to limiting and reversing sprawl.

The reconfiguration of large areas of the city into Superblocks will allow the expansion of the network of bicycle lanes and complementing the network of main routes with the development of secondary/proximity bike lanes, as well as incorporating parking facilities for bicycles. In parallel to space redistribution, Superblocks incorporate necessary efforts to better integrate bicycle and public transport use to ensure alternatives to car use (a necessary action discussed in more detail in Chapter 5). This includes adapting public transport for bicycle access (especially inter-city ones) and integrating bike parks at stations. Adapting the city for the use of electric bicycles is another objective of Superblocks, e.g. ensuring bike lanes are available in streets with slopes and implementing bike-sharing schemes that include electric bikes.

The implementation of Superblocks will also incorporate the reconfiguration and expansion of the bus network, in parallel to increasing frequencies. Interurban services will also be improved, including by integrating bus lanes into road infrastructure connecting different territories. Indeed, a distinguishing feature of Superblocks is the possibility to shift from a radial to an orthogonal system of buses. This allows more efficient services, which can be more accessible to the population (e.g. the goal is to have population that is at most 300 m away from a stop), and offer frequencies similar to those of the metro (4-5 min apart instead of 15 min). All of which contributes to shifting longer trips from car to public transport. Before the pandemic, the new orthogonal bus network (fully implemented at the end of 2018 following the perimeter of the superblocks) had increased the number of users by 15%. The bus network implemented at the end of 2009 in Vitoria-Gasteiz (the capital of the Álava Province), designed following the perimeter of the superblocks in the same way as in Barcelona, had increased, before the pandemic, by almost 100% the number of users (Rueda, 2019[52]).

Making street reconfiguration a wide-scale plan is also important to avoid gentrification and eviction. In addition to limiting benefits, when such projects are only implemented as pilots in reduced areas of cities, an important downside tends to be gentrification and eviction, as it creates better relative conditions in a constrained space and thus creates price differentials between the reconfigured area and other areas, making it unaffordable for current residents to stay. In Barcelona, the first Superblocks in the Eixample neighbourhood have been introduced in areas with social housing. Moreover, the fact that new amenities (e.g. quality public and green space) will be distributed throughout all of the 503 Superblocks avoids the risk of creating price differentials between areas (Rueda, 2019[54]); (Postaria, 2021[55]). That said, it is important to think about how to extend the model beyond the municipality of Barcelona, to avoid increasing price differentials and living conditions between Barcelona and the surrounding municipalities in the larger metropolitan area and region.

Figure 3.7. The changes brought about by the Superblocks model

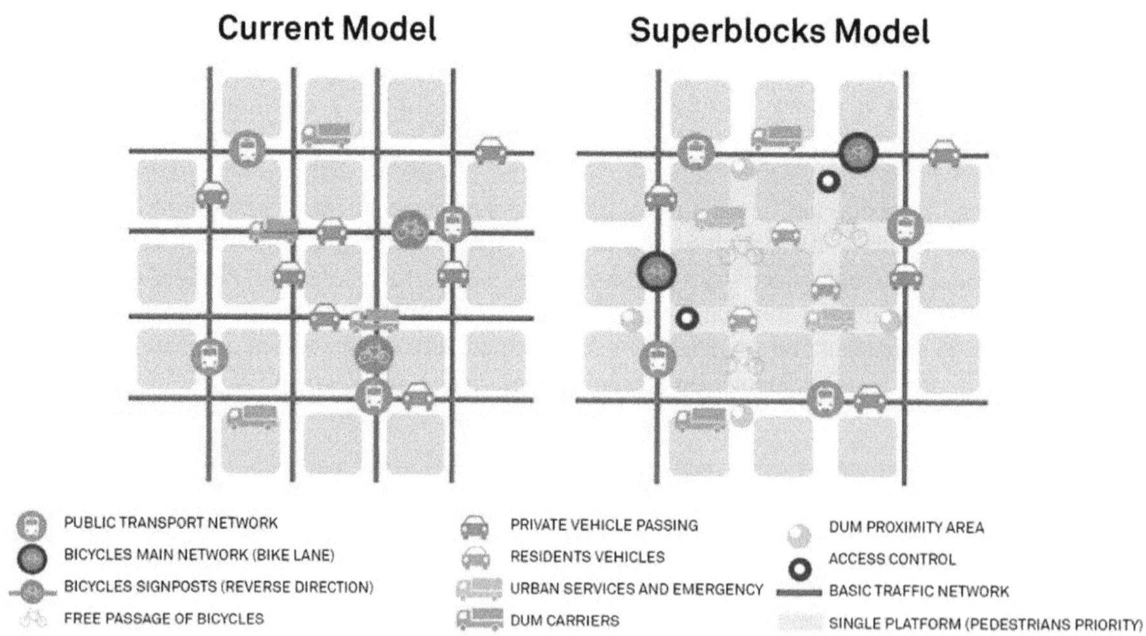

Source:BCnecologia and Ajuntament de Barcelona (2014[51]).

Although Superblocks have the potential to bring significant benefits, their implementation has not been free from challenges (Postaria, 2021[55]). Experience implementing them brings valuable insights on the role and importance of the political context and dynamics for the implementation of transformative projects, as well as on the challenges of obtaining public acceptability. These issues are discussed below, building on the experience of Barcelona's Superblocks as well as other international examples involving significant road reallocation and redesign.

Implementation challenges: Public acceptability and political process

Transformative interventions such as Superblocks in Barcelona tend to face push-back from the local population. Among other things, this is due to the fact that these interventions imply important changes in current lifestyles and even in the way people are used to thinking about their city landscape and the way public space is used. Literature focused on this topic identifies several relevant behavioural biases in individuals, such as loss aversion, which is the tendency to give more weight to losses than to gains, or *status quo* bias, which is a preference for the current state and opposition to change (Thaler and Sunstein, 2008[59]). In the case of Superblocks, for example, individuals might weigh the loss of the car more heavily than the gains from space reallocation. Groups also tend to exhibit collective conservatism and stick "to established patterns even as a new need arises" (Thaler and Sunstein, 2008[59]). Taken together, this means communities as a whole, as well as individuals, have collective inertia of opposition to such transformational change.

One way of overcoming these biases is for cities to use temporary projects, in many cases in the form of "tactical urbanism". Tactical urbanism consists of making quick and low-cost changes that do not involve any permanent infrastructure but can importantly provide a taste of what the new space would look like. Interventions can then be adapted (or removed) depending on the needs and views of the population. Temporary projects provide a non- (or less) threatening way for people to explore changes to road reallocation and overcome the initial opposition, which is rooted in individuals' loss aversion and *status quo* bias. It makes individuals, and the community as a whole, less apprehensive, open to possibilities and taking risks to see if their fears actually materialise, e.g. such as fears related to losing space for cars (Rowe, 2013[60]). Moreover, allowing people to see a new version of their street (or neighbourhood) offers the opportunity to experience the new situation as being the *status quo* and make this something they are then averse to losing (Rowe, 2013[60]). This allows people and communities to explore change and circumvent their defensiveness (Rowe, 2013[60]). Numerous cities have used temporary projects to reallocate road space, for example in Copenhagen in Nørrebrogade, the Plaza Program in New York City, the Yarraville Pop-up Park in Melbourne and the Parklet Program in San Francisco (Rowe, 2013[60]). Box 3.4 describes the use of tactical urbanism in Brussels during the lockdown and restoration of economic activity due to the COVID-19 pandemic to accelerate the implementation of the mobility ("Good Move") plan.

Box 3.5. Accelerating Brussels' redesign through tactical urbanism

The city of Brussels benefited from the COVID-19 lockdown to implement tactical urbanism projects. City authorities took advantage of the confinement in early 2020 to accelerate the implementation of the recently developed 2020-30 regional transport plan Good Move (Bruxelles Mobilité, 2020[61]).

Among the central aims of the plan is to transform Brussels into a " pleasant and safe city, made up by peaceful neighbourhoods, connected by intermodal structural axes, and centred around efficient public transport services and more fluid traffic flows" (Bruxelles Mobilité, 2020[61]). The Good Move plan is by and for the inhabitants of Brussels and is based on a participatory process. Residents were involved from the early stages. In 2017, the "Good Move for Citizens" was launched and a citizens' panel was formed for residents to present their own ideas. Recommendations from the panel were used in the creation of the new mobility plan (Pascal Smet, 2017[62]).

The Good Move plan takes a holistic approach and is centred around six axes:

1. Good neighbourhood: structure mobility within neighbourhoods and improve life quality for their inhabitants. The plan introduces 30 km/h speed limits within the areas to reduce accidents, creates space for pedestrians and cyclists, and restores the local character of the streets. It also includes the renovation of public spaces to prioritise the safety and comfort of citizens using these areas. The good neighbourhoods axis brings about space reallocation, and changes the function of space to turn the focus away from solely mobility purposes.
2. Good network: organise the transport network and ensure a highly performing service. The plan improves travelling conditions by developing networks for pedestrians, cyclists, heavy goods vehicles and public transport lines. The plan will also redevelop some roads into multimodal urban boulevards, develop cycle routes and create pedestrian lines to regional transport hubs.
3. Good service: offer inhabitants and users an array of service options. The interconnection of various services will be strengthened through the development of transport hubs.
4. Good choice: direct individual and collective choices, without restricting individual liberties. The plan links territorial development to mobility options. Activities including services, jobs, tourist attractions and shops will be established at central locations in accordance with the principles of a closer city. Special attention will be paid to the management of parking, pricing and traffic taxation to best prioritise mobility solutions focused on improving quality of life, health and the environment.
5. Good partner: ensure a governance framework that is inclusive of key stakeholders, including various levels of government, neighbourhoods, and public and private entities. The plan uses a participatory approach and opts for citizen implementation of key actions.
6. Good knowledge: continuously update mobility data and regularly evaluate the Good Move plan. Good Move will evaluate the regional mobility policy by acquiring, analysing and sharing mobility data to best understand the impacts of the plan, as well as conduct satisfaction surveys among all local users.

Seizing the opportunity to accelerate the Good Move transformation

Brussels used the confinement and post-confinement period to look for ways in which the transformation envisioned by the Good Move plan could be accelerated. This also offered a way for the population to experience how the changes envisioned in the new plan could transform their neighbourhoods and the city. In particular, according to authorities, the confinement period made it ever more evident the excessive amount of space that the city allocated to cars, and thus the multiple opportunities for reallocating this space in ways that can enhance residents' quality of life.

During the confinement in March 2020, the Mobility Minister of the Regional Government of Brussels provided support to municipalities to create areas denominated *zones de rencontre*. These are areas where pedestrians have the priority and the speed limit is set at 20 km/h. These areas were created to allow for joggers and pedestrians to coexist while ensuring safe distancing. Sixteen out of the 19 municipalities had engaged in the development of these areas by the summer, with a total of 100 km of road space dedicated to this type of area.

Many *zones de rencontre* were later made permanent (with some going through some type of adaptation for improvement). The approach was embedded in the so-called "tactical urbanism" (see definition above).

In addition, 40 extra bike corridors were created in the city. According to authorities, the aim was to provide public transport users with a way to avoid riding during peak hours, reducing overcrowding on public transport. In addition, this was also seen as a longer term opportunity to significantly increase the role of cycling, helping to reduce car dependency and avoiding its potential exacerbation as a consequence of the COVID-19 crisis.

Extra money for bike lanes and slow street installation is part of the recovery plan, as well as support for bike leasing. Implementation of bike parking facilities has also been provided as part of the recovery package.

Finally, the "Brussels en Vacances" programme provided funding for small projects (EUR 2 000-15 000) that focused on reconfiguring space in neighbourhoods to make neighbourhoods more appealing during holidays (as many people would not have money to travel or would be too scared to). Examples include boxes for gardening and playgrounds, which were developed instead of car parking space. The projects could be made permanent, if residents support this.

Source: Bruxelles Mobilité (2020[61]).

Tactical urbanism was also used in the case of Barcelona's Superblocks, showing a way forward to reduce the trade-offs between trying to gain acceptance up front and moving forward in implementing projects that aim at deep transformation. As documented by Roberts (2019[57]), the idea of Superblocks had been around in Barcelona for decades[17] before being implemented by the Colau administration in 2016. Indeed, the former administration had planned a first version of a Superblock for the Poblenou area. The administration had undertaken extensive consultation, but this took time, and the process was slow. In contrast, the Colau administration implemented its version of the project (see below) without undergoing extensive consultation or communication.[18] This came at the expense of strong protests from the population (later steered also by the press) and particularly from local businesses. For the first six months after its implementation, these protests importantly jeopardised the project. Nonetheless, an important asset was that because public space was quickly reallocated away from cars, people had this space at their disposal. The administration then steered public consultation towards choosing what to do with the space. In the words of Salvador Rueda, one of the main developers of the Superblock concept: "no one who gains public space ever asks to be rid of it. Never!" (Roberts, 2019[57]).. Nonetheless, the Colau administration did acknowledge the need to improve public participation for projects after Poblenau. Strengthening the framework for fostering Superblocks as a collaborative project with central involvement from residents is a priority for the new projects that will be developed in the short term (Postaria, 2021[55]).

In addition, as noted by the Deputy Mayor Sanz, finding the right balance between tactical and structural urbanism has been an important lesson from the Poblenou Superblock (Roberts, 2019[57]). As mentioned above, tactical urbanism does not involve the development of permanent infrastructure. On the one hand, increasing and consolidating public acceptance requires a transition towards developing the permanent infrastructure that can make people benefit the most from the new public space (i.e. playgrounds, outdoor sitting areas, changing the pavement level, etc.). At the same time, developing permanent infrastructure too early, before the population has had the time to reflect on what they want to do with the space, can also lead to discontent (Roberts, 2019[57]).

The Superblock example also shows that, if well designed, the benefits reaped by the population can be sufficient to outweigh initial resistance and political risk. As Deputy Mayor Sanz highlights, residents of other city areas are now asking for the development of Superblocks in their own neighbourhood (Roberts, 2019[57]). Moreover, while groups initially against Superblocks have, in some cases, continued with legal processes, demands have been progressively modified from the retirement of the Superblock to the adaptation of particular features (Roberts, 2019[57]).

The implementation of Superblocks has also not been independent from the political process, which in many ways also influenced public opinion. In their analysis, Zografos et al. (2020[49]) identify a number of political challenges that the Poblenau project had to overcome. The first was the fragility of the municipal authority represented by the new mayor in power. Major Colau, who came from a non-traditional, grassroots-based political party (contrary to the former administration which was a centre-right party), had a weak position in the city council. A visible and controversial project such as the Superblocks soon became a reason for discrediting the new regime. Second, given that the former administration had also made plans for the project, there was an important struggle for the credit behind it. The Colau administration decided to change the location of the project, which to an important extent increased the challenges for striking a balance between communicating with the new residents while also moving fast enough to be able to implement the project before the end of its political term.

As the Colau administration progressively developed its own vision of the project, a third challenge emerged, which was more about the clash between the two projects and the vision of the city they represented. The new project had a different spirit, which shifted the vision from one centred around business and economic growth to one focused on residents' quality of life and access to an affordable and liveable city (Zografos et al., 2020[49]). As such, the project was soon branded by critics of the administration as the representation of Colau's "anti-private vehicle obsession" (Zografos et al., 2020[49]).

Importantly, having a vision centred around quality of life does not mean that projects cannot benefit local businesses and even create new ones. Rather, higher pedestrian and cyclist flows have been associated with the creation of new businesses and jobs (Perk et al., 2015[17]); as well as other benefits for local businesses. For instance the pedestrianisation of Madero Street –a large and central street in the heart of Mexico City – increased commercial activity by 30%and reduced reported crime by 96% (C40, 2016[63]) in (ITF, 2021[64]). But unlocking the greatest benefits, and avoiding implementation challenges, requires the existing local business owners to be involved in the design of the project and for street re-design to be thought of in the context of enabling commercial activities and avoiding safety issues between these and other users (Box 3.6).

Box 3.6. Planning for freight and delivery services as part of Complete Streets

As discussed at a roundtable in April 2020 organised by the Institute for Transportation and Development Policy, it is essential to design for freight and delivery services as part of Complete Streets. Several negative impacts come to mind when thinking about truck delivery services. These include dangerous collisions, traffic congestion, lane obstruction, infrastructure damage and the challenges it presents for urban streets. However, freight services are integral to a well-functioning urban region and key in making urban-rural linkages. The movement of goods is critical to social and economic welfare; thus freight movement must be able to coexist with other modes of planned transport.

Common challenges with freight and delivery services include navigation challenges as the vehicles move through a community. A number of small design changes, e.g. adding a kerbside parking lane between the cycling or pedestrian lane and the street can help trucks turn, allowing the safe coexistence of freight and other users. Other possibilities include using speed humps instead of speed bumps, or avoiding roundabouts where large trucks are meant to navigate.

There are also conflicts between freight and vulnerable road users when freight and delivery services reach their destination (kerbside challenges). Designated infrastructure for bikes and pedestrians and clearly identified conflict areas is key to dealing with such challenges. This can include bike boxes to move cyclists ahead of drivers' blind spots, two-faced turn cues so that bikes don't have to travel across lanes of traffic to turn left, and painting sidewalks to clearly designate loading zones. In addition, when parking is eliminated in urban areas, it can result in trucks parking in places they shouldn't to offload goods. The type of truck and what is being offloaded also needs to be considered because offloading can spill into active travel lanes. Solutions to this problem include having transit bulbs to allow space for bus loading, while keeping parts of the kerb designated for truck offloading. As well, better management of delivery off streets is imperative to improve congestion. This can include creating centralised delivery locations, secure storage rooms, lockers and loading dock appointment systems.

Finally, demand management is also a key aspect for improving freight and truck delivery service. Utilising off-peak delivery hours, creating consolidation centres so that there are smaller trucks on the road, and densifying demand through pick up points all can assist in this process.

Source: https://www.itdp.org/event/complete-streets-space-for-freight.

Revisiting parking policies is crucial to redesign streets and improve management of public space

Parking policies hold significant emissions reduction potential. As such, they should be more central in climate strategies for the transport sector. Parking policies are often overlooked (Kodransky and Hermann, 2011[65])and, as signalled by (Franco, 2020[66]), "have significant environmental and economic implications, including effects on climate change, air pollution, energy consumption, traffic congestion, housing affordability and economic development".

Parking policies, as used (or not used) today, incentivise car use. Policies subsidising, under-pricing or providing an oversupply of parking space influence automobile use, land use and urban form (Franco, 2020[66]). Evidence from cities across the globe demonstrates that the parking space required could be reduced by 10-30% with efficient parking policies, and these could also reduce general vehicle traffic volumes (Litman, 2016[67]). The availability of parking space, in particular at residential and work sites, has been signalled as importantly related to vehicle ownership and use, showing that people tend to drive walkable or bikeable distances if parking is easily available (Franco, 2020[66]). For instance, Franco and

Khordagui (2019[68]) find that increasing on-street parking by 10% is associated with a 1.3% increase in the probability of driving. A back-of-the-envelope calculation by Russo, van Ommeren and Dimitropoulos (2019[69]) suggests that the provision of free parking at the workplace by employers may be responsible for 17 million tonnes of CO_2 emissions per year in the United States.

Subsidies are often in the form of "free parking". As (Franco, 2020[66])highlights, there is no such thing as free parking. Where parking is "free" or under-priced (which is often the case), its costs are being paid elsewhere and by someone else, for example through mortgages and rents in the case of off-street parking provided in buildings, or through general taxes in the case of on-street parking (Franco, 2020[66]). Subsidised or free on-street parking also incentives cruising, i.e. driving around the area waiting for a parking space to be liberated, which leads to congestion, emissions and air pollution (Franco, 2020[66]); (Russo, van Ommeren and Dimitropoulos, 2019[69]). People living in areas with free on-street parking tend to use this space instead of private parking (Scheiner et al., 2020[70]), occupying parts of the street that could be used for different functions (e.g. green areas to foster biodiversity, etc.) (Russo, van Ommeren and Dimitropoulos, 2019[69]).

Parking policies can instead be designed to regulate and discourage car use (Kodransky and Hermann, 2011[65]), positively contributing to emissions and pollution reduction efforts. This would imply a shift from current parking policies, which are mainly focused on accommodating cars and thus incentivise its use. Higher parking prices, smart parking meters, zoning and the revisiting of parking supply are some of the ways in which parking policies can play a role in the redesign of streets and the improved management of public space, with the ultimate goal of reducing emissions and improving life quality.

Higher parking prices have the potential to incentivise modal shifts away from private cars. In the city of Amsterdam, for example, it is estimated that a 10% increase of the parking price for residential parking would translate into an 8% reduction of car ownership (price elasticity of -0.8) (Groote, van Ommeren and Koster, 2016[71]). Note that this elasticity might be lower in cities with limited options for substituting car trips (e.g. public transport, walking or cycling), highlighting the importance of combining parking policies with policies to improve conditions for active and shared modes of transportation, such as the ones described in Chapter 5. In San Francisco, smart parking meters (SFpark) have enabled implementing real-time fare adjustments and have increased the effectiveness of variable-rate on-street parking prices (OECD, 2015[30]). Prices are set precisely to balance supply and demand to leave one or two spaces free per block (Pierce and Shoup, 2013[72]), which can "save time for parkers, reduce congestion, speed up public transit, and improve transportation for almost everyone" (Pierce and Shoup, 2013[72]).

Shifting parking costs from employer to employee can drive an important change in commuters' modal choices, as well as reduce incentives to move to the suburbs (Franco, 2020[66]) based on Breuckner and Franco (2018[73])). The authors propose that workers pay for parking at market rate, and that employers raise employee wages to offset the cost. A parking cash-out is another policy option: employers lease or partially subsidise parking for employees and offer them the choice of keeping their parking spot or trading it in for an equivalent cash payment. Employees that choose to forgo the cash payment are choosing to spend it on parking, while those who accept the payment can use the money however they see fit (Brueckner and Franco, 2018[73]). Allowing employees such choice sheds light on the parking cost and has resulted in less people driving to work. For example, in California, based on surveys carried out in the years following the implementation of the Cash-out Law (1992), the number of people driving to work alone decreased by 17%; carpooling, using public transportation and active travel increased by 64%, 50% and 33%, respectively (Franco, 2020[66]) based on (Shoup, 2005[74]).

The effectiveness of cash-out programmes is dependent on the accessibility of alternative transport modes, urban density and the amount of the cash subsidy (i.e. the parking price) (Brueckner and Franco, 2018[73]). Synergies can be made if revenues are used to develop alternatives to driving. The Nottingham City Council has introduced a Workplace Parking Levy (WPL), a type of annual congestion-charging scheme for employers providing workplace parking. All employers who provide workplace parking are legally required to license the spots, although employers with ten or fewer parking spots may qualify for a 100% discount. The central government releases the Retail Price Index, which is used to calculate the WPL charge. Employers must register for an annual license, which runs from April to March of the next year, with the cost of each parking spot set prior to 1 January. Nottingham has used the revenue from the WPL to fund the tram system extension (NET Phase Two), Nottingham Station and the Link Bus Network, while also incentivising employers to manage employee parking (Nottingham City Council, n.d.[75]).

Differentiating parking prices by zone can improve their efficiency and public acceptability. In Lisbon, three parking price zones exist. Zoning is determined according to the availability of public transport services and to the density of parking sought in the different areas. Red areas correspond to main transport corridors. In these areas, relatively high parking prices (EUR 1.6 per hour) and maximum parking duration limits (2 hours) are implemented. Contrastingly, in green zones, where there is relatively low public transport availability and where parking space is less scarce, parking prices are the lowest (EUR 0.8 per hour) and time limits are longer (4 hours). Yellow areas are central areas of the city that, while not on a transport corridor, have a relatively high availability of public transport. In these areas, the price of parking is EUR 1.2 per hour and the maximum time allowed for on-street parking is 4 hours (Government of Lisbon, 2018[76]; ELTIS, 2014[77]).[19] In the same vein, the three-zone parking pricing scheme in Copenhagen discourages car use and promotes the use of active transport modes such as biking in the city centre, with lower prices for parking in peripheral areas and higher ones in central areas of the city (Kodransky and Hermann, 2011[65]). In Strasbourg (France), a concentric three-zone parking pricing scheme imposes higher parking prices as well as shorter parking times in the city centre, compared to the periphery of the city as well. This policy has gone hand-in-hand with the replacement of on-street parking spaces in the city centre with cycling lanes and tramways, providing a good example of synergistic policy packages (as explained above, the elasticity of parking pricing correlates to the availability of alternative options to cars). Such a policy bundle seeks to reduce car use in the city centre and to concentrate long-term parking needs at park-and-ride and other off-street parking facilities in more residential areas on the outskirts of the city (General Commission for Strategy and Foresight, 2013[78]).

Parking policies can also promote the purchase of more efficient cars, by linking the parking price to the emissions efficiency of the car. For example, some boroughs in London differentiate the charges for permits of residential parking according to the type-approval[20] CO_2 emissions of the applicant's car (Kodransky and Hermann, 2011[65]). Moreover, the City of London introduced differentiated parking fees for on-street parking in the Square Mile in 2018. While low-emission vehicles (electric and hybrid) pay GBP 4 per hour, conventional cars are charged up to GBP 6.8 per hour (FleetNews, 2018[79]). In this case, however, careful attention is necessary to ensure that all cars pay what is needed to achieve an efficient use of space and trigger modal "shift" and encourage "avoid" effects, regardless of their technology. Embedding such a policy in a larger package of policies intended to reverse car dependency is key and if keeping a car-dependent system this could also have negative equity implications. In addition, electric and hybrid vehicles should not be given the same treatment (see Chapter 6 for a discussion).

Implementation challenges

Implementing parking pricing with the aim to regulate car use, as any change, does not come without challenges. The first is public acceptability of pricing something considered to be "free", and a "right", as explained in Section 2.2.1. The cash-out programme described above is a good example of a policy that sheds light on the actual cost of parking. Active communication efforts to make the potential alternative uses of space visible to people are also fundamental to increase policy acceptability and support. Parking Day is an example of citizen-led initiative aimed to raise awareness of the opportunity costs of using public space for car parking. Parking Day is a global[21] event, with the goal of mobilising citizens, artists and activists. The objective is to transform concrete street parking space into convivial, artistic and green places. The day is an opportunity to reflect on the role of shared space, to visualise urban uses for public places and to make proposals for future city planning. In some cases, the lock-down periods and the need for social distancing, as a result of theCOVID-19 crisis, increased awareness for the use of public spaces. In many instances, parking space has been converted into terraces allowing restaurants to increase the available space for seating people. See Chapter 7 for more information about COVID-19 and tactical urbanism.

The second challenge is data availability. Cities do not necessarily have complete inventories reflecting the total on-street and off-street parking supply available. This limits authorities' capacity to adjust parking pricing and co-ordinate on-street and off-street parking policies (Franco, 2020[66]). Strasbourg has been able to overcome this challenge and successfully co-ordinate on-street and off-street parking policies, in particular via public-private partnerships with private garage owners (Franco, 2020[66]).These partnerships, have facilitated the implementation of a harmonised pricing structure with differentiated tariffs (as described above) (Franco, 2020[66]).

Third, co-ordination among different authorities is needed to ensure that overall decisions on parking policy and regulation are consistent. Minimum parking requirement regulations, often the competence of planning authorities (whereas other parking policy tends to be in the hands of transport authorities) have, for instance, played a very relevant role in fostering car dependence. Minimum parking requirements determine the minimum number of parking spaces in new building constructions, and have, as other parking (e.g. pricing) policies, often been focused on accommodating cars rather than regulating their use. Minimum parking requirements can raise housing costs, reduce land value and foster urban sprawl, thus reducing urban density (Shoup, 1997[80]). Given their relevance to urban form and sprawl, the changes necessary in minimum parking requirements for these to contribute to emissions reductions are described in Chapter 4.

Road pricing focused on the efficient use of road space and embedded in street redesign plans can also be a powerful tool

Road pricing can contribute to shifting away from a "predict and provide" approach (see Chapter 2), the focus on expanding road capacity for cars as the way to fight congestion (the consequences of which are explained in Section 3.1), towards an emphasis on better managing the use of existing roads. Road-pricing schemes will better deliver climate goals if they are designed with the aim of efficiently using road space. Road-pricing schemes have often been set with the expectation of increasing traffic speeds and reducing time delays for motorists, often considered as congestion's most important disutility (van Dender, 2019[81]; ITF, 2018[82]). However, as explained above, climate and well-being goals do not depend on allowing people to travel as fast and far as possible, but on sustainably delivering accessibility, for which adequately allocating and managing public space (of which roads are a part of) is crucial. Thus, rather than looking at road pricing as a way of increasing speeds per se, schemes should be used with the view of efficiently using road space.

Crozet and Mercier (2018[83]) find that in urban areas, space use per car is more efficient at speeds between 20 km/h and 40 km/h, as within this range speed is high enough for the available road space to deliver significant access, while minimising the consumption of space per vehicle, as space needed for safe travel is less. Space consumption per car is just above 1 m^2h[22] within this speed range, compared to 4 m^2h at speeds of 130 km/h (Crozet and Mercier, 2018[83]). Such a speed range can be taken as a reference when designing road-pricing schemes. In Singapore, for instance, periodical updates on prices are realised to ensure average speed flows are within this "optimal" speed level.

In addition, as also suggested by Crozet and Mercier (2018[83]), road pricing could also contribute to incentivising shared mobility if pricing is differentiated by vehicle occupancy (see below for other criteria for differentiating pricing). This would not only create an efficient use of road space by minimising space consumed per vehicle, but would also create disincentives for low occupancy or even empty vehicles (in the case of autonomous cars in the future), to encourage efficiency on a per person basis.

Moreover, research suggests that fostering optimal average travel speeds, rather than the "highest-possible" speeds, may also be a more efficient way to reduce congestion per se (ITF, 2017[84]), which is associated with high levels of greenhouse gas emissions and pollution. In dense urban areas, speeds between 20 km/h and 40 km/h (which are in line with speeds that minimise space consumption per car) reduce the likelihood of bottlenecks and time delays (ITF, 2017[84]). Real-world emissions testing has revealed that "[T]he low velocity and the increased braking may double the [local pollutant] emissions per kilometre in congested urban situations" (ITF, 2017[84]). The smooth car traffic conditions enabled by keeping average speeds within shorter ranges are also associated with lower CO_2 emissions than stop-start conditions. Studies in the United States have shown a 40% reduction in CO_2 emissions when driving in smooth traffic at an average speed of 45 km/h rather than in congested, stop-start conditions (Grote et al., 2016[85]). While this is slightly above the threshold mentioned above, it provides a reference for comparing emissions under smooth and congested traffic. In addition, lowering speeds (in particular inside urban areas) is also relevant for road safety reasons (Litman, 2012[86]). For this, implementing and enforcing speed limits is also crucial.

The greatest gains will come if pricing road use by motorists is implemented in parallel to re-allocating space away from cars and towards other transport modes and uses (i.e. beyond transport) (see above). The same congestion levels can be associated with very different overall travel volumes and emissions. As such, introducing road pricing without revisiting an over dimensioned road space supply allocated for driving and parking (and without investing in public and active modes) could result in reduced congestion, but still very high total traffic volumes and emissions. On the other hand, introducing road pricing while adjusting the supply of road space for driving and parking, which at the same time liberates space for other modes and uses beyond transport, can provide greater incentives for modal shift, as well as the conditions for shorter distance trips. Reduced congestion levels in this case (which could be similar to those resulting from the case above) would be associated to much lower overall traffic and emissions. Thus, if embedded in comprehensive policy packages and investment programmes, road pricing can contribute to supporting transit-oriented development and to containing (or reversing) sprawl (ITF, 2018[82]), bringing much larger mitigation, air quality and other (e.g. equity) benefits.

Unlocking these benefits requires (once again) prioritising the need to correct the excessive allocation of public space for car use, which is a barrier to modal shift and the creation of proximity, over short-term congestion alleviation gains. Indeed, as shown in the London example below, implementing road-pricing schemes while reallocating road space away from cars can offset to an extent the congestion reductions in the short term. However, as explained above, only in this way can road pricing lead to congestion reductions that effectively deliver significant traffic and emissions reductions in the mid- and long run.

Importantly, focusing on the efficient use of road and public space, rather than higher car travel speeds, does not mean that motorists can't benefit as well, as these would both have quality alternatives for a number of trips as well as benefit from more fluid traffic and greater reliability of trips when they consider it is worth paying to drive (Litman, 2021[32]). Indeed, embedding road pricing into a larger package focused on shifting systems away from car dependency is key to limiting a relevant downside, which is that those who can afford to tend to drive more (ITF, 2021[10]). Improving the relative attractiveness of other modes *vis-à-vis* the car can help decrease the time cost threshold at which a motorist would be discouraged to drive (Litman, 2021[32]; 2014[87]). Thus, presumably it would also increase the price threshold at which motorists would rather pay than use alternatives. This will allow better channelling car use towards the trips where it will have more value than costs, which is what would happen in a system that is no longer car dependent (ITF, 2021[10]), and can reflect the "healthy" transport system depicted in Section 2.1.

Examples and good practice

Several authorities are considering road pricing in the context of a general shift from fuel to road pricing as a way to maintain revenue stability as fleets become increasingly electric (see discussion in (van Dender (2019[81])). However, current world examples are more focused on urban road-charging schemes, which only apply to vehicles entering a specific area. These are often referred to as congestion-charging schemes, which are implemented mostly inside urban areas, where space is particularly scarce and congestion tends to be worse. These schemes are implemented in a specific perimeter (although the size can vary widely), which can be an area or in some cases a (or several) corridor(s). Examples featured in this subsection focus on this type of scheme.[23]

While not yet widely used, urban road-pricing schemes are growing in number (ITF, 2018[82]). Cities like London, Stockholm, Milan and Singapore have congestion-charging schemes for specific areas. An important lesson from international experience is that the most efficient road-pricing schemes are those where prices vary according to the scarcity of space. This means that ideally, charges must be set according to the actual use within a given area (i.e. distance-based) rather than charging only when a cordon around that area is crossed. The price should also vary depending on levels of congestion at different times and in different places[24] (i.e. distance and place-based charging); and as suggested before, could be differentiated according to load factors. This type of differentiated pricing is also more efficient in dealing with bottleneck congestion, i.e. points of access to and exit from expressways, since it can help drive demand away from pinch points. It is also in line with the general principle of achieving optimal travel speeds, as the scarcer the land, the fewer vehicles will need to occupy the road space available in order to have smooth traffic conditions, and thus the higher the price needed to discourage all other drivers. Prices could also be differentiated by type of fuel or emissions profile and/or indexed to the availability of public transport.

The road-pricing scheme in Singapore applies several of the best practices described above. The scheme has electronically applied differentiated pricing based on time and location, and is implemented in both the central part of the city and for several highways (ITF, 2018[82]). The system has three daily pricing peaks: the morning and evening rush hours and a third peak at 2:30 pm due to the tendency for offices to schedule meetings during this time of day. Prices are set by an electronic road-pricing system to maintain speeds at 20-30 km/h on arterial city roads (which optimise space use in dense areas and contribute to road safety as discussed above), and 45-65 km/h on expressways. Prices are reviewed and adapted as needed on a quarterly basis.

The congestion-charging scheme, launched in 2003 in London, covers around 4% of the Greater London area. Charges are paid only once, when entering the covered zone, and prices are flat (rather than differentiated). This penalises short trips and may encourage car use once the charge has been paid (incentivising, for example, trips by car in areas well-deserved by public transportation). Experience in London also highlights that flat-rate pricing schemes may also be ineffective in managing fast-growing sectors, such as delivery vehicles for e-commerce, taxis and app-based ride services (ITF, 2018[82]). While the flat-rate nature of the scheme may not place London's congestion-charging scheme among the best examples, the scheme was interestingly undertaken in combination with wider street space reallocation towards active modes and public transport, as well as significant investment to improve conditions for the users of these modes. Among other things, bus capacity was increased by 24% on the routes that were affected by the congestion charge (ITF, 2017[84]). Having undertaken significant road reallocation away from cars had the impact of offsetting, to a certain degree, the positive impacts of reduced car use in congestion in the short-term (ITF, 2017[84]). However, the comprehensive package of policies and investment to improve public and active modes, of which the congestion-charging scheme is part of, has allowed London to importantly reduce journeys undertaken by cars over time in a more effective way than if congestion charging had been implemented on its own. Car use steadily decreased by 20% between 2001 and 2017. Conversely, bicycle journeys more than doubled and bus journeys increased by 60% over the same period. Indeed, London is the only urban area among the 120 analysed by the ITF (2019[88]) where accessibility by public transport is higher than by car. In addition, the investment in improving public transport and active modes also contributed to increased public acceptability (see below).

In the case of Stockholm, authorities implemented a cordon-charging scheme as in the case of London. This was due, to an important extent, to authorities searching for a balance between efficiency and clarity, as schemes with higher degrees of price differentiation can become complex, potentially requiring more sophisticated technologies and being more difficult to understand for users. Thus, authorities opted for a simple cordon charge, but tried to counteract some of the shortcomings by differentiating the charge during peak and off-peak hours (although with a maximum number of times that a user can be charged per day).

In Milan, a pollution charge in the central ring road of the city (the ECOPASS zone) exists since 2008 (ITF, 2017[84]). When launched, the cleanest (Class I and Class II) vehicles entered for free, and charges varied according to emissions levels for all other vehicles (ITF, 2017[84]). The scheme had initially also brought important congestion reductions, but these became marginal as vehicle technologies improved. With the objective of bringing both congestion and technological shift advantages, in 2012 the system[25] became a combination of a low-emission zone, banning entrance to the inner ring for the most pollutant vehicles, and a congestion charge zone, a (one-off) fee levied on all the vehicles entering the area, regardless to the vehicle's level of emissions (ITF, 2017[84]). In 2019, the scheme was extended to cover 72% of the municipal territory,[26] and banned the entrance to this area to Euro 0 gasoline-powered and Euro 0,1,2,3 and 4 diesel-powered vehicles weekdays from 7:30 am to 7:30 pm (ReVeAL, 2019[89]).

Unfortunately, a number of countries and cities have included the waiving (presumably temporary, but still not clear in many cases) of congestion charges and other fees for car ownership and use as part of their COVID-19 recovery package (Buckle et al., 2020[90]). This goes against any logic of placing climate at the centre of priorities for the sector. It creates unfortunate trade-offs between economic objectives (i.e. increasing disposable incomes) and climate and other (e.g. air quality, equity) goals.

Implementation challenges

A major implementation challenge for road-pricing schemes has historically been public acceptability. Claims of regressiveness and/or "unfairness"[27] of the schemes account for some of the unpopularity of such schemes.

The association of the car to positive notions such as a right, freedom or status (see Section 2.2.1), also adds to the opposition to road pricing, as even individuals that do not own a car aspire to having one, and higher costs of ownership and use make this possibility more remote. Moreover, when looked at from a car-oriented lens (in turn influenced by car-oriented narratives; see Box 2.2) roads' function is to accommodate cars rather than as public space that needs to accommodate a multiplicity of transport modes and functions beyond transport (see the discussion on Complete Streets and place-making concepts in Section 3.2.1).

The ITF (2017[84]) points out that communication strategies can play a crucial role in changing this perception if they raise awareness of the need to manage roads as part of public space and a common and scarce resource, and by explaining the advantages of congestion pricing schemes over other potential mechanisms. As discussed in Eliasson (2016[91]), surveys conducted in four cities (Lyon, Helsinki, Gutenberg and Stockholm) showed that respondents thought that introducing the charge was unfair until they were asked to recommend a better option (alternatives mentioned in the survey included queuing, government allocation and a lottery).

In addition, a better understanding of distributional impacts can help to better design road-pricing schemes, as well as to inform communication efforts and increase the public's understanding and acceptability of the scheme. Often, analysis has focused on determining whether road-pricing schemes are regressive or progressive,[28] but this is highly context-dependent. For example, in Beijing and Delhi, road-pricing schemes were found to be potentially progressive, as lower income residents, relying on public transport, were not impacted (ITF, 2017[84]). On the other hand, in Gothenburg, where most people travel by car, the scheme has been found to be regressive; although this is also because company cars (according to Swedish tax law) are exempt from paying the charges (Eliasson, 2016[91]). As discussed in Mattioli et al. (2019[92]) and Eliasson (2016[91]), framing discussions in terms of the regressive or progressive nature of road pricing and other measures is misleading to some extent. Because this analysis is based on averaging impacts by income group (i.e. average toll payment/average income per income group), it overlooks differences within each income group, which can be key to effectively understanding distributional impacts. For instance, high shares of low-income groups may not own a car, and thus the payment recorded for that group corresponds in reality to a sub-group that carries a higher burden than reflected when averaging for the whole group (Mattioli et al., 2019[92]).

More comprehensive analysis (e.g. including horizontal equity analysis) is better suited for distinguishing the overburden borne by groups with still relatively low incomes and who are car-dependent (which can be very vulnerable to the toll) (Mattioli et al., 2019[92]). In addition, identifying spatial vulnerability, and in particular adaptive capacity, by analysing accessibility through alternatives to car use in different locations is also relevant (Mattioli et al., 2019[92]). Furthermore, recognising the heterogeneity of current car users depending on their value of time is also useful to understand the winners and losers (Crozet and Mercier, 2018[83]). In this respect, Crozet and Mercier (2018[83]) show that acknowledging differences in the value of time allows us to see that only a fraction of current car users (those with a higher value of time) will benefit from a toll. Introducing congestion pricing together with significant improvements to public transport alternatives can indeed improve the picture. In this case, car users with a high value of time will pay, but be better-off. Others can switch to a quality alternative option and be better-off, or at least have only small well-being reductions, compared to the drastic worsening of travel conditions that would occur where public transport options are kept poor. Increasing the options for shifting away from the car would indeed also increase the behavioural change targeted by the policy in the first place, and thus its positive environmental effects.

In addition, the perceived objective of the scheme is key to the public's support or opposition (Eliasson, 2016[91]). Schemes tend to be unpopular if seen as a tax or a way to raise revenue[29] (and more so where trust in government is weak) (Eliasson, 2016[91]). Effective communication that provides clarity that the reason for implementing the measure is to fulfil other objectives (e.g. climate, air quality, etc.) is extremely important. In London as in Stockholm, authorities invested in campaigns to prepare citizens, making it clear that introducing the scheme was part of a wider long-term plan (in those cases to reduce air pollution) (ITF, 2017[84]). While making it clear that the main objective is not to raise revenues, using revenues in ways that are well accepted by the population can also be useful. For instance, half of the revenues from the congestion price in London go to offsetting the cost of the system put in place to manage and monitor the system. The remainder is allocated to TfL (accounting for about 5% of TfL's budget) and used for investing in public transport (ITF, 2017[84]). Having communicated on this, and actually having started delivering improvements in the bus network even before the congestion-charging scheme was implemented, also helped gain public acceptance (ITF, 2017[84]).

Finally, as for road reallocation, introducing a congestion pricing scheme as a temporary measure can help to better overcome the loss aversion and *status quo* biases discussed above. In Stockholm, the congestion pricing scheme was first introduced as a seven-month trial, that was then made permanent after having positive results in a referendum (ITF, 2017[84]).

References

(n.a.) (n.d.), *RijnWaalpad - a cycle highway with (almost) no interruptions | ECF*, https://ecf.com/news-and-events/news/rijnwaalpad-cycle-highway-almost-no-interruptions (accessed on 27 October 2021). [44]

Ajuntament de Barcelona (2014), *Metropolitan Area Urban Mobility Plans (PMU).* [51]

Ajuntamient de Barcelona and BCNecología (2020), *PMUS 2018-2024.* [48]

Anciaes, P., P. Jones and J. Mindell (2015), "Community severance: Where is it found and at what cost?", *Transport Reviews*, Vol. 36/3, pp. 293-317, http://dx.doi.org/10.1080/01441647.2015.1077286. [6]

Berlin.de (n.d.), "Facts and figures on transport", Senate Department for the Environment, Transport and Climate Protection, Berlin, https://www.berlin.de/sen/uvk/verkehr/verkehrsdaten/zahlen-und-fakten (accessed on 19 July 2021). [12]

BiTiBi (2017), *WHY BiTiBi?.* [45]

Brueckner, J. and S. Franco (2018), "Employer-paid parking, mode choice, and suburbanization", *Journal of Urban Economics*, Vol. 104, pp. 35-46, http://dx.doi.org/10.1016/j.jue.2017.12.002. [73]

Bruxelles Mobilité (2020), "Good Move: The Regional Mobility Plan for 2020-2030", web page, Brussels Regional Public Service, https://mobilite-mobiliteit.brussels/en/good-move (accessed on 24 March 2021). [61]

Buckle, S. et al. (2020), "Addressing the COVID-19 and climate crises: Potential economic recovery pathways and their implications for climate change mitigation, NDCs and broader socio-economic goals", *OECD/IEA Climate Change Expert Group Papers*, No. 2020/04, OECD Publishing, Paris, https://dx.doi.org/10.1787/50abd39c-en. [90]

C40 (2016), "Benefits of Climate Action Piloting A Global Approach To Measurement APPENDIX CONTENTS", http://www.c40.org/researches/measuring-benefits (accessed on 24 September 2021). [63]

Cairns, S., S. Atkins and P. Goodwin (2002), "Disappearing traffic? The story so far", *Municipal Engineer*, Vol. 151/1, pp. 13-22, http://dx.doi.org/10.1680/muen.151.1.13.38856. [47]

Chester, M. et al. (2015), "Parking infrastructure: A constraint on or opportunity for urban redevelopment? A study of Los Angeles County parking supply and growth", *Journal of the American Planning Association*, Vol. 81/4, pp. 268-286, http://dx.doi.org/10.1080/01944363.2015.1092879. [95]

City of Amsterdam (2021), *Policy: Cycling - City of Amsterdam*, https://www.amsterdam.nl/en/policy/policy-traffic/policy-cycling/ (accessed on 27 October 2021). [42]

Colville-Andersen, M. (2018), *Copenhagenize: The Definitive Guide to Global Bicycle Urbanism*, Island Press, Washington, DC, http://dx.doi.org/10.5822/978-1-61091-939-5. [13]

Creutzig, F. et al. (2020), “Fair street space allocation: Ethical principles and empirical insights”, *Transport Reviews*, Vol. 40/6, pp. 711-733, http://dx.doi.org/10.1080/01441647.2020.1762795. [11]

Crozet, Y. and A. Mercier (2018), “Urban toll: Rethinking acceptability through accessibility”, presentation at the "Round table on Social Impacts of Time and Spacebased Road Pricing", Auckland, 30 November-1 December 2017, https://www.itf-oecd.org/urban-toll-rethinking-acceptability-through-accessibility (accessed on 21 August 2019). [83]

Dolin, M. et al. (2014), *Complete Streets, Complete Networks: Rural Contexts*, Active Transportation Alliance. [29]

EIT Urban Mobility (n.d.), “Solving the mobility changes facing our cities”, website, https://www.eiturbanmobility.eu (accessed on 26 March 2021). [9]

Eliasson, J. (2016), “Is congestion pricing fair?: Consumer and citizen perspectives on equity effects”, *International Transport Forum Discussion Papers*, No. 2016/13, OECD Publishing, Paris, https://doi.org/10.1787/79123657-en. [91]

ELTIS (2014), “Complete overhaul of Lisbon’s parking policy (Portugal)”. [77]

European Commission (2009), *Reclaiming City Streets for People: Chaos or Quality of Life?*, Publications Office of the European Union, https://op.europa.eu/en/publication-detail/-/publication/94a8a003-be86-467a-9a85-63a5d52bf7ae (accessed on 24 August 2020). [46]

FleetNews (2018), “City of London introduces emissions-based parking charges”, web page, https://www.fleetnews.co.uk/news/car-industry-news/2018/08/15/city-of-london-introduces-emissions-based-parking-charges (accessed on 26 March 2021). [79]

Franco, S. (2020), *Parking Prices and Availability, Mode Choice and Urban Form Discussion Paper*, ITF, http://www.itf-oecd.org (accessed on 9 July 2021). [66]

Franco, S. and N. Khordagui (2019), “Commute mode choices and the role of parking prices, parking availability and urban form: Evidence from Los Angeles County”, *UCI Working Paper*, University of California, Irving. [68]

General Commission for Strategy and Foresight (2013), *Towards a User-Oriented Parking Policy*, General Commission for Strategy and Foresight, Paris, https://www.strategie.gouv.fr/english-articles/report-towards-user-oriented-parking-policy (accessed on 26 March 2021). [78]

Government of Lisbon (2018), *Sítio da Câmara Municipal de Lisboa: Estacionamento.* [76]

Groote, J., J. van Ommeren and H. Koster (2016), “Car ownership and residential parking subsidies: Evidence from Amsterdam”, *Economics of Transportation*, Vol. 6, pp. 25-37, http://dx.doi.org/10.1016/j.ecotra.2016.07.001. [71]

Grote, M. et al. (2016), “Including congestion effects in urban road traffic CO2 emissions modelling: Do local government authorities have the right options?”, *Transportation Research Part D: Transport and Environment*, Vol. 43, pp. 95-106, http://dx.doi.org/10.1016/J.TRD.2015.12.010. [85]

Happy City (n.d.), “Happy City”, website, https://thehappycity.com/about (accessed on 8 July 2021). [26]

Healthy Streets (2021), "Healthy Streets", website, https://healthystreets.com (accessed on 24 March 2021). [24]

Iracheta Carroll, J. (2020), *Air Quality, Mobility and Metropolitan Policy: Empirical Evidence from Mexico City, Los Angelos and San Francisco*, Doctoral Thesis, Indiana University, https://scholarworks.iu.edu/dspace/handle/2022/25377. [4]

ITDP (2016), *Street Design and Management Policy*, Institute for Transportation and Development Policy, https://go.itdp.org/download/attachments/36570663/Street%20Design%20and%20Management%20Policy_ITDP_161212.pdf?api=v2 (accessed on 19 August 2019). [38]

ITF (2021), *Avoiding Car Dependency*. [64]

ITF (2021), *Reversing Car Dependency: Summary and Conclusions*, ITF Roundtable Reports, No. 181, OECD Publishing, Paris, https://doi.org/10.1787/bebe3b6e-en. [10]

ITF (2020), *Road Safety Annual Report 2020*, OECD Publishing, Paris, https://dx.doi.org/10.1787/f3e48023-en. [7]

ITF (2019), "Benchmarking accessibility in cities: Measuring the impact of proximity and transport performance", *International Transport Forum Policy Papers*, No. 68, OECD Publishing, Paris, https://doi.org/10.1787/4b1f722b-en. [88]

ITF (2019), "Improving transport planning and investment through the use of accessibility indicators", *International Transport Forum Policy Papers*, No. 66, OECD Publishing, Paris, https://doi.org/10.1787/46ddbcae-en. [5]

ITF (2018), *The Social Impacts of Road Pricing: Summary and Conclusions*, ITF Roundtable Reports, No. 170, OECD Publishing, Paris, https://dx.doi.org/10.1787/d6d56d2d-en. [82]

ITF (2017), *Income Inequality, Social Inclusion and Mobility*, ITF Roundtable Reports, No. 164, OECD Publishing, Paris, https://doi.org/10.1787/g2g7ae77-en. [98]

ITF (2017), "Strategies for mitigating air pollution in Mexico City", *International Transport Forum Policy Papers*, No. 30, OECD Publishing, Paris, https://doi.org/10.1787/bb049481-en. [84]

Jones, P. (2009), *Link and Place: A Guide to Street Planning and Design*, Landon Publishing, London, https://es.slideshare.net/EngineersAustralia/link-and-place-a-guide-to-street-planning-and-design-by-prof-peter-jones-2400681 (accessed on 15 January 2021). [36]

Jones, P. (2009), "'LINK' AND 'PLACE': A NEW APPROACH TO STREET PLANNING AND DESIGN". [23]

Jones, P. et al. (2018), *Urban Mobility: Preparing for the Future, Learning from the Past*, CREATE, https://www.researchgate.net/publication/329168103_Urban_Mobility_Preparing_for_the_Future_Learning_from_the_Past (accessed on 16 March 2021). [8]

Jones, P., S. Marshall and N. Boujenko (2008), "Creating more people-friendly urban streets through "link and place" street planning and design", *IATSS Research*, Vol. 32/1, pp. 14-25, https://doi.org/10.1016/S0386-1112(14)60196-5. [27]

KiM (2018), *Cycling Facts 2018 | Report | Government.nl*, https://www.government.nl/documents/reports/2018/04/01/cycling-facts-2018 (accessed on 27 October 2021). [41]

Kodransky, M. and G. Hermann (2011), *Europe's Parking U-Turn: From Accommodation to Regulation*, Institute for Transportation & Development Policy, New York, NY, https://www.itdp.org/2011/01/18/europes-parking-u-turn-from-accommodation-to-regulation (accessed on 25 March 2021). [65]

Litman, T. (2021), *Evaluating Public Transit Benefits and Costs: Best Practices Guidebook*, Victoria Transport Policy Institute, Victoria, British Columbia, https://www.vtpi.org/tranben.pdf. [32]

Litman, T. (2016), *Parking Management: Strategies, Evaluation and Planning*, Victoria Transport Policy Institute, Victoria, British Columbia, https://www.vtpi.org/park_man.pdf (accessed on 26 March 2021). [67]

Litman, T. (2015), *Evaluating Complete Streets: The Value of Designing Roads For Diverse Modes, Users and Activities*, Victoria Transport Policy Institute, Victoria, British Columbia, https://www.vtpi.org/compstr.pdf. [19]

Litman, T. (2014), "Evaluating public transportation: Local funding options", *Journal of Public Transportation*, Vol. 17/1, pp. 43-74, https://www.nctr.usf.edu/wp-content/uploads/2014/03/JPT17.1_Litman.pdf. [87]

Litman, T. (2012), "Pricing for traffic safety", *Transportation Research Record: Journal of the Transportation Research Board*, Vol. 2318/1, pp. 16-22, http://dx.doi.org/10.3141/2318-03. [86]

Litman, T. (2008), *Evaluating Accessibility for Transport Planning*, Victoria Transport Policy Institute, Victoria, British Columbia, https://www.vtpi.org/access.pdf. [31]

López, I., J. Ortega and M. Pardo (2020), "Mobility infrastructures in cities and climate change: An analysis through the superblocks in Barcelona", *Atmosphere*, Vol. 11/4, p. 410, http://dx.doi.org/10.3390/ATMOS11040410. [50]

Mattioli, G. et al. (2019), "Vulnerability to motor fuel price increases: Socio-spatial patterns in England", *Journal of Transport Geography*, Vol. 78, pp. 98-114, http://dx.doi.org/10.1016/j.jtrangeo.2019.05.009. [92]

Ministry of Territorial, Agrarian and Urban Development (2020), *Movilidad 4s para México: Saludable, Segura, Sustentable y Solidaria – Plan de Movilidad para una Nueva Normalidad*, Government of Mexico, https://www.gob.mx/sedatu/documentos/movilidad-4s-para-mexico-saludable-segura-sustentable-y-solidaria-plan-de-movilidad-para-una-nueva-normalidad (accessed on 24 March 2021). [20]

Mock, P. et al. (2012), "Discrepancies between type-approval and "real-world" fuel-consumption and CO2 values: Assessment for 2001-2011 European passenger cars", Working Paper 2012-02, International Council on Clean Transportation, https://theicct.org/sites/default/files/publications/ICCT_EU_fuelconsumption2_workingpaper_2012.pdf (accessed on 20 July 2021). [96]

Mueller, N. et al. (2020), "Changing the urban design of cities for health: The superblock model", *Environment International*, Vol. 134, p. 105132, http://dx.doi.org/10.1016/j.envint.2019.105132. [56]

Municipality of Groningen (2021), *Leef-En Klimaatstraten: Een nieuw perspectief op de straat*, Municipality of Groningen, Groningen. [94]

Nello-Deakin, S. (2019), "Is there such a thing as a "fair" distribution of road space?", *Journal of Urban Design*, Vol. 24/5, http://dx.doi.org/10.1080/13574809.2019.1592664. [14]

Netherlands, G. (2021), *Ways of encouraging bicycle use | Bicycles | Government.nl*, https://www.government.nl/topics/bicycles/bicycle-policy-in-the-netherlands (accessed on 27 October 2021). [43]

Netherlans, G. (2021), *Bicycles | Government.nl*, https://www.government.nl/topics/bicycles (accessed on 27 October 2021). [39]

Nottingham City Council (n.d.), "Workplace Parking Levy", web page, https://www.nottinghamcity.gov.uk/wpl (accessed on 9 July 2021). [75]

OECD (2015), *OECD Territorial Reviews: Valle de México, Mexico*, OECD Territorial Reviews, OECD Publishing, Paris, https://dx.doi.org/10.1787/9789264245174-en. [30]

Pascal Smet (2017), "Good Move, the plan for a Brussels on a human scale", Pascal Smet, https://pascalsmet.brussels/en/project/good-move-en (accessed on 20 July 2021). [62]

Perk, M. et al. (2015), *Capturing the Benefits of Complete Streets*, Florida Department of Transportation, Tallahassee, FL, https://www.nctr.usf.edu/2016/01/capturing-the-benefits-of-complete-streets-2 (accessed on 25 November 2020). [17]

Petit, S. (2017), "World vehicle population rose 4.6% in 2016", web page, Wards Intelligence, https://wardsintelligence.informa.com/WI058630/World-Vehicle-Population-Rose-46-in-2016 (accessed on 13 August 2021). [97]

Pierce, G. and D. Shoup (2013), "Getting the prices right", *Journal of the American Planning Association*, Vol. 79/1, pp. 67-81, http://dx.doi.org/10.1080/01944363.2013.787307. [72]

Postaria, R. (2021), "Superblock (Superilla) Barcelona – A city redefined", Cities Forum, https://www.citiesforum.org/news/superblock-superilla-barcelona-a-city-redefined (accessed on 8 July 2021). [55]

ReVeAL (2019), "Milan launches Area B, Italy's largest low-emission zone", ReVeAL, https://civitas-reveal.eu/uvar-in-europe/milan-launches-area-b-italys-largest-low-emission-zone (accessed on 10 July 2021). [89]

Roberts, D. (2019), "Barcelona, Spain, urban planning: What the city learned from the first superblocks", Vox, https://www.vox.com/energy-and-environment/2019/4/9/18273894/barcelona-urban-planning-superblocks-poblenou (accessed on 23 June 2021). [57]

Rowe, H. (2013), *Smarter Ways to Change: Learning from Innovative Practice in Road Space Reallocation*, State of Australian Cities Research Network, https://apo.org.au/node/59916 (accessed on 20 July 2021). [60]

Rueda, S. (2020), *Debats in the Official College Arquitects of Catalonia (COAC). Superilles, cap a un nou model de ciutat.*. [58]

Rueda, S. (2020), *Regenerating the Cerdà Plan. From Cerdà's Block to the Ecosystemic Urbanism Superblock*. [53]

Rueda, S. (2019), *Superblocks as the Base of New Urban Mobility and a New Model of Public Space: Barcelona as a Case Study.*. [54]

Rueda, S. (2019), "Superblocks for the Design of New Cities and Renovation of Existing Ones: Barcelona's Case", in Nieuwenhuijsen, M. and H. Khreis (eds.), *Integrating Human Health into Urban and Transport Planning*, Springer. [52]

Russo, A., J. van Ommeren and A. Dimitropoulos (2019), "The Environmental and Welfare Implications of Parking Policies", *OECD Environment Working Papers*, No. 145, OECD Publishing, Paris, https://dx.doi.org/10.1787/16d610cc-en. [69]

SACTRA (1994), *Transport and the economy: full report*, http://moz-extension://cdd8ccd8-cf3a-4a04-885d-b1b9fc022324/enhanced-reader.html?openApp&pdf=https%3A%2F%2Fwebarchive.nationalarchives.gov.uk%2F20050304041634%2Fhttp%3A%2F%2Fwww.dft.gov.uk%2Fstellent%2Fgroups%2Fdft_econappr%2Fdocuments%2Fpdf%2Fdft_econappr_pdf_022512.pdf (accessed on 26 March 2021). [3]

Savills (2016), *Completing London's Streets*, Savills, https://pdf.euro.savills.co.uk/uk/residential---other/completing-london-s-streets-080116.pdf. [22]

Scheiner, J. et al. (2020), "What's that garage for? Private parking and on-street parking in a high-density urban residential neighbourhood", *Journal of Transport Geography*, Vol. 85, p. 102714, http://dx.doi.org/10.1016/j.jtrangeo.2020.102714. [70]

Shoup, D. (2005), "The High Cost of Free Parking", *Journal of Planning Education and Research*. [74]

Shoup, D. (1997), "The high cost of free parking", *Journal of Planning Education and Research*, Vol. 17/1, pp. 3-20, http://dx.doi.org/10.1177/0739456x9701700102. [80]

Sterman, J. (2000), *Business Dynamics: Systems Thinking and Modeling for a Complex World*, Irwin/McGraw-Hill, http://jsterman.scripts.mit.edu/Business_Dynamics.html (accessed on 8 March 2021). [1]

TfL (2017), "Healthy Streets", web page, Transport for London, https://tfl.gov.uk/corporate/about-tfl/how-we-work/planning-for-the-future/healthy-streets (accessed on 19 March 2021). [34]

TfL (n.d.), *How Green Infrastructure Contributes to the Healthy Streets Approach*, Transport for London, London, https://content.tfl.gov.uk/contributions-of-gi-to-healthy-streets-approach.pdf. [33]

Thaler, R. and C. Sunstein (2008), *Nudge: Improving Decisions About Health, Wealth, and Happiness*, Yale University Press. [59]

Tour de Force (2021), *Home - Fietsberaad*, https://fietsberaad.nl/Tour-de-Force-English/Home (accessed on 27 October 2021). [40]

Tower Hamlets Council (n.d.), "Liveable streets", web page, Project Centre, https://www.pclconsult.co.uk/liveablestreets (accessed on 15 January 2021). [25]

UCL (2014), "A new approach to urban street planning and design", web page, University College London, https://www.ucl.ac.uk/impact/case-studies/2014/dec/new-approach-urban-street-planning-and-design (accessed on 26 March 2021). [35]

UN-Habitat (2016), *The Fundamentals of Urbanization: Evidence Base for Policy Making*, United Nations Human Settlements Programme, Nairobi, https://unhabitat.org/sites/default/files/download-manager-files/Global%20Report%20H%20III%20UN-Habitat%202016%C6%922.pdf. [15]

US Department of Transportation (n.a.), "Traffic calming to slow vehicle speeds", web page, US Department of Transportation, Washington, DC, https://www.transportation.gov/mission/health/Traffic-Calming-to-Slow-Vehicle-Speeds (accessed on 19 March 2021). [21]

van Dender, K. (2019), "Taxing vehicles, fuels, and road use: Opportunities for improving transport tax practice", *OECD Taxation Working Papers*, No. 44, OECD Publishing, Paris, https://dx.doi.org/10.1787/e7f1d771-en. [81]

Waka Kotahi NZ Transport Agency (2021), "Movement and place classification", web page, Waka Kotahi NZ Transport Agency, https://www.nzta.govt.nz/roads-and-rail/road-efficiency-group/one-network-framework/movement-and-place-classification (accessed on 4 August 2021). [37]

Welle, B. et al. (2018), *Cities Safer By Design: Guidance and Examples to Promote Traffic Safety through Urban and Street Design*, World Resources Institute, Washington, DC, https://publications.wri.org/citiessafer (accessed on 15 January 2021). [16]

WRI (2018), *Sustainable & Safe: A Vision and Guidance for Zero Road Deaths*, World Resources Institute, Washington, DC, https://files.wri.org/s3fs-public/sustainable-safe.pdf. [28]

WSP and RAND Europe (2018), *Latest Evidence on Induced Travel Demand: An Evidence Review*, Department for Transport, London, https://assets.publishing.service.gov.uk/government/uploads/system/uploads/attachment_data/file/762976/latest-evidence-on-induced-travel-demand-an-evidence-review.pdf. [2]

Yu, C. et al. (2018), "Assessing the economic benefits and resilience of complete streets in Orlando, FL: A natural experimental design approach", *Journal of Transport & Health*, Vol. 8, http://dx.doi.org/10.1016/j.jth.2017.11.005. [93]

Yusuf, J. et al. (2016), "Becoming more complete", *Public Works Management & Policy*, Vol. 21/3, http://dx.doi.org/10.1177/1087724X15624694. [18]

Zografos, C. et al. (2020), "The everyday politics of urban transformational adaptation: Struggles for authority and the Barcelona superblock project", *Cities*, Vol. 99, p. 102613, http://dx.doi.org/10.1016/j.cities.2020.102613. [49]

Notes

[1] Globally, the number of cars is estimated to have doubled every 20 years since 1976: from 342 million in 1976, to 670 million in 1996, to 1.3 billion in 2016 (Petit, 2017[97]).

[2] The area occupied by parking is not negligible. Chester et al. (2015[95]) find that, in Los Angeles, the area dedicated to parking is 1.4 times more than the area dedicated to the roadway system.

[3] A feedback loop is a non-linear cause-effect relationship. See Annex A.

[4] Or at least large areas within them.

[5] The Mexico City Metropolitan Area (Valle de México) includes the 16 *delegaciones* (boroughs) of Mexico City, 59 municipalities from the state of Mexico and 1 municipality from the state of Hidalgo.

[6] As highlighted by the ITF (2019[5]), "projects that make significant improvements to non-motorised trips compare poorly with those that cut travel time on motorised transport. This is due to the conventional approach to cost-benefit analysis that relies on travel time savings as a proxy for most of the benefits associated with transport investment. This traditional focus on travel time savings often leads to prioritisation of schemes that are misaligned with increased sustainable mobility goals. All else being equal, cars are indeed faster than public transport, serving a larger area in the same amount of time. As such, improving a link in a fast network like a road is likely to generate more travel time savings than a comparable improvement in a slower public transport network".

[7] Chapter 2, uses the food pyramid analogy and describes "healthy" transport systems as those where motorised, and especially private vehicles (the sugar and the fat) are only used for a reduced number of trips.

[8] Community severance "describes the effects of transport infrastructure or motorised traffic as a physical or psychological barrier separating one built-up area from another built-up area or open space". It "occurs when transport infrastructure or motorised traffic divides space and people" (Anciaes, Jones and Mindell, 2015[6]). Community severance is also described as the "barrier effect" resulting from transport systems that limits, rather than facilitates, people's mobility (Anciaes, Jones and Mindell, 2015[6]).

[9] This statistic does not include changes during the COVID-19 pandemic.

[10] Public transport accounts for 27% of trips. Information on the space attributed to public transport was not specified.

[11] "Street intersection density – the number of intersections per one square kilometre of land. The more intersections there are in a street network, the more walkable the streets are deemed to be" (UN-Habitat, 2016[15]).

[12] Buses running in dedicated lanes.

[13] The comparison of five case studies of Complete Streets in Florida, Ohio and North Carolina with control areas without a Complete Streets design found economic benefits including increased property values, higher tax collections and increased business activity (e.g. the creation of new businesses and jobs) (Perk et al., 2015[17]). Another study performed in Orlando assessed the impact on housing values before and after Complete Streets projects during the housing market boom (2000-07) and during the economic crisis and housing market crash (2007-11). It concluded that, on average, houses that were in Complete Streets design had an 8.2% higher home value appreciation and a 4.3% higher home value resilience (i.e. capacity

to maintain their value during the economic crisis) than similar houses in adjacent areas that did not have a Complete Streets design (Yu et al., 2018[93]).

[14] It must be recognised that a number of countries have increasingly incorporated impact assessments into policy decision frameworks, which is also important. For instance the new climate law in Sweden mainstreams the use of these tools, and in addition to measuring climate impacts also report a number of expected co-benefits from policy proposals.

[15] Renamed as "movement and place".

[16] It was central to the Urban Mobility Plan for 2013-18 and continues to be key to the Urban Mobility Plan for 2019-24.

[17] An earlier and simpler version (with a focus on traffic calming measures) of Superblocks was implemented in two different areas in 1993 and 2003 (Roberts, 2019[57]).

[18] For example, via brochures distributed to the population.

[19] In other European cities (e.g. Amsterdam, London), where incomes and opportunity costs are higher, prices are multiple times this amount.

[20] Type-approval is the process the manufacturer must follow before being allowed to sell a new vehicle model on the market. The manufacturer must determine the CO_2 emissions level and the fuel consumption of the vehicle (Mock et al., 2012[96]).

[21] Parking Day projects have taken place in Argentina, Belgium, Canada, France, Germany, Italy and the United States and people are invited to join from all over the world (https://www.myparkingday.org).

[22] m^2h refers to "space-time consumption", which combines surface (m^2) and the duration of the consumption (h).

[23] If existing schemes were to be integrated into a general taxing scheme, then ideally driving through these areas would be taxed more to continue reflecting the relatively scarce space, higher congestion problems and higher density.

[24] Importantly, levels of exposure to local air pollution in different areas can also be mirrored by road-charging schemes if these are differentiated by density or congestion levels (both correlated with exposure) (van Dender, 2019[81]).

[25] Renamed "Area C" scheme.

[26] And was called "Area B".

[27] While it could seem this way, the notion from the general public that something is unfair is not always linked to the fact that its impacts are effectively regressive.

[28] While often these comparisons are not made, the distributional impact of road pricing is not higher than that related to fuel taxes, and it is less significant than generalised consumption taxes such as value-added tax (ITF, 2021[64]).

[29] As discussed by the ITF (2017[98]), urban or congestion charging schemes are not a cost-effective measure for raising revenue in any case, and thus should not be implemented for these reasons. Road pricing would have a greater fiscal advantage if envisaged as a general shift from fuel prices to maintain revenue stability as a systems shift to electric car use. Van Dender (2019[81]) discusses this subject in depth and highlights that charges could be set to recover infrastructure costs of driving even where

congestion is not an issue. Even in this case, revenue objectives should not blur or override the potential of this instrument to attain environmental and social benefits. Thus, careful analysis and co-ordination between fiscal and transport authorities is important to align these different agendas in this case.

4 Transformational change #2: from sprawl to proximity

This chapter explains the dynamic of urban sprawl and how to integrate spatial planning into climate strategies to reverse sprawl and recreate proximity between people and places. It makes recommendations for improving governance, planning frameworks and regulations for revisiting new development as well as urban renewal plans to improve life quality and create sustainable territories.

4.1. Why cities sprawl

Like traffic volumes, decisions on where to live are endogenous to the system. As investments in roads increase their capacity (B1 in Figure 4.1), the radius accessible within a certain time budget by car (e.g. 30 minutes) increases.

This new car-dependent "proximity" to city centres, coupled with lower housing prices in peripheries (and other advantages that less dense areas may have compared to city centres), incentivises people to move to the suburbs. To take an example, Resnik (2010[1]) describes the way in which urban sprawl in the United States has increased since the 1950s, as individuals moved out of urban centres to evade noise, crime and traffic. The draw of larger homes and more space – at least partially fuelled by the widely disseminated American Dream narrative – accelerated this flight to the suburbs, where zoning regulations created single-use developments (Resnik, 2010[1]) (see below for more on why this type of development was prioritised). This resulted in large, low-density residential areas interconnected by roads, where residents typically commuted by vehicle (Resnik, 2010[1]).

In the preceding paragraph, the word proximity is in quotation marks as road expansion, rather than creating "real" proximity, compensates for the lack of proximity (or "fake" proximity) with more mobility. Furthermore, once people move to car-dependent areas, they may have incentives to move even further away, further reducing proximity and increasing the need for more mobility, bringing us back to the dynamic of induced demand (B1, B2 and B3). Moving further away may allow people to benefit from lower housing prices with a similar time budget to the city centre (e.g. five or ten additional minutes by car), without losing much in terms of alternative transport modes, as they already did not have many options other than the car. While in theory public transport could expand to remote places (benefiting from new roads), the rapid and scattered expansion of development limits the extent to which public transport networks can keep up, since a minimum density of demand is important for public transport to be viable and attractive (see below[1]).

Figure 4.1. Road capacity expansion incentivises urban sprawl

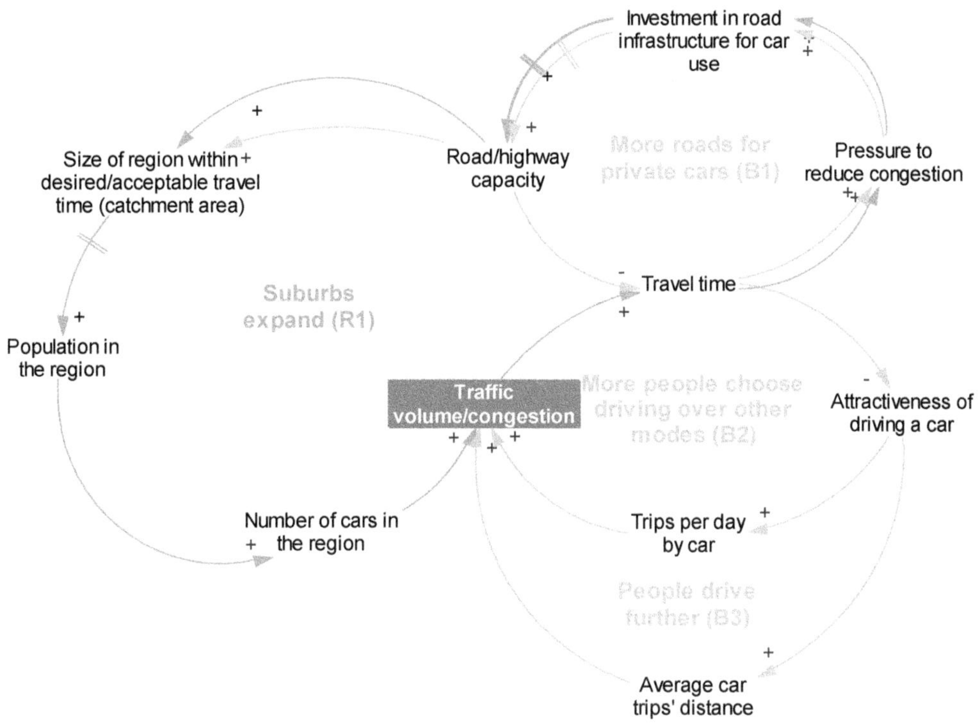

Notes: Arrows with a "+" mean that both variables move in the same direction (when one increases, the other increases and vice versa). Arrows with a "–" mean that the variables move in opposite directions (when one increases, the other decreases and vice versa). The two lines on the arrow denote a delay. The figure can be read as follows: as investments in road infrastructure for car use increase, road/highway capacity increases. This leads to an expansion of the region accessible within a desired/acceptable travel time (e.g. 20 minutes by car to the city centre), which increases the population in the region, and the number of cars. Note that a bigger radius with access to city cores within a certain time budget fosters urban sprawl. As the number of cars increases, traffic volume/congestion also increase, increasing travel time. As the gap between the desirable and actual travel time widens (not shown in figure), the pressure to reduce congestion also increases, leading to higher investments in roads, higher road/highway capacity, further expanding the size of the region accessible within a reasonable travel time, etc.
Source: Adapted from Sterman (2000[2]).

As more people move to the suburbs and become car dependent, congestion starts to appear, increasing the average travel time for trips from the suburbs to the city centre, thus potentially slowing or *balancing* the urban sprawl dynamic (B4 in Figure 4.2). Housing prices in the periphery (not shown in Figure 4.1) also start to increase as demand increases, further reducing immigration and the development of those suburbs (Sterman, 2000[2]).

Figure 4.2. Congestion reduces the attractiveness of suburbs

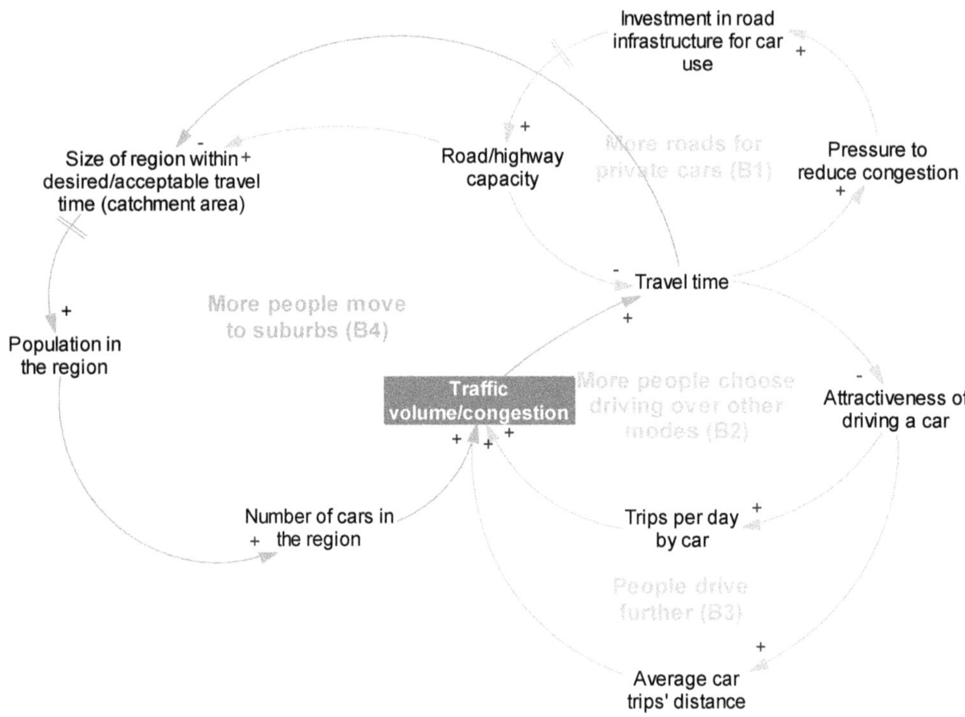

Notes: Arrows with a "+" mean that both variables move in the same direction (when one increases, the other increases and vice versa). Arrows with a "–" mean that the variables move in opposite directions (when one increases, the other decreases and vice versa). The two lines on the arrow denote a delay. As travel time decreases thanks to investments in road/highway capacity expansion, the size of the region accessible within an acceptable travel time also increases. This, however, leads to an increase in traffic volume/congestion that increases travel time, and may discourage people from moving further away (said differently, the higher the travel time, the smaller the region accessible within an acceptable travel time becomes).
Source: Adapted from Sterman (2000[2]).

What can be observed is, however, that suburban development tends to continue. This can be the result, at least in part, of the now car-dependent population's pressure for authorities to build more roads to reduce congestion and time travel, bringing us back to the induced demand dynamic (B1, B2 and B3). As housing prices increase, there is also an incentive for the construction industry to build in the new suburbs further away from cities. Building away from cities is a way for the construction industry to accelerate market expansion, since space is limited in places that are already developed and construction permitting may be slow due to the higher density of affected neighbours and greater complexity of the infrastructure.

While suburban development is not always an issue in itself, the way this expansion has taken place is a barrier to sustainable transport systems. The expansion of suburbs has followed a single-use or siloed logic, in which each area focuses on a specific use: suburbs tend to be residential neighbourhoods, places of interest are often concentrated in city centres or in other specific areas (e.g. shopping malls), and offices are clustered in working districts. The resulting development pattern is low density and often scattered. This leads to clusters of badly connected, most often only by roads, built-up areas, and increases the need to travel long distances (Figure 4.3). The fact that suburban expansion is privileged over infill development[2] (to a great extent due to the reasons outlined above) is also problematic, as it contributes to the conversion of green areas.

Figure 4.3. Single-use development increases traffic

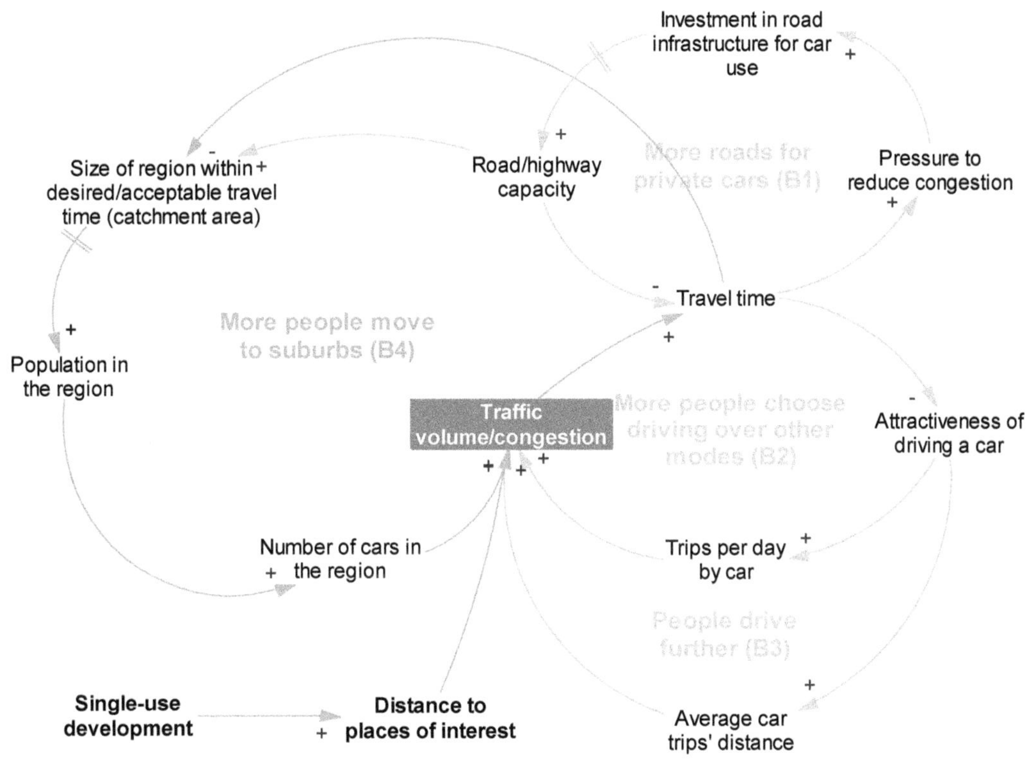

Notes: Arrows with a "+" mean that both variables move in the same direction (when one increases, the other increases and vice versa). Arrows with a "–" mean that the variables move in opposite directions (when one increases, the other decreases and vice versa). The two lines on the arrow denote a delay. As development follows a single-use logic, the distance to places of interest increases (as people need to travel to meet many of their needs), which increases traffic volume/congestion.
Source: Adapted from Sterman (2000[2]).

Decades of policies focused on mobility, "blind" to the importance of creating proximity and delivering accessibility (see more in Chapter 2), are part of the reason why suburban development has followed this single-use logic. When the objective is to increase mobility and speed up travel, then expanding the size of the built-up area to areas with cheaper prices may not seem directly problematic – as long as more roads are built to connect the different areas and accommodate the increased traffic volume. The externalities of such expansion, if recognised at all, are also accepted as "necessary and inevitable costs". Greenhouse gas emissions, air pollution, habitat and biodiversity loss, overconsumption and resource waste are some of these costs (McDonald et al., 2019[3]; Mahendra and Seto, 2019[4]). Dependence on cars is not seen as problematic either, as long as road capacity expansion "reacts" (or "predicts" and "provides") to maintain the average speed of travel within an acceptable range. The privilege given to emission- and space-intensive modes of transportation like private cars is also not seen as an issue through a mobility lens, as the fact that using so much space to accommodate cars leaves less space for other modes and urban functions (green space, centrally located housing, etc.) is also ignored. Note that considering certain impacts as "externalities" or "side effects" reflects that a greater importance is given to certain outcomes relative to others. As explained by Sterman, Forrester and Standish (2002[5]), "There are no side effects – only effects. Those we thought of in advance, the ones we like, we call the main, or intended, effects, and take credit for them. The ones we did not anticipate, the ones that came around and bit us in the rear – those are the 'side effects'".

Narratives supporting car-dependent lifestyles have also played a significant role in increasing the attractiveness of suburbs. Communication efforts to associate the car (and the detached houses described above) with notions such as freedom, rights or status (Norton, 2011[6]; Gössling, 2020[7]), also contributed to normalising car dependency and associating it to increased well-being (Freund and Martin, 1993[8]) (see Figure 4.3).

The logic of single-use development described above significantly constrains the scope for climate action. In single-use or siloed urban areas, people need to travel, often long distances, for almost every need: to work, to the bakery, to the cinema, to school or to the park. Longer distances imply that active modes of transport are less and less of an option. The attractiveness of public transport is also negatively affected, both further increasing car dependency.

With a scattered population that needs to travel long distances and depend on cars to meet its daily needs, climate policies such as carbon prices also become politically unfeasible. In car-dependent, single-use urban systems, the behavioural shift that is intended by the introduction of carbon pricing is simply not possible (or its scope is very narrow) due to the limited or lack of alternatives to car use. Carbon taxes at the rate needed to meet ambitious emissions reduction targets are unlikely to be accepted by the population, potentially leading to social upheavals such as the Yellow Vests (Gilets Jaunes) movement in France. If not accepted by the population, the implementation of such policies will be unlikely or will be rolled in and out periodically, thus ineffective. Chapter 6 further develops this topic.

Scattered and single-use development, and the resulting car-dependent systems, can also greatly affect well-being more broadly. For example, children's freedom is affected as they become dependent on their parents to get to places until they can drive a car. Parents' time availability (to do other things than take children places) is also greatly affected by this trend.

The next section discusses what it would entail to reverse the dynamic of urban sprawl in terms of the types of policies, measurement frameworks and governance mechanisms.

4.2. How to reduce sprawl via spatial planning and design

Chapter 3 identified the need to shift from a "predict and provide" mind-set, which is narrowly focused on providing roads to allow for car travel, towards holistic approaches to design and manage public space. How to manage and design public space is at the core of Complete Streets and Place-making approaches, and Chapter 3presented examples of how these approaches could be implemented to transform and better manage streets (including by reallocating space, improving parking policy and using road pricing). It must be emphasised that this is a first step towards reversing car dependency by reversing induced demand.

This section goes beyond the design and management of public space and focuses on changes needed to rethink territories as a whole (beyond public space) to contain and reverse urban sprawl. A number of specific policies and actions (e.g. zoning regulations, housing policy, etc.) are crucial for the redesign of territories. A detailed analysis of these policies is beyond the scope of this report. This analysis focuses rather on the necessary changes in governance, planning and regulatory frameworks guiding spatial planning (including those policies mentioned). The focus is on how these changes can help shift policy away from "proximity blindness" (see Chapter 2), by linking transport and land-use decisions, and make the sustainable delivery of accessibility central to decision making.

While the policies in Chapter 3 (e.g. Superblocks) can be implemented, and lead to positive impacts in the short term, the changes presented in this section are deeper, longer term changes. They are, however, necessary for the transition towards sustainable-by-design systems. Importantly, longer-term changes do not necessarily mean several decades. For instance, according to Savills (2016[9]), implementing the type of large-scale renewal projects proposed for London, which build on Complete Streets (see below), would take around ten years to be fully implemented. In addition, as shown by the example of Pontevedra described below, a number of benefits (e.g. reduced traffic and pollution, road safety improvements) are progressively unlocked as territories transform.

A number of synergies between the actions in Chapter 3 and the objective of redesigning territories addressed in this chapter can be made. For instance, redesigning streets can liberate space not only for other public use, but also for other uses (e.g. new or expanded areas for local businesses). In the mid- and longer run, liberated space can be used even for new development (e.g. bringing housing to more centrally located areas). Similarly, revisiting parking policy can help avoid future sprawl and rather foster compact development, in addition to its shorter term impact on modal shift (Franco, 2020[10]).

Moreover, new development and urban renewal strategies can build on and benefit from Complete Streets and Place-making approaches to rethink spatial development more generally (i.e. beyond public space). Place-making refers to "the production of liveable and sustainable places… [and thus it] …should be included in the missions of the various disciplines that address the organization and management of the built environment" (Palermo, 2014[11]) . Thinking of territories in terms of Complete Streets and Place-making can allow planning for development (or redevelopment) innovatively. For instance, it can allow planning with a different balance between space used for mobility and space used for other urban functions, and shed light on the importance of infrastructure connectivity to increase territories' attractiveness (Palermo, 2014[11]).

A study in London sheds light on the potential of applying these concepts to city renovation projects (Savills, 2016[9]). The study focuses on the redesign of an area dedicated to social housing (1750 housing) that could, via a Complete Street-based redesign, provide additional and better quality[3] housing (Figure 4.4). The redesign project aims to "increase the supply of housing in popular, high quality, mixed-use and street-based neighbourhoods, which reflect the urban form of London's best-loved places" (Savills, 2016[9]). Cost-wise, the report estimates that urban renovation using the Complete Streets urban layout would be less costly per hectare of renovated land (GBP 19.9 million) compared to what the report refers to as "contemporary renovation" (i.e. a business-as-usual approach) (GBP 21.8 million). The value of real estate would, instead, be higher in the former: total end-value per hectare was estimated at GBP 48.1 million for renovation under a Complete Streets approach, against GBP 40 million for contemporary renovation (Savills, 2016[9]).

A design based on Complete Streets would allow the provision of between 54 000 and 360 000 additional housing units. The author explains the estimation of this range as follows: "the bottom of the range is based on an assumption that density is increased from 78 homes per hectare to the bottom end of the range achieved on the six example estates (109 homes per hectare). The top end of the range assumes that the density is increased from 78 homes per hectare to the top end of the range achieved on the six examples (279 homes per hectare)" (Savills, 2016[9]).

Figure 4.4. Street patterns for London's city renovation project

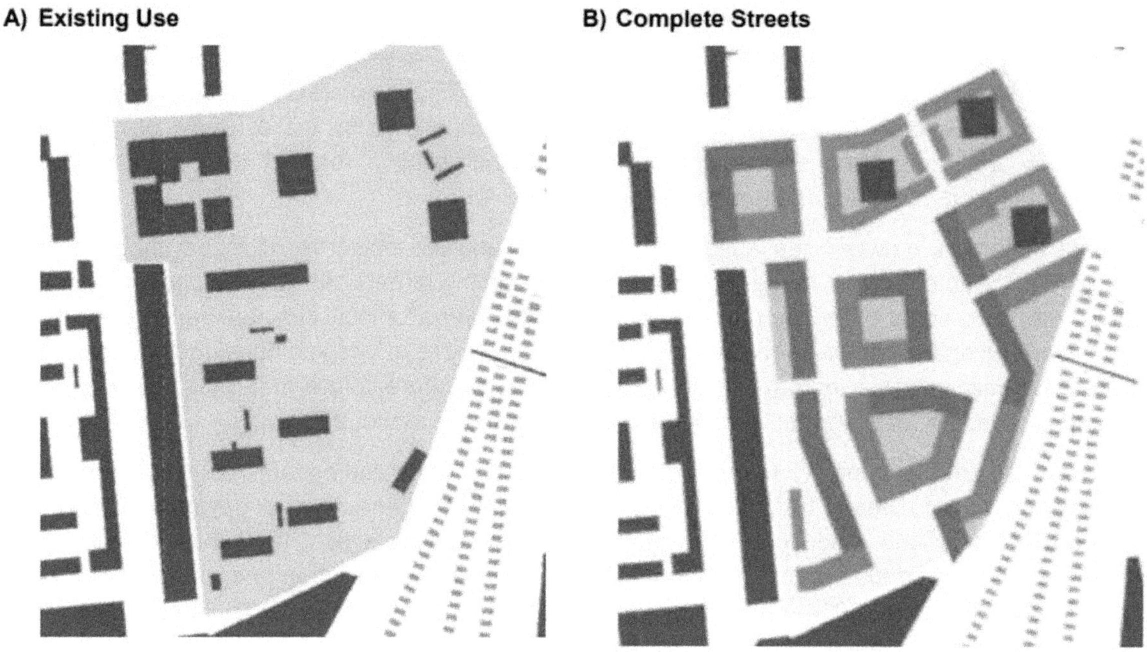

Source: Savills (2016[9]).

Urban redesign based on Complete Streets and place-making approaches is often associated to large urban areas, and seen as irrelevant for smaller cities or towns. Pontevedra, a city of 83 000 inhabitants in Spain (Galicia region), demystifies such a belief and provides a concrete example of how these ideas can be applied beyond large metropoles (Figure 4.5).

Figure 4.5. Street redesign in Pontevedra: Before and after

Source: Concello de Pontevedra, accessed from Burgen (2018[12]).

Pontevedra undertook a number of initiatives in line with Complete Street and Place-making approaches, with the aim of reversing sprawl by increasing the attractiveness of the central areas of the city. A Pontevedrian public official explains that "to encourage people to return to live in the city, it was necessary to improve the quality of life, reduce traffic, and create a human city. By acting quickly, we have stopped urban sprawl" (Burgen, 2018[12]). Moreover, in line with one of the key messages in this report, the transformation of Pontevedra was carried out with the logic that the solution to urban mobility is beyond mobility; thus, instead of the city being conditioned by the need to improve mobility, mobility should be conditioned by the need to improve the city (IEEE, 2020[13]).

In terms of street redesign and management, the basis was laid down by recognising public space as a universal right (IEEE, 2020[13]). Measures implemented included the banning of road traffic and the pedestrianisation of the central area of the city, which progressively extended to other areas (in total 6.7 km^2) (Jiao, He and Zeng, 2019[14]) ; limiting speeds to 20-30 km/h; and the doubling of pedestrian space, where benches, green spaces and playgrounds were installed. In fact, the general rule has been to allocate to pedestrians half of the space in streets that are more than 2.5 m wide, and all of the space in streets that are less than 2.5 m wide (IEEE, 2020[13]). Since car drivers looking for parking spots were identified as one of the main sources of congestion, parking spots were limited to 15-30 minutes, and on-street parking was eliminated and partly replaced by underground and periphery parking. For the new parking regulation to be enforced, the number of police officials was increased, and parking fines of up to EUR 200 are given for not respecting the parking rules.

Pontevedra's changes go beyond street redesign. The changes are a concrete example of a mental shift from a single-use logic towards mixed land-use planning. A landmark policy in this regard has been the withholding of planning permits to shopping centres in the periphery in benefit of local businesses, with the aim of incentivising local economic activity, creating jobs, and increasing the attractiveness of walking and cycling as well as social interactions.

The city also undertook communication and educational campaigns. A metro-like map, called the Metrominuto, shows the services and shops available by foot (Figure 4.6). The local government Pasominuto programme provides 20 walking itineraries with information such as calories burnt to promote walking. A map with bike paths within a 20-kilometre radius around the city is currently under development (Burgen, 2018[12]).

Figure 4.6. A map to highlight proximity to places by foot

Source: Concello de Pontevedra, accessed from Burgen (2018[12]).

The benefits of Pontevedra's strategy are numerous. Overall, the central area of the city has become more attractive, and has welcomed 12 000 new inhabitants (Burgen, 2018[12]).

The results achieved in Pontevedra are an example of the notion of "disappearing traffic" discussed in Chapter 3: there is 69% less traffic in the city centre and 90% less in the downtown core compared to 2013, meaning that 7 (or 9) out of 10 cars have "disappeared". Thanks to the creation of proximity, the majority of people's trips are made by active or shared transport (70% by foot, 22% by vehicle, 6% by bike and 3% by public transportation) (Burgen, 2018[12]), positioning Pontevedra on the right-hand side of Figure 2.1. Pollution and CO_2 emissions decreased by 61% and 70%, respectively, over the same period. The improvements in terms of road safety were also impressive. Where 30 people died due to traffic accidents from 1996 to 2006, on the same street, only 3 died over the next 10-year period, and there have not been any traffic fatalities since 2009 (Burgen, 2018[12]).

The example of Pontevedra highlights that approaches that aim to restore a balance between mobility and proximity are relevant and can be applied in small cities. The example also sheds light on the multiple synergies created through the initiatives described above. In terms of trade-offs, one main drawback of Pontevedra's strategy has been a certain increase in traffic in the peripheries. Such a drawback can be linked to the fact that the initiatives were mainly carried out at the city centre level, and do not reach peripheral areas (as discussed in Section 4.2.1).

Importantly, the Complete Streets and place-making approaches can also be applied in suburbs. In Canadian suburbs and cities, malls are being transformed into mixed-use developments (CBC, 2019[15]). For example, the parking lots of the Square One Shopping Centre in Toronto's suburb of Mississauga will be converted into 37 towers including residential space, retail, offices and green spaces. The goal of the project is to create a transit mobility hub and connect the space to the Hurontario LRT (a light-rail line currently under construction) (CBC, 2019[15]).

In the case of rural areas, which can in many cases be part of the larger commuting zone of a city, a Complete Street and place-making logic can also help to create commercial corridors and revitalise economies that have suffered from scattered and single-use development (which have also made these territories highly dependent on cars). As discussed by the US EPA (2012[16]), rural regions can plan and encourage the development of their commercial base. This can help strengthen the town centre and solidify revenue sources for communities to support their schools, roads and emergency services. Using mixed zoning to incorporate commercial and residential buildings reduces driving distances and increases the use of active transportation for residents' daily travel. Converting warehouses or light-industrial buildings to mixed-use developments, for instance, can revitalise an area. Commercial growth along corridors can reduce scattered development, create a sense of community, increase the tax base for the municipality and active travel, and create jobs (US EPA, 2012[16]).

The rest of this section discusses changes in governance, planning and regulatory frameworks that are necessary for redesigning territories. Section 4.2.1 discusses the case of metropolitan transport authorities (MTAs), an institutional set-up that has proven instrumental for transitioning urban territories (including cities and their larger commuting regions) towards more sustainable transport and urban systems. Section 4.2.2 introduces frameworks and indicators that can help authorities systematically guide development according to accessibility criteria and which are consistent with the Complete Streets and Place-making notions. Finally, Section 4.2.3 illustrates the important role that new development regulations can play in redesigning territories. The section presents two regulations currently misaligned with the transition towards car-independent territories – minimum parking requirements and traffic-oriented transport assessments – and provides recommendations to correct them.

4.2.1. Better governance: The case of metropolitan transport authorities

Authorities in charge of transport, land-use, urban planning and housing are key actors in the transition towards more sustainable transport and urban systems. Redesigning territories is particularly challenging, as it implies integrating decisions from all these actors (among others) and focusing on the whole of territories, which seldom coincide with administrative boundaries and include areas with distinct characteristics and needs. Evidence suggests that focusing only on inner cities (often a small share of current built-up city areas and their commuting zones) has contributed to increasing accessibility gaps and pricing differentials in housing costs between these inner areas and more peripheral ones, potentially accelerating sprawl (Siripanich, 2019[17]).

In the process of decentralisation, relevant powers over transport and urban spatial authorities have often been granted to the local level of government. This has led to more informed local decisions, but also to fragmentation and a multiplicity of not-necessarily co-ordinated or aligned plans and strategies for territories that are part of a same metropolitan area or Functional Urban Area (FUA) (see Box 4.1)

MTAs are an institutional set-up with the potential to strike a balance between decision making that is decentralised enough to reflect actual local needs, and co-ordination, as centralised enough as to ensure coherence at the metropolitan area and/or FUA level (ITF, 2018[18]).

Box 4.1. Functional Urban Areas (FUAs) based on the joint OECD-EU methodology

The OECD and the European Union have developed a joint methodology for analysing cities and their commuting zone. The methodology builds on the analysis of density and commuting patterns, rather than on administrative boundaries, offering a unit of analysis that better reflects the economic and social interactions in a given area (often going beyond administrative boundaries). Because they are based on density and commuting patterns, these units of analysis also offer a territorial unit that is comparable across countries and cities.

According to this methodology, urban areas can be seen as comprised of the following territories:

- **Urban centre:** "a set of contiguous, high-density (1 500 residents per square kilometre) grid cells with a population of 50 000 in the contiguous cells".
- **City** (referred to in this report as a metropolitan area as well) incorporates an urban centre, and any contiguous local unit (e.g. municipality, district) that has at least 50% of its population inside the urban centre identified. This scale is thus **much larger than inner cities** (often the original city, for example the inner-city area of Paris), and includes suburban areas.
- **Commuting zone**: includes "a set of contiguous local units that have at least 15% of their employed residents working in the city".
- **Functional urban area** (also referred to in this report as a metropolitan region) integrates a city and its commuting zone. Importantly some rural areas can be part of functional urban areas.

Figure 4.7. Key concepts of functional urban areas

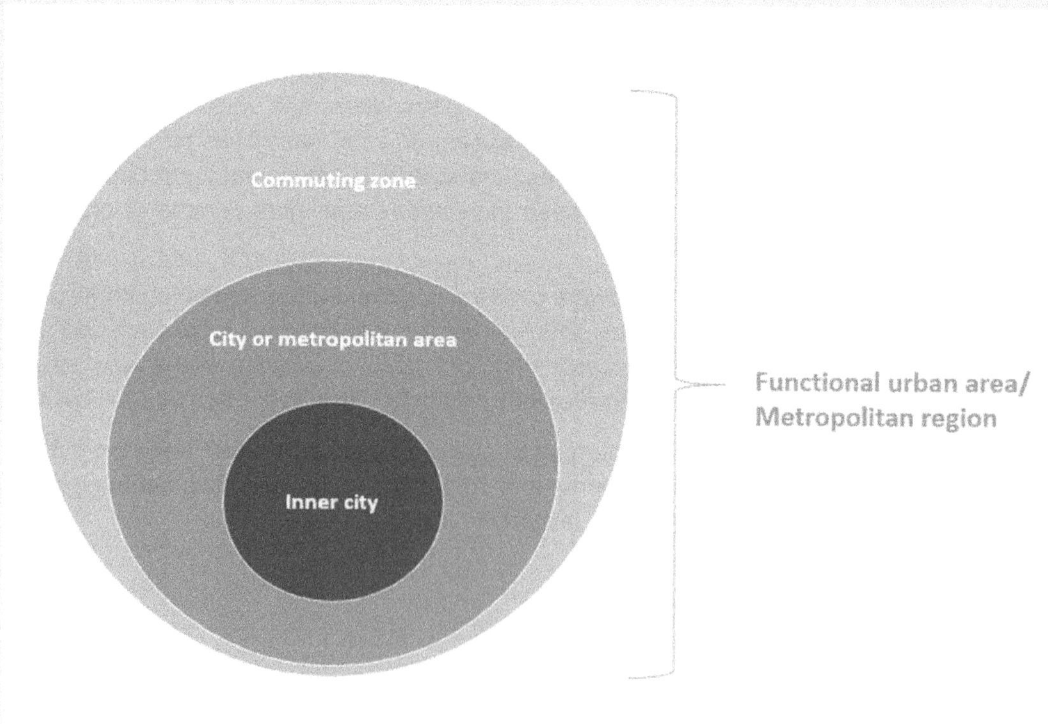

Source: Authors based on Dijkstra, Poelman and Veneri (2019[19]).

MTAs have proven to be successful in managing the needs of wider city areas and in many cases their commuting zones as well (depending on how they are set-up) (ITF, 2018[18]). This allows better connecting and integrating different areas (e.g. inner cities and suburbs or rural areas that are part of larger commuting zones). They have also played a key role in fostering the co-ordination of transport and spatial planning, in particular when the institutional set-up is such that MTAs coexist within metropolitan bodies that also plan at this level for land use. Such co-ordination is central to striking a balance between mobility and proximity, which is in turn fundamental for the delivery of more equitable and sustainable accessibility.

The ITF (2018[18]) highlights best practices based on in-depth analysis of the Paris, London and Barcelona MTAs. The authors associate the following characteristics to functional MTAs (further discussed below):

- formal authority with legal backing over a specified territory, with clearly defined responsibilities
- authority over strategic-level planning
- regulatory capacity
- competence over wide multimodal transport modes, i.e. competence including roads, and planning for active modes, rather than only public transport
- predominant role of subnational authorities in the decision-making process (e.g. through a predominant role on the governing board or similar body)
- dedicated funding and decision-making authority over the use of the transport budget
- dedicated and highly skilled staff.

The MTAs analysed have legal backing for their competence over transport planning at different territorial scales. For example, the Paris area's MTA (Ile-de-France Mobilités) covers the entire region of Île-de-France, which is a territory that coincides well with the metropolitan region or functional urban area linked to Paris, as defined by the EU-OECD methodology presented in Box 4.1 (ITF, 2018[18]). Transport for London (TfL), on the other hand, covers the Greater London area, which coincides with the city or metropolitan area; i.e. a much larger area than London's inner city (which was the original city), but smaller than the entire functional urban area or metropolitan region. In Barcelona, two MTAs coexist and co-ordinate with each other: the Autoritat del Transport Metropolità (ATM) is in charge of transport infrastructure across the metropolitan region (i.e. including the city and its commuting zone), while Àrea Metropolitana de Barcelona (AMB) covers Barcelona and its 32 adjacent municipalities (metropolitan area or city). Barcelona's case is a particularly interesting institutional set-up: AMB covers the continuous built-up area and can thus plan the network of local buses, bicycle lanes and pedestrian facilities in a way that makes sense for the entire area. ATM covers the city plus the larger commuting zone (i.e. the metropolitan region) and plans for the commuting trains and regional buses. Both institutions co-operate and co-ordinate so that planning and investment between the two scales is coherent (ITF, 2018[18]). In the case of the Paris region, the City of Paris (City of Paris, n.d.[20]) has embraced the 15-minute city framework (see next section), which can importantly facilitate planning development (and redevelopment) along Complete Streets and Place-making principles. An important challenge will be to find ways to include other territories in the larger city area and the commuting zone. The fact that no authority holds power over transport planning at the level of the wider city (i.e. Paris and its near periphery), can hinder or make such integration difficult.

Authority over strategic-level planning (i.e. the development of a vision with which infrastructure and policy need to be consistent as well as the long-term plans to implement it), is also identified as a key characteristic of successful MTAs. Importantly, such planning is facilitated by MTAs being embedded in larger metropolitan bodies with land-use planning competencies. For example, TfL is embedded within the Greater London Authority[4] and AMB in Barcelona not only has power for transport, but also over land use and environment. Overall, it is important that the strategic plans for transport policy and infrastructure developed by the MTAs are co-ordinated and consistent with urban plans. For example, Ile-de-France Mobilités is in charge of the Mobility Master Plan for the region (PDUIF), which directly influences the Local

Urban Master Plan (PLU). TfL develops the Mayor's Transport Strategy for the Greater London Area in coordination with the London Plan (the spatial plan for London). In the case of Barcelona, ATM develops the Mobility Master Plan for the metropolitan region (PDM), while AMB develops the Urban Mobility Plan for the metropolitan area (PMMU), which is closely linked to the Metropolitan Urban Master Plan (ITF, 2018[18]). In all cases, such strategies are embedded in important processes of public participation and consultation, in addition to the participation of the various local governments. These planning documents are also embedded in multi-level planning frameworks, guiding plans for lower government levels (e.g. boroughs or municipalities) and ensuring consistency with national goals and planning (ITF, 2018[18]). Showing consistency of projects with such plans is also a requisite for eligibility for several national funds dedicated to mobility and urban infrastructure (ITF, 2018[18]).

Having regulatory capacity over transport services is also a key condition for MTAs to be able to make the vision and long-term strategy described above operational. For example, MTAs operating in fully deregulated transport settings may develop ambitious long-term strategies, but without the capacity to set standards for services or plan for routes, their capacity to implement the strategies will be very limited (see Chapter 5). Regulatory capacity has been key for TfL and AMB to improve bus concessions and regulate service through public tendering, for instance.

Implementing comprehensive strategies (including Complete Streets and Place-making approaches) also requires MTAs to have competence over multiple transport modes and policy levers, i.e. beyond public transport to include road use and allocation, as well as the capacity to plan for active modes. TfL has improved public transport, walking, and cycling conditions through a combination of actions, such as improving tendering processes to incentivise better bus services by private providers, road reallocation in favour of public and active modes, the development and improvement of active and public transport infrastructure, and congestion charging. Part of TfL's ability in doing so is its regulatory capacity over different modes (including taxis and private-hire services), as well as competence over road safety and a major influence on road management and design.

The predominant role of subnational authorities in the decision-making body (e.g. board of directors, council, etc.) is also fundamental to ensure a shared vision for the area. In addition, this is a crucial condition for making the establishment of such entities possible in places where decentralisation has already occurred. Because transferring some of the capacity already granted to local entities (e.g. municipalities, boroughs, etc.) needs to be transferred to the MTA, it is normal that such entities will only come on board if their effective representation in the decision-making process is ensured.

Dedicated funding and decision-making authority over the use of the transport budget is key for MTAs to create well-integrated and competitive transport networks. As discussed in Chapter 5, setting up an MTA can also serve to put in place financial frameworks that can help enlarge the sources of funding of transport networks, reducing pressure over transport budgets.

Finally, dedicated and highly skilled staff is another crucial characteristic of fully functional MTAs. Staff with data analysis skills, for example, can allow MTAs to gather data to inform decisions, and better respond to users' needs while shifting metropolitan areas and regions away from car dependency. MTAs with data-skilled staff (and the funding to ensure those positions) can also establish partnerships with on-demand service providers and other institutions (e.g. universities) for the development of innovative platforms and information services that better foster the integration of private and public services in the pursuit of better alternatives to car use.

4.2.2. Better planning, guided by better metrics

Better spatial planning (including, but beyond, public space) and design are at the core of finding a balance between mobility and proximity, thus increasing the attractiveness of active and shared modes, and ensuring equitable, quality and sustainable accessibility. This section presents planning frameworks and metrics that can support the enhancement of spatial planning, with the potential to guide decisions towards achieving these goals and in this way become central to reducing transport-related emissions.

The "15-minute city" framework is a good example of a framework that can play a key role in guiding, and co-ordinating, planning decisions towards rebalancing mobility and proximity, leading to "healthier" territories. In 15-minute cities, urban development is centred on accessibility, so that people can get to (many) places by walking and cycling in less than 15 minutes. As such, planning is systematically guided towards creating proximity (especially to basic services and opportunities that people need the most frequently). At the same time, it creates the conditions so that connections by walking and cycling between people and those services can ensure that these modes are the most convenient. While the 15-minute city builds on the notion of denser cities, it looks beyond the creation of density, integrating the notions of mixed land uses and diversity of opportunities as well. Because the priority in planning is given to accessibility by sustainable modes, and on people having access to the places they need and like, the framework is useful for integrating Complete Streets and Place-making notions to urban development and planning.

Planning in this framework focuses on looking at a scale often neglected: a territory larger than the neighbourhood but smaller than the metropolitan region (Duany and Steuteville, 2021[21]). Nonetheless, the model allows rethinking the entire urban area or region. The idea is that, rather than having inner cities surrounded by car-dependent suburbs and towns, territories could be redesigned as networks of 15-minute cities (and smaller towns), reversing urban sprawl and unlocking enormous opportunities for emissions reductions and better daily lives. Importantly, this can be used to redesign large metropolitan areas, but can also be implemented in small cities (as the case of Pontevedra illustrates) and rural towns.

The framework defines three radii accessible by foot and bike within which authorities need to ensure proximity to a certain number of services (Duany and Steuteville, 2021[21]):

- A first five-minute walk (around 0.4 km) radius where people have access to ordinary daily needs: small businesses, and a central square or a main street with a minimum level of mixed land uses. An indicative population within this radius is around 2 600 people.
- A second radius determined by a 15-minute walk (around 1.2 km) contains a full mix of services, i.e. grocery store, pharmacy, general consumption places and public schools. It also contains larger parks (serving multiple neighbourhoods) as well as larger employers (compared to the small businesses above). An indicative population within this radius is about 23 000 people.
- A third radius determined by a 15-minute cycle (around 3 km) contains major cultural, medical and education (e.g. higher education) centres. This radius also allows access to regional parks and regional transit stations. This would include a population of around 350 000.

By encouraging planning that consciously brings people, opportunities and places of interest closer together, the 15-minute city framework can lead to "healthy" territories (right panel in Figure 2.1) in which the bulk of trips are made by foot, bike, micro- or shared mobility modes that excel in short distances. Not being space-intensive, these transport modes reduce the space needed for mobility purposes, further allowing the creation of proximity (creating a virtuous cycle). This does not mean that people will not go further than these radii, but the idea is that they do not need to for most needs. Micro-mobility (including electric bicycles) and public transport should be encouraged as the most competitive alternative beyond the 15-minute radii, leaving car use for very specific trip purposes. For instance, an electric bicycle can allow a much larger perimeter than a normal bike in a 15-minute period (Duany and Steuteville, 2021[21]). In addition, public transport and micro-mobility can also provide an alternative for occasions where walking and cycling are not adequate (e.g. when people are in a hurry), in this way helping to avoid car use. For instance, an electric bicycle can allow reaching a perimeter of around 2.6 km (i.e. between the second and third radii) in five minutes (Duany and Steuteville, 2021[21]).

Accessibility metrics can also be incorporated into specific planning tools to ensure that new development and urban renewal fosters increased proximity between people and places and that better connections through sustainable modes are prioritised. The Public Transport Accessibility Level indicator (PTAL) used by TfL in London, and the Housing plus Transport (H+T) Affordability Index used in the United States are two examples (discussed below) of indicators that have in the past been effectively linked to decision making for guiding spatial planning and development. The radii described in the 15-minute framework could also be used as an important reference for setting minimum accessibility levels by walking and cycling and to different types of opportunities and services as standards to guide new development and urban renewal.

TfL uses the PTAL indicator (among others) as a standard for linking urban development location to public transport accessibility, and PTAL is an important element in the London Plan (London's spatial plan). It also uses the PTAL to guide the permitted density of development and for linking maximum parking requirements for new development (see below) to public transport availability (ITF, 2019[22]). TfL introduced WebCAT,[5] an open web portal for connectivity assessment, in order to make its data and analysis available to boroughs, developers, planners and other key stakeholders. As part of this, an interactive mapping tool provides users with PTAL values in any location across London. Users can also see PTAL levels that would result from different scenarios (e.g. the development of a certain infrastructure) and create their own PTAL maps (ITF, 2019[22]).

WebCAT has importantly contributed to making regulation linked to PTAL (e.g. planning obligations, land-value capture mechanisms) transparent for developers and raising acceptability. While more sophisticated indicators have been developed by TfL over time, PTAL remains an important tool for policy design and communication with different stakeholders (e.g. developers) due to its simplicity, transparency and broad use. PTAL has also served as a basis for identifying and redeveloping "opportunity areas" in London. Opportunity areas are large areas of brownfield land that either have good public transport access or where, due to its characteristics (e.g. location), good public transport connections could be easily developed (ITF, 2019[22]). Linking redevelopment strategies for these areas to analysis and criteria based on the analysis of PTAL helps ensure that their redevelopment contributes to environmental, social and economic goals.

The Housing plus Transport (H+T) Affordability Index[6] is another example of an indicator that has helped to integrate transport and land-use decisions more systematically. In a number of US states (e.g. Illinois and El Paso, Texas), the index allowed prioritising funding[7] for subsidised housing for the most location-efficient projects (i.e. the selection process prioritised projects located near public transport or with good access to job centres) (ITF, 2017[23]). As a result, the funds supported the development of affordable housing close to public transport, which helps align climate and equity goals (CNT, 2018[24]).

Similar indicators have been developed to help prospective homeowners factor in both housing and transport costs while exploring household choices. In the San Francisco Bay Area, the H+T Affordability Index was adapted to help prospective homeowners understand the overall financial impact of living closer to, or farther from, work (ITF, 2017[23]). Similarly, the *coût résidentiel* developed in France combines the cost of housing and transport to inform public policy and household choice (Mattioli, 2015[25]). The *coût résidentiel* is a publicly available indicator consisting of the breakdown of all household expenses due to residential location, including travel and accommodation (Cerema, 2020[26]).

4.2.3. Better regulation for new developments: Parking standards and multimodal transport assessments

Both parking regulations and transport assessments for new developments, such as residential buildings and offices, importantly impact urban form. In most countries, law for new building developments requires a minimum number of parking slots. Such minimum parking regulations incentivise car use (Ajuntament de Barcelona, 2014[27]) and increase housing costs (Litman, 2016[28]), by requiring space – that could be used for other uses (e.g. more housing units, green or recreational spaces) – to be allocated to car parking (Brueckner and Franco, 2018[29]). This can make it financially unviable to develop more affordable housing units and often consumes valuable land near public transport; it also implies cross-subsidisation from non-car to car users.

Shifting away from minimum requirements is a key step for supporting sustainable and equitable developments. London, San Francisco, Seattle and Mexico City changed their parking policy from minimum requirements to maximum requirements (Franco, 2020[10]). London, for example, managed to halve the number of parking spaces in new residential buildings with such a reform (Guo and Ren, 2013[30]). In San Francisco, downtown parking is limited to 7% of the building's floor area, while in Seattle the maximum allowed in office space downtown is one parking space/1 000 ft². In Mexico City, minimum parking requirements were abolished in 2017 and were substituted for maximum parking requirements. In addition, for developments in the area of the city denominated as Area 1, where there is access to formal public transport services[8] at an average distance of 1 km, developers need to pay a fee per parking place developed, as they approach the maximum allowed number of slots (Government of Mexico City, 2017[31]). Parking constructed is free from this fee up to 50% of the established maximum, but starts to be priced after reaching this threshold (Guzmán, 2020[32]). The fee goes to a mobility fund and is used for investing in public transport (Government of Mexico City, 2017[31]). In addition, minimum parking requirements for bicycles were also introduced as part of this legal reform (Guzmán, 2020[32]).

Transport assessments, when required; tend to focus on road availability and the impact of the new development on traffic congestion. Requiring developers to produce multimodal transport assessments, e.g. assess the availability of facilities for walking, public transport, shared-mobility services (including micro-mobility and bicycles), and infrastructure for users of these modes, instead of only roads, can help prioritise construction permits in areas that are less car dependent. It can also allow authorities to assess whether the projects are well-suited for ensuring that an important share of the travel that they generate can be undertaken in a sustainable manner, and are thus contributing to (rather than jeopardising) sustainable transport goals. Where this is not the case, developers can also be given the possibility to contribute to key transport infrastructure for sustainable modes (in alignment with long-term strategic infrastructure plans) to make the project viable (as in the case of the United Kingdom) (ITF, 2019[22]). In the United Kingdom, two types of multimodal assessment exist: 1) transport assessments, required when projects are expected to have high transport impacts; and 2) transport statements, a simplified report identifying the main transport issues and potential mitigation strategies (OECD, 2015[33]) (Box 4.2).

As discussed in Sevtsuk (2021[34]), and Sevtsuk, Basu and Chancey (forthcoming[35]), introducing requirements and guidance for the development of pedestrian impact assessments (included in transport assessments in the ULK; see below) is particularly important. After studying the impacts of annual changes in the built environment on pedestrian flows in Melbourne, for instance, Sevtsuk, Basu and Chancey (forthcoming[35]) conclude that these changes can have significant and measurable impacts on the spatial distribution of pedestrian flows. Pedestrian impact assessments for development projects are therefore an important tool for better understanding the potential impacts on pedestrian flows to ensure that planning is steered towards the promotion of walking. "Pedestrian impact assessments" can be used to produce a "pedestrian census" where pedestrian volumes during different times can be tracked. These data can be useful to identify areas where investment can be the most impactful in terms of promoting walking. Models used for the development of pedestrian assessments can also support multi-stakeholder discussions around development projects, providing an accessible platform for developers, community members and city officials to better integrate pedestrian-oriented concerns in the policy-making and planning processes (Sevtsuk, Basu and Chancey, forthcoming[35]).

Box 4.2. Transport assessments and transport statements in the United Kingdom

Transport statements and transport assessments are required from developers in the United Kingdom. The different information and analysis required is intended to ensure that any new development contributes to (rather than hinders) increasing multimodal accessibility and shifting trips from car towards sustainable modes of transport.

Transport statements and assessments require a different level of transport and land-use information from developers. Transport assessments, which are required for larger development projects, require more comprehensive analysis, including a number of specific mode assessments (see Table 4.1, which summarises the elements required in each case).

Table 4.1. Minimum requirements in transport statements and assessments in the United Kingdom

<table>
<tr><th colspan="2">Type of evaluation</th></tr>
<tr><th>Transport statement</th><th>Transport assessment</th></tr>
<tr><td colspan="2">Existing site information</td></tr>
<tr><td colspan="2">• A site location plan of the proposed development site in relation to the surrounding area and transport system
• The permitted and existing use of the site
• A detailed description of the existing land uses in the vicinity of the site
• Whether the location of the site is within or near a designated air quality management area (AQMA)
• Any abnormal load uses of the current site</td></tr>
<tr><td colspan="2">Baseline transport data</td></tr>
<tr><td>• Qualitative description of travel characteristics, including pedestrian and cyclist movements and facilities
• Existing public transport provision
• Description and functional classification of the highway network
• Analysis of the injury accident records on the public highway of the site</td><td>• Quantification of trips and modal distribution
• Existing public transport facilities
• Parking facilities
• Pedestrian and cyclist traffic
• Description and functional classification of the road network
• Current traffic flows on links and at junctions
• Current personal injury accident records for the study area
• Summary of planned transport improvements (including type, implementation schedule and sponsoring agency)
• Current peak periods on adjacent road network
• Levels for air quality and noise for the highway network
• Baseline carbon emissions data, by mode</td></tr>
<tr><td colspan="2">Additional detailed evaluations</td></tr>
<tr><td>Not needed</td><td>Public transport assessment</td></tr>
<tr><td>Not needed</td><td>Walking/cycling assessment</td></tr>
<tr><td>Not needed</td><td>Road network assessment</td></tr>
<tr><td>Not needed</td><td>Traffic data and forecast</td></tr>
<tr><td>Not needed</td><td>Safety consideration and accident analysis</td></tr>
<tr><td colspan="2">Proposed development</td></tr>
<tr><td>• Plans and drawings showing site location, layout and use
• Proposed land use
• Scale of development
• Main features (layout and access points)
• Trip generation and modal distribution
• Qualitative and quantitative analysis of travel characteristics proposed
• Proposed improvements to site accessibility via sustainable modes of travel
• Transport impacts of site construction works
• Proposed parking strategy</td><td>• Plans and drawings showing site location, layout and use
• Proposed land use
• Scale of development and site area in hectares
• Hours of operation
• Proposed access and servicing arrangements
• Traffic impacts of site construction works
• Proposed parking strategy
• Development phases</td></tr>
</table>

Source: OECD (2015[33]).

References

Ajuntament de Barcelona (2014), *Metropolitan Area Urban Mobility Plans (PMU)*. [27]

Brueckner, J. and S. Franco (2018), "Employer-paid parking, mode choice, and suburbanization", *Journal of Urban Economics*, Vol. 104, pp. 35-46, http://dx.doi.org/10.1016/j.jue.2017.12.002. [29]

Burgen, S. (2018), ""For me, this is paradise": Life in the Spanish city that banned cars", *The Guardian*, https://www.theguardian.com/cities/2018/sep/18/paradise-life-spanish-city-banned-cars-pontevedra (accessed on 20 July 2021). [12]

CBC (2019), "Transforming cities can start with transforming malls, say planners", https://www.cbc.ca/news/canada/edmonton/mall-urban-planning-redevelop-transform-1.5278366 (accessed on 20 July 2021). [15]

Cerema (2020), *Les outils de sensibilisation à l'impact des choix résidentiels: Une étude du Cerema*, Cerema, https://www.cerema.fr/fr/actualites/outils-sensibilisation-impact-choix-residentiels-etude-du (accessed on 20 July 2021). [26]

City of Paris (n.d.), "Paris ville du quart d'heure, ou le pari de la proximité", web page, https://www.paris.fr/dossiers/paris-ville-du-quart-d-heure-ou-le-pari-de-la-proximite-37 (accessed on 28 March 2021). [20]

CNT (2018), "Center for Neighborhood Technology", website, https://www.cnt.org (accessed on 3 July 2019). [24]

Dijkstra, L., H. Poelman and P. Veneri (2019), "The EU-OECD definition of a functional urban area", *OECD Regional Development Working Papers*, No. 2019/11, OECD Publishing, Paris, https://doi.org/10.1787/d58cb34d-en. [19]

Duany, A. and R. Steuteville (2021), "Defining the 15-minute city", *Public Square: A CNU Journal*, https://www.cnu.org/publicsquare/2021/02/08/defining-15-minute-city (accessed on 8 March 2021). [21]

Franco, S. (2020), *Parking Prices and Availability, Mode Choice and Urban Form Discussion Paper*, ITF, http://www.itf-oecd.org (accessed on 9 July 2021). [10]

Freund, P. and G. Martin (1993), *The Ecology of the Automobile*, Black Rose Books, London, https://www.researchgate.net/publication/289117639_The_Ecology_of_the_Automobile (accessed on 24 June 2021). [8]

Gössling, S. (2020), "Why cities need to take road space from cars – and how this could be done", *Journal of Urban Design*, Vol. 25/4, pp. 443-448, http://dx.doi.org/10.1080/13574809.2020.1727318. [7]

Government of Mexico City (2017), *Nueva Norma de Estacionamientos*, Government of Mexico City, http://www.aducac.mx/web/images/descargas/NormaEstacionamiento.pdf. [31]

Guo, Z. and S. Ren (2013), "From minimum to maximum: Impact of the London parking reform on residential parking supply from 2004 to 2010?", *Urban Studies*, Vol. 50/6, pp. 1183-1200, http://dx.doi.org/10.1177/0042098012460735. [30]

Guzmán, J. (2020), “De mínimos a máximos: Cómo los estacionamientos en Ciudad de México están cambiando”, Transecto, https://transecto.com/2020/12/de-minimos-a-maximos-como-los-estacionamientos-en-ciudad-de-mexico-estan-cambiando (accessed on 17 July 2021). [32]

IEEE (2020), *Las Ciudades: Agentes Críticos para una Transformación Sostenible del Mundo*, Instituto Español de Estudios Estratégicos, Madrid, http://www.ieee.es/publicaciones-new/cuadernos-de-estrategia/2020/Cuaderno_206.html (accessed on 20 July 2021). [13]

ITF (2019), “Improving transport planning and investment through the use of accessibility indicators”*, International Transport Forum Policy Papers*, No. 66, OECD Publishing, Paris, https://doi.org/10.1787/46ddbcae-en. [22]

ITF (2018), “Policy directions for establishing a metropolitan transport authority for Korea’s Capital Region”*, International Transport Forum Policy Papers*, No. 61, OECD Publishing, Paris, https://doi.org/10.1787/8b87cefc-en. [18]

ITF (2017), *Income Inequality, Social Inclusion and Mobility*, ITF Roundtable Reports, No. 164, OECD Publishing, Paris, https://dx.doi.org/10.1787/g2g7ae77-en. [23]

Jiao, J., S. He and X. Zeng (2019), *An investigation into European car-free development models as an opportunity to improve the environmental sustainability in cities: The case of Pontevedra*, https://uniqueca.com/archives/proceedings/Papers%20HUSO2019%20.pdf (accessed on 30 September 2021). [14]

Litman, T. (2016), *Parking Management: Strategies, Evaluation and Planning*, Victoria Transport Policy Institute, Victoria, British Columbia, https://www.vtpi.org/park_man.pdf. [28]

Mahendra, A. and K. Seto (2019), “Upward and outward growth: Managing urban expansion for more equitable cities in the global South”, World Resources Institute, Washington, DC, https://www.wri.org/research/upward-and-outward-growth-managing-urban-expansion-more-equitable-cities-global-south (accessed on 12 July 2021). [4]

Mattioli, G. (2015), *Contemporary Societies Faced with Energy Transitions*, Université François Rabelais, Tours, https://eprints.whiterose.ac.uk/87866/1/Mattioli%202015%20Energy%20related%20economic%20stress.pdf. [25]

McDonald, R. et al. (2019), “Research gaps in knowledge of the impact of urban growth on biodiversity”, *Nature Sustainability*, Vol. 3/1, pp. 16-24, http://dx.doi.org/10.1038/s41893-019-0436-6. [3]

Norton, P. (2011), *Fighting Traffic: The Dawn of the Motor Age in the American City*, The MIT Press, https://mitpress.mit.edu/books/fighting-traffic (accessed on 19 March 2021). [6]

OECD (2015), *OECD Territorial Reviews: Valle de México, Mexico*, OECD Territorial Reviews, OECD Publishing, Paris, https://dx.doi.org/10.1787/9789264245174-en. [33]

Palermo, P. (2014), “Place-making and urban development: new challenges for contemporary planning and design”. [11]

Resnik, D. (2010), “Urban sprawl, smart growth, and deliberative democracy”, *American Journal of Public Health*, Vol. 100/10, pp. 1852-1856, http://dx.doi.org/10.2105/AJPH.2009.182501. [1]

Savills (2016), *Completing London's Streets*, Savills, https://pdf.euro.savills.co.uk/uk/residential---other/completing-london-s-streets-080116.pdf. [9]

Sevtsuk, A. (2021), "Estimating pedestrian flows on street networks", *Journal of the American Planning Association*, pp. 1-15, http://dx.doi.org/10.1080/01944363.2020.1864758. [34]

Sevtsuk, A., R. Basu and B. Chancey (forthcoming), "We shape our buildings, but do they then shape us? A longitudinal analysis of pedestrian flows and development activity in Melbourne". [35]

Siripanich, A. (2019), "Interaction of public transport accessibility and residential property values using smart card data", *Sustainability*, Vol. 11/9, http://dx.doi.org/10.3390/su11092709. [17]

Sterman, J. (2000), *Business Dynamics: Systems Thinking and Modeling for a Complex World*, Irwin/McGraw-Hill, http://jsterman.scripts.mit.edu/Business_Dynamics.html (accessed on 8 March 2021). [2]

Sterman, J., J. Forrester and J. Standish (2002), "All models are wrong: Reflections on becoming a systems scientist", *System Dynamics Review*, Vol. 18/4, pp. 501-531, http://dx.doi.org/10.1002/sdr.261. [5]

US EPA (2012), *Essential Smart Growth Fixes for Rural Planning, Zoning, and Development Codes*, United States Environmental Protection Agency, Washington, DC, https://www.epa.gov/sites/default/files/documents/essential_smart_growth_fixes_rural_0.pdf. [16]

Notes

[1] Chapter 5 also discusses how to improve the provision of public transport even in lower density areas, although reversing sprawl (and thus reducing the areas falling into this category) should be a central aim.

[2] Infill development refers to the process of developing vacant or underused parcels within developed urban areas.

[3] Between 190 000 and 500 000 homes could be improved according to the study.

[4] The Greater London Authority is the administrative body in charge of the Greater London area. The Greater London area includes the centre of London; parts of the counties of Middlesex, Surrey and Kent (incorporated in 1851), and parts of the counties of Surrey, Essex, Hertford and Kent (incorporated in 1963). The Greater London area has remained mostly unchanged since 1963 (ITF, 2018[18]).

[5] Web-based Connectivity Assessment Toolkit.

[6] The H+T Affordability Index provides an estimate of the typical cost of housing and transportation in different neighbourhoods and compares this estimate to a household or typical household's income. The Center for Neighbourhood Technology deems a neighbourhood affordable if a given household would spend 45% or less of its income on housing and transportation costs. This number reflects an existing rule of thumb that households should spend 30% or less of their income on housing and adds another 15% for transportation costs (ITF, 2017[23]).

[7] Via the low-income housing tax credit, the largest source of funding for constructing and maintaining subsidised housing in the country.

[8] I.e. excluding semi-formal services: *microbuses*.

5 Transformational change #3: From eroded to attractive sustainable transport modes

This chapter focuses on the dynamics underlying the erosion of shared and active modes of transport, including public transport. It then discusses policies to foster the development of multimodal networks to reverse such erosion, and thus reduce car dependency, lower emissions, improve accessibility and increase people's well-being.

This chapter focuses on the erosion of shared and active modes of transport, including public transport. This erosion is, to a great extent, a result of the induced demand and urban sprawl dynamics discussed in Chapters 3 and 4. The chapter also discusses policies with the potential to accelerate the development of multimodal networks to reverse such erosion, and thus reduce car dependency, lower emissions and improve accessibility.

5.1. Why sustainable transport modes are not attractive to people

Public transport's quality of service - and thus its attractiveness – largely depends on the frequency, fare and the reliability of service. The enabling conditions for public transport to provide a good service include high interconnectivity between public transport modes and other modes such as walking, cycling or the use of micro-mobility (ITF, 2014[1]), and a minimum density of people and places of interest.[1]

As explained in Chapters 3 and 4, investments in road expansion capacity and the priority given to private motorised vehicles in terms of public space allocation has resulted in induced demand and urban sprawl. Such prioritisation has also led to the erosion of public transport. On the one hand, the *attractiveness of driving a car* increases vis-à-vis other modes as congestion decreases, potentially reducing *public transport ridership* (Figure 5.1). On the other hand, the prioritisation of investments in road infrastructure to accommodate private vehicles may result in lower investments in public transportation infrastructure, and thus a reduced quality of service and attractiveness, further reducing *ridership* (not shown in Figure 5.1) (Sánchez-Atondo et al., 2020[2]; Taylor and Fink, 2013[3]). Indeed, while a number of governments earmark funding for public transportation, budgets dedicated to roads are often significantly higher than those dedicated to public transport (Public Transport Users Association Victoria Australia, 2009[4]; Leahy, 2020[5]).

The vicious cycle described in Figure 5.1 limits the opportunities to transition to clean, efficient and safe public transport networks, and increases the attractiveness of driving a car *vis-à-vis* public transport, thus exacerbating climate mitigation, pollution, road safety and equity[2] challenges. As *public transport ridership* drops, *public transport revenue* decreases and the *public transport budget deficit* increases, potentially pushing authorities to increase fares (not shown in Figure 5.1). When public transportation fares increase, the attractiveness of driving a car also increases, as it becomes relatively less expensive. Often, however, public transportation fare increases are politically difficult to implement. Thus, instead of increased fares, deficits may result in lower investments in the public transport network and service, resulting in poor infrastructure quality, and routes and frequency cuts, further eroding the *quality of service of public transport* and its attractiveness[3] (Sterman, 2000[6]) (Figure 5.1).

Figure 5.1. The erosion of public transport and the privilege given to cars

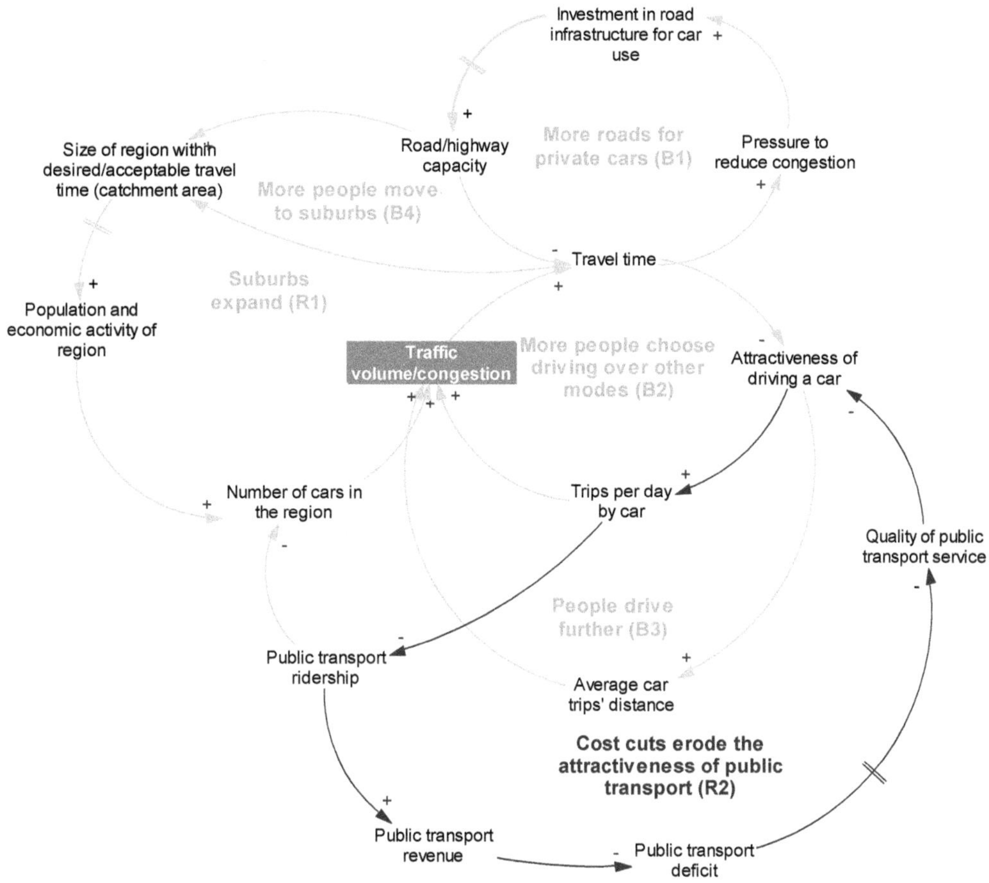

Notes: Arrows with a "+" mean that both variables move in the same direction (when one increases, the other increases and vice versa). Arrows with a "–" mean that the variables move in opposite directions (when one increases, the other decreases and vice versa). The two lines on the arrow denote a delay. The figure can be read as follows (purple arrows): As the *attractiveness of driving a car* increases (thanks to *investments in road/highway capacity expansion*), the number of *trips per day by car* increases (because of more people choosing to drive a car), which reduces *public transport ridership*. As *public transport ridership* shrinks, *public transport revenue* shrinks as well, which may increase *public transport deficit*. The higher the deficit, the less investments are possible to ensure a good quality of service (not shown in figure), and thus the *quality of public transport service* decreases. As the *quality of transport service* decreases, the *attractiveness of driving a car* increases, which increases the number of people choosing cars rather than public transport, etc.
Source: Adapted from Sterman (2000[6]).

The attractiveness of public transport becomes further eroded in the context of high sprawl and suburbanisation, for which *investments in road capacity expansion* is an important enabler (see Figure 5.2). This has a number of implications. First, with sprawl, the average length of trips increases, resulting in higher emissions. Second, low-density expansion exacerbates the challenges of providing *quality public transport services* in terms of proximity to stations/stops across the entire built-up area and commuting zone. Third, lower density of demand hinders the financial viability of expanding services, increasing the share of places not reachable by public transport. Figure 5.2 illustrates this dynamic: as the *size of the region accessible by road/highway* increases, density tends to decrease (not shown in figure) and the *number of places conveniently accessible by public transport* decrease (Figure 5.2), increasing the *attractiveness of driving a car* and further eroding the quality of public transport service.

Figure 5.2. Further erosion of public transport due to urban sprawl

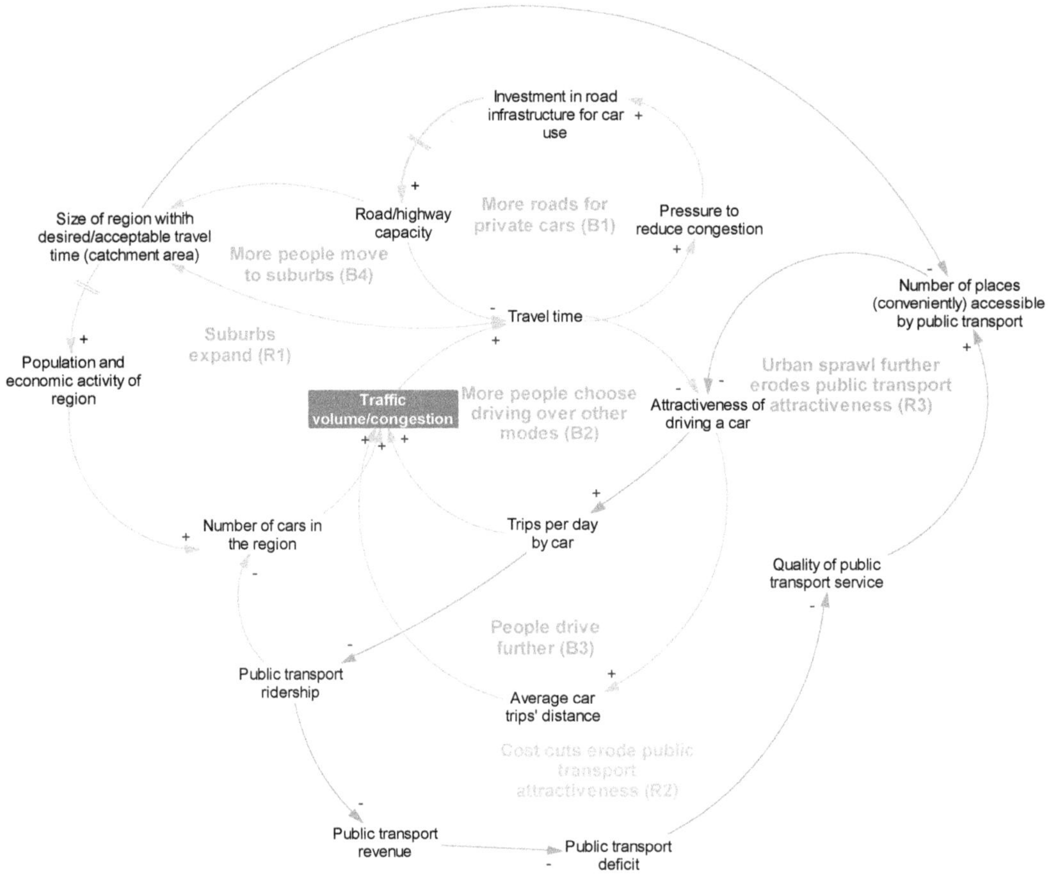

Notes: Arrows with a "+" mean that both variables move in the same direction (when one increases, the other increases and vice versa). Arrows with a "–" mean that the variables move in opposite directions (when one increases, the other decreases and vice versa). The two lines on the arrow denote a delay. The figure can be read as follows (orange arrows): as the *size of the region accessible by road/highway* increases, density tends to decrease (not shown in figure) and the *number of places conveniently accessible by public transport* decrease. Thus, as the region expands, places may be less well deserved by public transport, reducing the attractiveness of public transport and increasing the attractiveness of its alternative: the car.
Source: Adapted from Sterman (2000[6]).

This is, indeed, what can be observed in most regions: cars perform better than public transport in terms of travel time and access to places of interests[4] (ITF, 2019[7]). For example, the ITF (2019[7]; forthcoming[8]) finds that, despite congestion, in European and Latin American cities (with the exception of London), driving a car provides greater access compared to public transport (Figure 5.3), and is sometimes the only option available. A study by Liao et al. (2020[9]) compared travel times between a car and public transportation in São Paulo, Brazil; Stockholm, Sweden; Sydney, Australia; and Amsterdam, Netherlands and found that public transportation takes on average 1.4-2.6 times more than driving a car. The study used real-world data to estimate travel time by both car and public transport, and compared their performance by travel distance and time of day (Liao et al., 2020[9]). The study also finds that cars allow those living in the commuting zone (see Annex A) greater access to goods and services, e.g. restaurants, shops, schools. Three out of ten high school students living in the commuting areas of the 120 European cities studied depend on cars to get to school, and walking is not a viable option for 40% of primary school students and 65% of high schoolers. Within cities, where density is higher, 3 out of 4 students are able to walk and 19 out of 20 are able to bike to school within 15 minutes or less. In cities in developing countries, the gap between access by car and public transport tends to be even wider (ITF, 2019[7]; forthcoming[8]).

Figure 5.3. Access of private cars vs. other modes of transport: Evidence from selected cities*

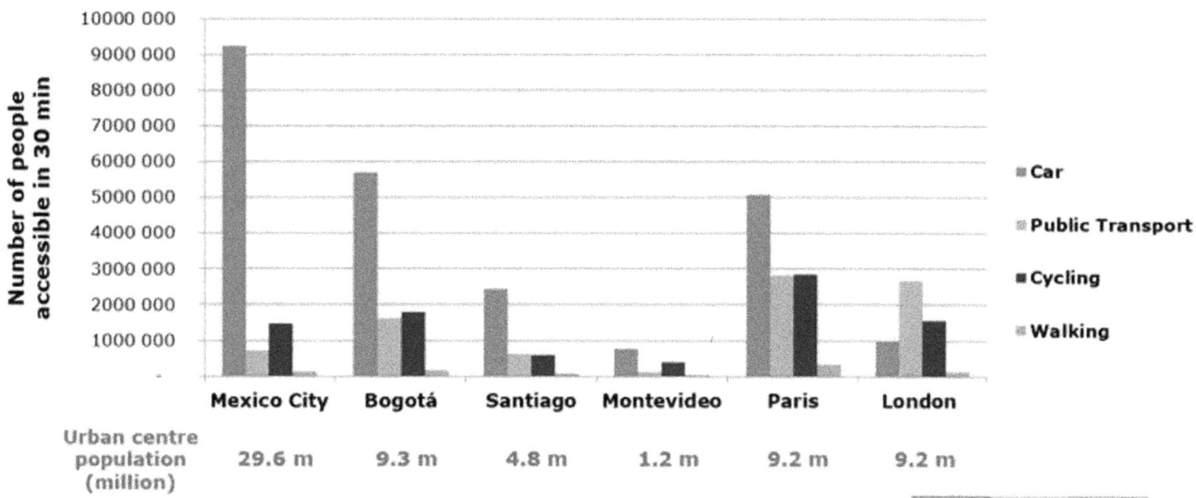

* Data reflect the territory that corresponds to cities (see Annex) rather than only inner cities. Cities consist of a high-density cluster of contiguous grid cells of 1 km² with a density of at least 1 500 inhabitants per km² (referred to as an urban centre) and any local unit with >50% of its population living in the urban centre (Dijkstra, Poelman and Paolo, 2019[10]).

Note: The number of people accessible in 30 minutes is used in this figure as a proxy for accessibility. "m" stands for million.

Sources: ITF (2019[7]; forthcoming[8]).

Public transport is not the only sustainable transport mode which attractiveness is compromised due to the car-dependent nature of urban and transport systems. Figure 5.4 illustrates the erosion of active and shared modes (including micro-mobility): as *investments in road infrastructure for car use* increase and *road/highway capacity* expands, the *share of space allocated to active modes* decreases, which reduces the *attractiveness of active modes*, as it may not be safe, or pleasant, to walk, ride a bike or an eScooter.

In addition to the amount of space allocated, the continuity of infrastructure is fundamental. While roads for car use form a connected and continuous network, walking and biking infrastructure in most cities is discontinuous, rendering them unsafe and, thus, unattractive. Furthermore, with the majority of road space allocated to car use, people walking, cycling and using micro-mobility[5] must "compete" for the same small share of space, often also shared with public transport and taxis, e.g. bus and taxi lanes shared with bikes or bike lanes in narrow sidewalks. The safety and convenience of active modes is, as a result, further eroded.

Figure 5.4. The erosion of active, shared and micro-mobility modes of transport

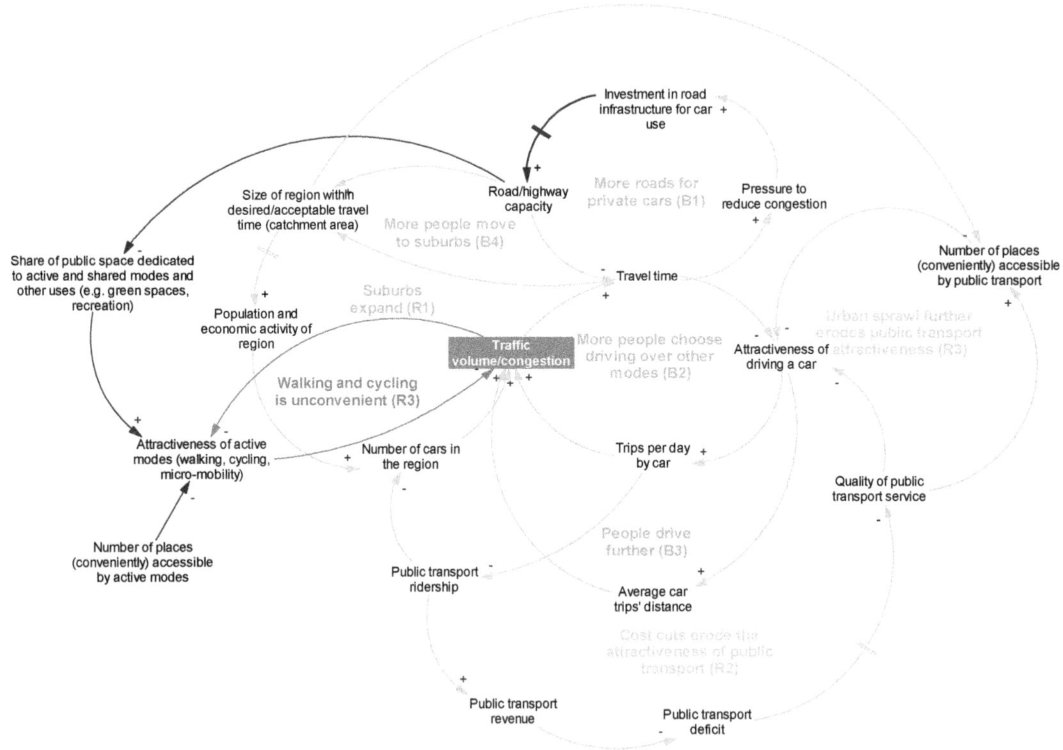

Notes: Arrows with a "+" mean that both variables move in the same direction (when one increases, the other increases and vice versa). Arrows with a "–" mean that the variables move in opposite directions (when one increases, the other decreases and vice versa). The two lines on the arrow denote a delay. The figure can be read as follows (blue and green arrows): as traffic volume/congestion (in red) increases as a result of induced demand (B1, B2 and B3) and urban sprawl (R1 and B4), and as the share of public space for accommodating cars at the detriment of other modes increases, active modes become less attractive (blue arrows). The less attractive these modes are, the more people may choose to drive a car (given that the attractiveness of public transport is also eroded), driving traffic volume and congestion up.
Source: Adapted from Sterman (2000[6]).

As for public transport, urban sprawl following a single-use logic contributes to the erosion of active modes and micro-mobility (Figure 5.5). While active modes and micro-mobility are particularly suited for short- and medium-length trips, respectively, urban sprawl increases the *average distance to places of interests*, reducing the *number of places conveniently accessible by active modes*, and thus their *attractiveness* and the number of people that choose them.

Figure 5.5. Further erosion of active and micro-mobility modes of transport due to urban sprawl

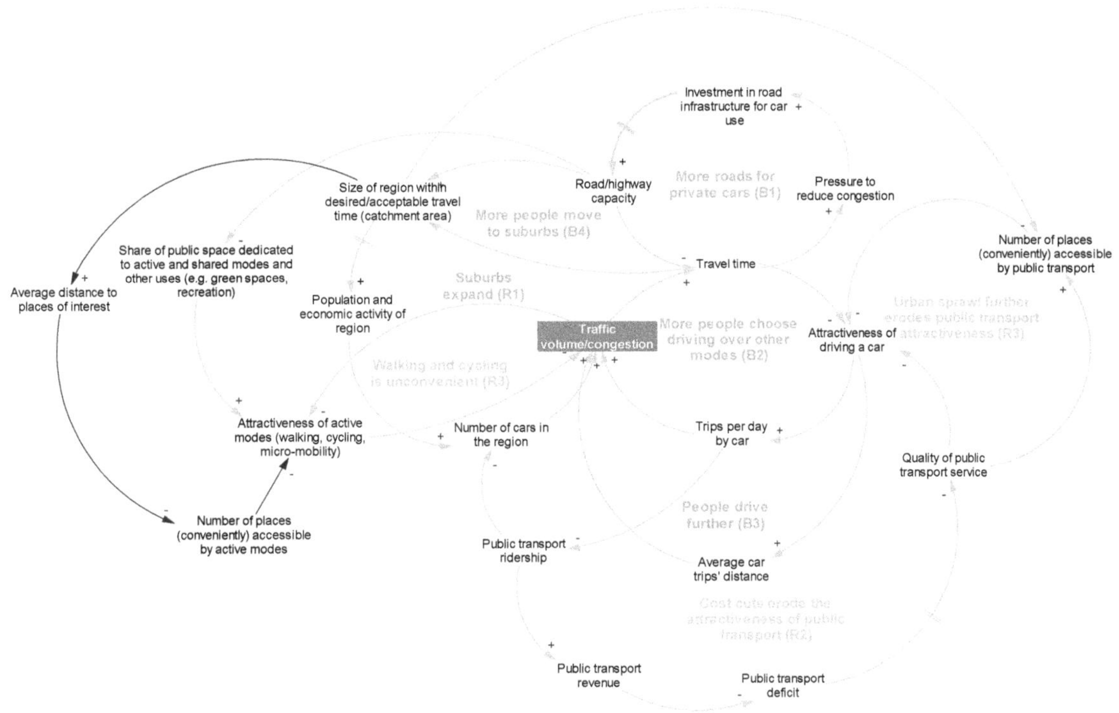

Notes: Arrows with a "+" mean that both variables move in the same direction (when one increases, the other increases and vice versa). Arrows with a "–" mean that the variables move in opposite directions (when one increases, the other decreases and vice versa). The two lines on the arrow denote a delay. The figure can be read as follows (dark green arrows): as people move further away to single-use areas (encouraged by the dynamics R1 and B4), the average distance to places of interest increases, which reduces the number of places conveniently accessible by walking or cycling. As the number of places accessible decreases, the attractiveness of active modes also decreases, and so thus the number of people that choose them.
Source: Adapted from Sterman (2000[6]).

The next section deeps dive on ways forward to reverse the dynamics illustrated in Figures 5.1-5.5 as to increase the attractiveness of active and shared modes, and thus the number of people that choose these modes for the bulk of their trips.

5.2. How to increase the attractiveness of sustainable transport via the development of multimodal networks

Climate strategies have the potential to reverse the systematic erosion of sustainable modes of transport described above and foster the development of multimodal networks of sustainable transport options. On the one hand, this requires important efforts for increasing the quality and convenience of public transport, which needs to be the backbone of transport systems (and shared mobility). This contrasts with strategies based on making public transport cheap or free for everyone, which can hinder investment, and thus limit possibilities for improving the quality of services (UITP, 2020[11]; ITF, 2017[12]). As will be discussed later, the possibility of subsidising services must not be excluded, but targeted subsidies (based on careful analysis of the socio-economic conditions of beneficiaries) should be the preferred option. There can also be grounds for cross-subsidising services (e.g. in lower density areas) due to environmental and social objectives (Mattioli et al., 2020[13]).

In addition, there is enormous potential to develop multimodal networks of sustainable alternatives if public transport is integrated with other shared mobility services. New technologies have provided an opportunity to upscale these services (e.g. by facilitating on-demand services). But it is necessary to provide wider scope and support for the development of innovative business models and vehicles (e.g. cargo bikes or new forms of micro-mobility) and to implement policies that can effectively encourage shared mobility to become the norm.

This section describes the type of policies that, if they are at the core of climate strategies, can unlock significant emissions reduction opportunities while improving people's well-being through the development of multimodal and integrated networks of sustainable modes of transport. Section 5.2.1 focuses on how to increase the attractiveness, and thus use, of public transport, while Section 5.2.2 focuses on active modes and micro-mobility.

5.2.1. Making public transport an attractive option

This section focuses on how governments can increase the attractiveness of public transport so that it is, along with other shared modes, one of the modes of transport that most people choose for their longer trips. It introduces the importance of regulatory power capacity, then discusses the role of funding. It goes on to focus on how the existing capacity of public transport systems can be used the most efficiently.

Regulatory power capacity

The first condition for enhancing the attractiveness of public transport requires that authorities have adequate regulatory power to oversee the sector. This includes setting quality standards for services (whether provided by public or private actors) and planning for the network of routes and services to ensure that public transport and other services are well co-ordinated and serve origin-destination needs. Importantly, having the staff with the right skills to carry out regulation is indispensable. As discussed in Chapter 4, metropolitan transport authorities are good institutions for carrying out this task, since they can oversee the public transport system (and its connections with other modes) in the light of a metropolitan-wide vision.

Where this is not the case and public transport is deregulated, authorities need to work towards setting the right governance and legal frameworks for regaining such powers. For instance, in places like Santiago, Bogotá and Mexico City, bus rapid transit services have been introduced in a way that not only increases the offer of mass transit, but also helps to renegotiate the public-private equilibrium to advance in re-regulating the bus system.[6] This includes by creating new regulatory bodies (OECD, 2015[14]; ITF, 2017[15]). In the United Kingdom, bus services were deregulated in the 1980s except in London, which is nowadays an important reference for having introduced (via its metropolitan transport authority, Transport for London) one of the best tendering processes. In 2016, the Cities and Local Government Devolution Act reintroduced the possibility for cities, towns and counties to decide upon the transport sector regulation again (Jones, 2016[16]) and cities like Manchester are re-regulating the regional bus network (Box 5.1). Importantly, building regulatory capacity within government administrations is also key.

Box 5.1. Re-regulating public transport: The case of the United Kingdom

During the 1980s and 1990s, many governments in both developed and developing countries deregulated public transport services (Sohail, Maunder and Cavill, 2006[17]). Worldwide experience shows that among other problems, deregulation can result in reduced reliability, poor connections, poor driver behaviour on the road to win passengers (bus wars), as well as business models which look to bring in excessive profits, via declining standards (Sohail, Maunder and Cavill, 2006[17]). Another shortcoming can be the absence of services in marginal areas if these are not seen as profitable, which can reduce the accessibility of poorer groups to jobs and other opportunities (Sohail, Maunder and Cavill, 2006[17]). In some contexts, and especially in developing countries, this has also given rise to informal or semi-formal modes of public transport, which even when they sometimes may bring some benefits (e.g. jobs for low-skilled workers), have also generated important costs (e.g. increased traffic congestion, air and noise pollution, and traffic accidents) (Cervero and Golub, 2007[18]). Overall, treating public transport as a deregulated private service has shown to lead to a number of shortcomings for ensuring that services meet the public interest.

The UK case

The transport sector in the United Kingdom was deregulated in the 1980s and privatised across the country with the objective of reinvigorating the bus industry and simultaneously reducing public expenditure (Bayliss, Mattioli and Steinberger, 2020[19]; Phillipson and Gilfillan, 2015[20]). London was an exception: having just reorganised public transport, the city was not yet ready for deregulation (Phillipson and Gilfillan, 2015[20]).

Transport deregulation initially led to lower fares, driven down by the opening of competition. Single operators and agreements between operators, coupled with the removal of public subsidies lead, within a few years, to fare increases, a decline of passenger numbers, followed by a decline in the quality of services (Phillipson and Gilfillan, 2015[20]). This, in turn, further reduced passenger numbers and funding for improving the services, trapping the sector in a vicious cycle.

In London, the public sector kept the possibility to regulate transport. Transport for London (TfL), created in 2000, is the lead agency in the city and is responsible for a majority of the transport network as well as strategic planning, transport policy planning, fare setting, and infrastructure and service planning (Kumar and Agarwal, 2013[21]).

Within TfL, London Bus Services Limited manages bus services by planning routes and determining the conditions for service provision. Contracts are granted to private bus operators fulfilling such conditions via public tendering. It is estimated that 15-20% of the total bus service is retendered every year (TfL, 2015[22]). In 2001, London Bus Services introduced quality incentive contracts,* a tendering and contracting system that incentives bus operators to improve service quality (TfL, 2015[22]). This structure provides incentives, as operators can receive bonuses based on their wait times and punctuality in comparison to the standard, or deductions for mileage not operated (ITF, 2018[23]). Between 2001 and 2015, bus ridership grew by 70% (TfL, 2015[22]). A number of countries around the world are considering similar changes to their tendering processes (TfL, 2015[22]).

At the national level, the Cities and Local Government Devolution Act 2016 allowed cities, towns and counties to decide upon the transport sector regulation again (Jones, 2016[16]). In March 2021, the Greater Manchester Combined Authority (GMCA) voted in favour of re-regulating the regional bus network after a public opinion poll found that 83% of respondents were in favour of it (King, 2021[24]). Manchester will implement a London-style franchising system, following the recommendation from Transport for Greater Manchester (BBC, 2021[25]). Transport for Greater Manchester will now have local control of buses on behalf of the GMCA and the Greater Manchester Mayor. The changes will allow the

GMCA to set standards, price caps, fares, timetables and routes instead of private companies (BBC, 2021[25]; GMCA, 2021[26]). Moreover, the GMCA will be able to co-ordinate and invest in the bus network and there will be integrated ticketing across the network of buses, trains and trams (BBC, 2021[25]; GMCA, 2021[26]).

* Unlike the net cost contracts or the gross cost contracts which were implemented prior to 2000, the quality incentive contracts include minimum performance standards (ITF, 2018[23]). Minimum performance standards are indicators that measure the performance of the operator (ITF, 2018[23]). The operator's annual reliability performance is compared to the minimum performance standards to calculate the reliability performance payment (ITF, 2018[23]). Measurements differ between high- and low-frequency routes and are based on the area type, journey time and congestion level (ITF, 2018[23]).

Improving financial capacity for increasing quality

Free public transport or very low public transport prices are often seen as a way of incentivising a modal shift from cars to public transport. Experience in cities that have tested free public transport shows, however, that while generating some modal shift from cars to public transport, the larger effect is an undesired modal shift away from walking and cycling (ITF, 2017[15]). Proost (2018[27]) highlights that for every new 100 passengers attracted by low public transport prices, only 15-35 are former car users.

Moreover, improvements in the quality of public transport have higher demand elasticity than public transport price changes. Analysis of underground rail networks across the globe shows that on average, a 10% reduction in fare levels will result in a 3% increase in patronage. In contrast, demand would increase by more than 5% due to a 10% increase in the capacity of a fixed network (UITP, 2014[28]).

By causing large deficits and reducing the scope to invest in public transport networks, low public transport prices are more problematic for attracting car users than higher public transport prices accompanied by investment. In other words, a strategy that aims at improving the competitiveness of public transport based on low prices reinforces the dynamics of low fares, low revenue, low investment and low quality illustrated in Figure 5.1. The fact that the cost of car use is often too low (i.e. not reflecting its negative social impact) contributes to "second-best pricing" solutions for public transport, i.e. public transport prices being set at even lower levels with the rationale of making them more competitive (ITF, 2018[29]).

An alternative strategy to move public transport systems away from this pervasive cycle is needed more than ever, as public transport has been hard hit financially due to the COVID-19 pandemic. In most cases, allowing for social distancing has meant providing a lot more capacity than would normally be required for the current level of ridership. In Milan, for instance, public transport services during lock-down ran at 75% of capacity while having only 5% of pre-COVID ridership (UITP, 2020[30]). By the end of 2020, the expected loss of revenue from fares in European public transport systems, for instance, was around EUR 40 billion (UITP, 2020[30]).

Shifting away from generalised subsidies and flat rates and towards differentiated rates with targeted subsidies[7] (see Box 5.2) can help strike a better balance between affordability and the financial sustainability of quality services. This will help to increase fare-box revenues and the capacity to invest in public transport networks. Flat fares (as opposed to distance-based fares, for instance) are used in many places, since distance-based fares tend to be seen as unfair, e.g. for low-income residents in the peripheries who travel longer distances. However, flat fares are not cost-effective and result in subsidising and incentivising sprawl (ITF, 2018[29]). Combining distance-based rates with subsidies targeted at lower income residents can help to make people's decisions more sensitive to the distance between a given location and the rest of the city while at the same time addressing equity concerns (ITF, 2017[15]).[8]

Box 5.2. Targeted subsidies for public transport

Implementing targeted subsidies (as opposed to generalised ones) is one way of striking a better balance between affordability and financial sustainability. Moreover, technological improvements such as smart cards and improved data management tools allow improving methodologies for targeting vulnerable users. Granting subsidies to groups like the elderly or students results in inclusion and exclusion errors, since there is a frequent mismatch between these categories and vulnerable groups (ITF, 2017[15]).

Instead, schemes targeting users by using affordability data will result in better outcomes from expenditure on subsidies (ITF, 2017[15]). The case of Bogotá, Colombia, is a good example. A targeted subsidy scheme for the integrated public bus system was introduced in 2014. The scheme benefited from the introduction of smart cards, which facilitated differentiating public transport fares for beneficiaries. At the same time, identification of the population that was subject to the subsidy was built on the System for Selecting Beneficiaries of Social Spending (SISBEN). SISBEN is a stratification instrument that was already used by the national as well as by local governments for programmes related to subsidies for water and electricity, among other things. The system classifies neighbourhoods and rural areas based on various socio-economic related characteristics of houses and neighbourhoods (Peralta-Quiros and Rodríguez Hernández, 2016[31]).*

* While doing this at the neighbourhood level can still lead to a certain mismatch between affordability and eligibility, these spatial categories reflect better socio-economic conditions than, for instance, age groups.

Even if improving fare-setting methods, fare-box revenues are often not enough for public transport to provide a high-quality services[9] (ITF, 2017[15]), and this was already the case before the health crisis. Importantly, public transport needs to be regarded as a "social [...and environmental]" investment (Cervero, 2011[32]), and co-ordinated action between different levels of government will need to concentrate on increasing the budget dedicated to providing better public transport services and wider coverage. An important part of this is to improve the appraisal methodologies that today bias investment towards projects for car use (see Chapter 3 and OECD (2019[33])).

Governments can also pave the way by making investment in public transport central to recovery packages (Box 5.3). As discussed in Chapter 7, public transport investment has a very high impact on jobs. In addition, when looking at capital cost (USD/km) per capacity created (Buckle et al., 2020[34]; IEA, 2020[35]) (persons/hour/direction carried), public transport (as well as infrastructure for active modes) has much lower capital cost per capacity than car infrastructure. The capital cost per capacity of a dual highway or an urban street dedicated entirely to cars ranges between USD 5 000 and USD 10 000 for a dual highway and USD 5 000 and USD 10 000 for an urban street. In comparison, the capital cost per capacity of metro and commuter rail is USD 2 000-5 000 and USD 2 000, respectively. Capital costs per capacity for bus rapid transit and lanes for regular buses is much lower (between USD 200 and USD 250 for bus rapid transit and between USD 300 and USD 500 for regular buses). Capital cost per capacity of bicycle lanes and pedestrian walkways is USD 30 and USD 20, respectively (IEA, 2020[35]).

Box 5.3. Making public transport central in recovery packages

A number of authorities have provided funds for supporting public transport services, which go beyond the logic of simply helping them survive the COVID-19 crisis and its aftermath.

- **Finland** assigned one-quarter of the EUR 5.5 billion recovery package to the development of railway and tramway infrastructure and the support of public transport operators. The investment is embedded in other plans (supported by housing, land-use and transport agreements) that focus on ensuring accessibility to public transport services of new housing development projects (IISD, 2020[36]).
- In the **United Kingdom**, the Department for Transport announced a second recovery package (worth GPB 256 million) in support of public transport operators outside London. Funding reflects a vision in which public transport is seen as key to a sustainable recovery, providing a way forward to reduce air pollution, support social equity and provide citizens with an alternative to private vehicle use (IISD, 2020[36]).
- In **London**, the central government has provided emergency funds to Transport for London (TfL), and negotiations for the upcoming period between the central government and the city are still ongoing. In addition, London authorities have used the current situation to rethink current funding mechanisms and have come up with a number of proposals and strategies that could allow TfL to reduce its reliance on fare-box revenues and enlarge its financial base. Among the options proposed is that London would be allowed to keep GBP 500 million from the vehicle excise duty paid by its residents every year. Another alternative proposed is charging a "boundary" tax to cars that enter the Greater London area (London City Hall, 2020[37]; Thicknesse, 2021[38]).

Overall, rethinking budgets for public transport is needed. As discussed in Chapter 4, metropolitan transport authorities can serve to rethink and improve governance. Establishing these types of authorities can also serve to put in place advantageous frameworks for diversifying and increasing the budgets needed to improve, maintain and expand public transport, making it part of an integrated and sustainable transport network that can fully serve metropolitan areas and their hinterlands. Importantly, such frameworks need to be the result of co-operation and co-ordination between national and subnational governments. The ITF (2018[23]) highlights the following examples:

- In the case of France, a dedicated business tax (*versement transport*,[10] VT) can be levied by municipalities that are part of a metropolitan transport authority, and funds are channelled directly to this institution. In the case of the Paris region, in 2016, the VT constituted 50% of the metropolitan transport authority's (Ile-de-France Mobilité) total budget. Another 30% came from fare-box revenues, and 20% from municipal and departmental contributions.
- In London, TfL uses land-value capture mechanisms, namely the community infrastructure levy, and planning obligations as tools for raising funds for transport projects. Business rate supplements[11] are also applied to raise funds for transport projects that can promote economic development.
- Both TfL and Ile-de-France Mobilités secure some funds from charges on private vehicles. For instance, 50% of driving offences and fines in Île-de-France go directly to Ile-de-France Mobilités. In the case of TfL, funding collected through parking fines, congestion charging and the low-emission zone, and the new toxicity T-Charge[12] are part of TfL's budget.

Making the best use of existing capacity

Public authorities also need to make the best from existing capacity by managing crowding, which became a particular problem during the pandemic, but has been an important problem of public transport services for decades. When travelling in crowded conditions people have, for instance, a perceived burden that is equal to having a 25% increase in their (in-vehicle) travel time. Thus crowding is an important element behind the inconvenience of public transport (Wardman, 2014[39]).

A number of governments have implemented actions during the COVID-19 pandemic that can serve as good examples for managing crowding in a post-pandemic situation as well. For example, in London, to ensure that staff from the National Health Service Nightingale Hospitals travelled safely, public transport services made use of additional staff to manage passengers without exceeding safe occupancy levels. This type of strategy has been used in other (pre-COVID occasions) to reduce crowding. Some cities also made important use of digital technologies to reduce crowding. For instance, Beijing introduced digital booking solutions and Catalonia rolled out an app that gives occupancy in real time (Lozzi et al., 2020[40]). In addition, the need for social distancing also led to rethinking supply in different services and routes. For instance, in Hamburg, part of the strategy to reduce crowding was based on rebalancing services provided in high-demand and low-demand routes.

Differentiating public transport pricing and frequencies during peak and non-peak hours can also be important for better spreading users throughout the day[13] and reducing crowding. Combining this with targeted subsidies, as explained above, can help deal with potential equity concerns as well.

At the same time, one of the most important lessons learnt by the need for social distancing is that active and micro-mobility modes can play a key role in easing the pressures on public transport. A number of authorities have increasingly acknowledged the importance of improving conditions for walking, cycling and micro-mobility. In addition to many other benefits (e.g. physical and mental health, potential public space liberated, increased accessibility, etc.), these modes could carry a number of shorter distance trips, leaving public transport with a more manageable demand while also avoiding car use. A number of countries introduced incentives for bicycle purchase (e.g. a grant of up to EUR 500 for bicycle and e-bicycle purchases in Italy), as well as direct provision of bicycles (e.g. for students in Amsterdam) (Lozzi et al., 2020[40]). This is in addition to the roll out of dedicated lanes for bicycles and micro-mobility modes (see Chapter 7). Importantly, integrating transport and land use and rethinking territories (as discussed in Chapter 4) is crucial to increase the scope for shorter trips and thus the use of active and micro-mobility modes (see the next section).

Using accessibility criteria and designing multimodal networks that allow seamless transfers from and to public transport through active and micro-mobility modes is also crucial. According to Wardman (2014[39]),[14] the convenience of public transport depends, among other things, on: access and egress time, and in particular walking time at any stage of the public transport journey; waiting time, including transfer time between services or modes; services available at desired times; transfers; travel time variability; and information (in addition to crowding). In Rotterdam, city authorities partnered with a number of micro-mobility companies after the COVID-19 outbreak to provide 1 500 shared bikes and 1 500 e-scooters that were available at 25 different transport hubs (Lozzi et al., 2020[40]).

The pandemic has also generalised teleworking. Teleworking has been incentivised and/or imposed in different countries and cities during the pandemic and it is likely that at least a more hybrid model (than that found before the COVID-19 pandemic) will define future work patterns (Lozzi et al., 2020[40]). It is logical to think that teleworking can help moderate the demand for public transport, particularly at peak hours. Nonetheless, there is uncertainty in terms of the effects of telework on non-commuting trips or decisions to move further from the work place.[15] Ravalet and Rérat (2019[41]) suggest that public transport authorities will need to understand well the changes in trip patterns and include these in service planning (Buckle et al., 2020[34]). Box 5.4 discusses the potential role of increased teleworking.

Box 5.4. The potential role of increased teleworking

While the emissions reduction potential of teleworking may seem obvious, its impact on emissions is less straightforward than it seems (Buckle et al., 2020[34]). According to Crow and Millet (2020[42]), additional emissions from electricity use at home may offset commuting-related emissions. The extent to which this is the case depends on the length of the commuting trip, the mode of transport and the level of additional emissions from electricity use. This thus substantially varies across regions. Teleworking may also not result in overall travel reductions, as it can increase non-commuting trips (Lin et al., 2006[43]; Moeckel, 2017[44]), and may, in the long term, reduce the need to live close to work, thus contributing to sprawl. Such mixed effects and uncertainties suggest that the potential impacts from increased telework should be treated with caution.

Increasing the chance that teleworking could play a role in reducing emissions calls for implementing it in combination with other policies (e.g. road pricing, parking pricing and management, fuel taxes, etc.) (Lin et al., 2006[43]). This would increase certainty that it serves the purpose of reducing car dependency and thus that reductions from peak-hour commuting are not compensated (thus effectively reducing congestion, emissions and air pollution) (Bojovic, Benavides and Soret, 2020[45]). Bojovic, Benavides and Soret (2020[45]) highlight the importance of combining teleworking with road space allocation and city redesign (see Chapters 3 and 4).

The risk of increased sprawl due to teleworking also calls attention to the role of land-use policy and territorial planning. Careful analysis of regulations for new developments (see Chapter 4) can help avoid the expansion of low-density areas (e.g. detached houses with big private green spaces), which make the development of dense and multimodal transport networks difficult, and increase travel distances and car dependence. As discussed above, even if commuting trips are reduced, other trips may compensate and increase emissions if more people become car dependent. Strategic and integrated planning at the metropolitan level (see Chapter 4) can importantly help align incentives and planning at the municipal and metropolitan levels. As highlighted by Zenkteler et al. (2019[46]), flexible land-use zoning is also key for transforming current residential areas into multi-purpose neighbourhoods, increasing their attractiveness.

Overall, the complex impacts of teleworking on transport, land use, energy consumption and ultimately greenhouse gas emissions call for carefully monitoring and understanding of new trends and the drivers behind them. The causal loop diagrams used in this report provide an overview of the dynamics that teleworking may trigger, and can be useful tools for taking more informed decisions on the policies needed to avoid the undesired dynamics that may arise from it.

5.2.2. Shared on-demand modes: The untapped potential of technology

While sharing rides or vehicles is not a novelty, new technologies such as apps to geolocalise and book rides/vehicles open up enormous opportunities for increasing the attractiveness of shared (including active) modes of transport. By facilitating cycling and micro-mobility[16] (e.g. shared (e)bicycles, cargo (e)bikes, e-scooters), and shifting trips from low-occupancy private vehicles to shared and high-occupancy vehicles (e.g. on-demand micro-transit services), ride and vehicle sharing can significantly reduce emissions (ITF, 2017[47]; 2017[48]; 2020[49]), while also liberating road space devoted to car parking and use. This can, in turn, increase the scope of the street redesign policies discussed in Chapter 3, and facilitate whole-territories redesign, as discussed in Chapter 4.

This section sheds lights on policies that could allow climate strategies to leverage the potential of shared mobility, orientating it to increasing the role of more sustainable modes. It first focuses on shared bicycles and micro-mobility services, then on on-demand micro-transit.

Mainstreaming shared bicycles and micro-mobility services

If mainstreamed into transport systems, shared bikes and micro-mobility schemes (which as of today remain marginal) could bring important emissions reductions and other benefits. Shared (electric) bikes (docked and dock less) and micro-mobility services (e.g. e-scooters) exist in numerous cities, provided by private companies or public authorities. These services have the potential to encourage a modal shift away from cars, in particular in dense urban areas (but not only). Bike-sharing schemes have, for example, been associated with greenhouse gas emissions reductions, reduced fuel consumption, lower expenditures for households, increased accessibility to public transport and increased physical activity, for instance (Buck, 2012[50]). Modelling results also suggest that a "systemic, electric, shared, and integrated" roll out of micro-mobility services by 2030 in Europe (i.e. assuming that 50% of trips under 8 km could be made by using micro-mobility modes) would result in 30 million tonnes of emissions reductions, 127 terawatt hours of energy savings, while creating nearly 1 million direct and indirect jobs every year. It could also liberate 48 000 hectares of inner-city land (the equivalent to 4 times the area of Paris) (EIT and McKinsey, 2019[51]).

Emissions reductions will, however, depend on various conditions. The first (as with any electric vehicle) is on the carbon intensity of electricity. But beyond this, as shown by de Bortoli (2020[52]) when analysing the introduction of e-scooters in Paris (where electricity is low-carbon), longer vehicle lifespans and sustainable servicing is key. In Paris, an important shortcoming has been that servicing is done with high-emitting (gas-powered) vehicles and involves long distances (since warehouses are located outside Paris) (de Bortoli, 2020[52]). As discussed by EIT and McKinsey (2019[51]), fostering of higher quality parts (which would allow longer lifespans); more local manufacturing and recycling of vehicle parts and batteries; and the development of battery swapping stations and charge and lock stations at mobility hubs (see Chaper 6), which could reduce the need for transporting vehicles and make servicing more sustainable, are all important to ensure sustainable micro-mobility service and make these more viable.

In addition, mainstreaming shared bicycle and micro-mobility services will require overcoming a number of barriers and calls for a comprehensive set of actions (in addition to those mentioned above). Without comprehensive strategies to effectively increase their role, the potential that new apps and technologies have opened up for these types of services will remain mostly untapped.

Overcoming negative perceptions and fostering co-operation between authorities and providers

Concerns over undesired negative impacts have hindered the development of shared bikes and micro-mobility, in particular regarding dock less bikes and e-scooters. The most prevalent concern relates to parking and safety considerations, especially in the case of e-scooters relative to pedestrians.

The "wild" parking of e-scooters is a reality, but tends to be overstated in the public debate compared to, for example, improper car parking, which is much more common but taken for granted and normalised. Many of the commercial providers' commercial strategies, which have consisted in "flooding'" markets (i.e. streets or sidewalks) to achieve economies of scale, have played an important role in creating parking issues (ITF, 2019[53]). Nonetheless, the negative perceptions related to micro-mobility, including about parking, are also an important reflection and example of the *status quo* and loss aversion biases discussed in Section 3.2, pointing to the need for effective communication efforts. Brown et al. (2020[54]) analysed vehicle parking practices[17] in selected commercial streets in five cities in the United States (Austin; Portland; San Francisco; Santa Monica; and Washington, DC). They found that motor vehicles impede sidewalk access due to improper parking much more than bicycles or scooters. While 25% of motor vehicles were improperly parked, only 0.8% of bicycles and scooters were. Ride-hailing, taxis, commercial and delivery services accounted for 64% of vehicle violations from motorised vehicles.

Safety issues between micro-mobility users and pedestrians are exacerbated when space is not specifically allocated to bikes or micro-mobility, pushing users to ride on the sidewalk (due to safety considerations of riding next to cars). The redistribution and redesign of road space, the provision of dedicated infrastructure, as well as traffic-calming measures and speed limits for cars and trucks (see Chapter 3) are central to fostering the use of shared bikes and micro-mobility while also reducing safety risks from their use (see more on addressing safety concerns from micro-mobility below). Quality infrastructure for both pedestrians and bikes/e-scooters is also important to avoid conflict between pedestrians and micro-mobility users, and to unlock the potential of the latter as sustainable alternatives to car use, e.g. bikes and e-scooters can provide access to public transport covering distances that would be too long on foot. A transport system where less space-consuming modes are the norm allows space to be liberated, which can be used to enhance living environments (e.g. increasing green, commercial, housing, leisure space). With dedicated infrastructure, these services could be widely implemented in peripheral areas with mass transit (e.g. light rail) connections, but with a poor connection between people's residence and mass transit stations (e.g. when mass transit stations are not within walking distance, e-scooters or e-bikes could reduce the dependence on cars). Creating such transport options could be a key component of redesigning suburban areas, in complement with spatial planning to increase proximity and street redesign.

Collaboration and co-ordination between authorities and providers and a "softer" regulatory approach, are needed. The response of many authorities has been to cap (e.g. Mexico City in the case of e-scooters) or temporarily ban (e.g. Amsterdam in the case of dock less bikes) these services. Another common response has been to impose high fees (ITF, 2019[53]). There is a strong case for these services to contribute to the cost of the infrastructure that they use (e.g. cycle lanes and parking space). However, aggressive policies to ban or cap these vehicles contribute to the perception that these are detrimental to social objectives. In addition, very high fees (through licences and/or per vehicle fees) imposed by some authorities make the business model unviable for many operators (ITF, 2019[53]). The level of these fees has, in many cases, also been inconsistent with their contribution to achieving modal shift and environmental goals. For instance, Mexico City organised auctions for bikes and e-scooter licences that yielded fees of USD 68-137 for bike licences and USD 370-736 for e-scooter licences, which are higher than those paid by taxis. In addition, in the case of bikes, a floor price of USD 53 was estimated, taking into account space consumption and other "externalities", discounted by the modal shift benefit, which shows that the fees imposed are higher than the social costs generated (ITF, 2019[53]). As highlighted by the ITF (2019[53]), regulatory action needs to be judged in light of public policy objectives, e.g. higher accessibility via sustainable modes. Docherty, Marsden and Anable (2018[55]) also caution that governance structures must set clear and overarching goals and considerations for the long term to enhance public value while enabling innovation to flourish, as there is the risk of public policy becoming solely reactionary if governance structures fail to act. A way forward is to foster collaboration and take a "softer" regulatory approach to shared bikes and micro-mobility, based on: data requirements to help understand modal shift and accessibility effects; surveillance of supply levels matching existing demand; minimum safety standards and promotion of safety education; respect of designated parking spaces and cooperation between providers and authorities to embed parking and use in street redesign objectives; and incentives/regulations for the optimisation of servicing and lifespan characteristics in line with climate goals (as discussed above). Providers and governments can also work together to create partnerships and jointly communicate on the ways in which these vehicles can support environmental and social policy objectives. This will very likely yield better results in terms of social value than the current trend of "hard" regulation based on bans, caps and high fees.

Using a wide range of incentives and increasing financial support

Shared bikes and micro-mobility modes could also be fostered via financial incentives (e.g. tax breaks) to companies incentivising modal shifts from high-emitting modes. This could also be combined with teleworking incentives (see below). Tax credits for providers of shared services could also incorporate shared bikes, e-bikes and e-scooter providers. Scrapping schemes could also include the possibility of switching from car use to public transport and/or other shared modes, as well as active modes.

In addition, as discussed by EIT and McKinsey (2019[51]), the offer of micro-mobility services needs to be enlarged so that it responds to various trip purposes and populations. While some cities (e.g. Freiburg) have introduced e-cargo bikes, these types of services remain quite limited. Shared electric (and regular) bike schemes in most places do not offer options for families (e.g. baby seats, bicycles for kids, etc.). Moreover, micro-mobility could offer a range of new types of vehicles beyond e-bikes and scooters that could also offer better options for different purposes (e.g. buying groceries, transporting kids or the elderly, etc.). EIT and McKinsey (2019[51]) point out that wider financing options for supporting innovation for micro-mobility are needed, as currently, financial institutions other than venture capital do not support innovation for this segment. Different models for users (e.g. leasing and different subscription models) are also needed for these services to expand.

Addressing barriers for low-income users

As in the case of micro-transit and on-demand services (discussed in the next section), direct subsidies for bike sharing and micro-mobility can help achieve "desired connectivity improvements at lowest cost and highest quality" (ITF, 2019[53]), and also contribute to equity considerations. Subsidies for micro-transit and shared bikes or micro-mobility should be considered based on a careful analysis of operational costs (for which competitive processes are necessary). They also need to be designed using targeted subsidies (preferably based on an affordability analysis rather than on age or occupation, e.g. students, groups). These are the same principles recommended for formal public transport subsidies (see the discussion above).

The cost of shared bikes and micro-mobility is, however, not the only barrier for low-income households to benefit from these services. In a study in the United States, Kodransky and Lewenstein (2014[56]) identify a number of other barriers. Among other things, the authors point to government's role for overcoming these barriers, for instance by including requirements for serving low-income communities when granting rights to operate. This has been done in Washington, DC, where the local transport department required car-share companies to place vehicles in low-income areas. In the case of Boston, the municipality offered grants to bike-sharing services (e.g. Boston's Hubway) in exchange for service expansion and reporting focused on low-income users (Kodransky and Lewenstein, 2014[56]). Additional recommendations from the authors include: designing pilot projects based on increased knowledge of low-income residents' mobility needs (including needs beyond commuting, i.e. to access education, health and childcare); expanding research on business models for better understanding the needs for financial support and subsidies; and making shared mobility modes part of long-term planning tools and exercises (with an emphasis on integrating services with formal public transport) (Kodransky and Lewenstein, 2014[56]). Box 5.3 describes in detail the barriers identified, as well as the examples of programmes and measures put in place in different cases to address them.

Box 5.5. Barriers to introducing shared mobility strategies to enhance accessibility for low-income groups and how to address them

Analysis in the United States based on a literature review and interviews with academics, government officials and industry professionals reveals that the use of shared mobility services (including car-sharing, ride-sharing and bike-sharing, but excluding transportation network companies) is very scarce. The study finds barriers to low-income usage of the three types of services, and identifies three main categories of barriers: 1) structural; 2) financial; and 3) informational/cultural. Among the main structural barriers are physical access, since stations are not often located in low-income areas, and logistical access, since users need Internet access and access to smartphones. In terms of financial barriers, there are user costs, since many times these services require lump sum payments in addition to user fees and impose overuse fines, all of which often prices out lower income users. Another financial barrier is the lack of a bank account (a situation that in 2012 included 1 in 12 households in the United States). Finally, informational/cultural barriers include a lack of information and even language barriers for low-income communities with foreign backgrounds and distrust or discomfort with shared services. On the side of providers, barriers include limited profitability when providing these services in low-income areas and increased costs due to liability issues, as there are often perceptions of higher risks.

Examples of governments that have addressed these barriers include:

Physical access: The department of Public Works in Denver introduced explicit regulation for car-share companies with requirements to place vehicles in areas (designated as "opportunity areas") with at least 30% of the population living below the poverty line. The New York Department of Transportation, collaborated with CitiBike to gather recommendations from the public for the placement of the new stations.

Logistical access: Ithaca car share (in New York City) rolled out an Easy Access plan to facilitate the enrolment of population without or with only limited Internet access.

User costs: The Boston Hubway bike-share system in New York introduced a reduced fee (USD 5 instead of USD 85) for low-income populations. The company has a significantly higher (11%) share of low-income users compared with other bike-share systems (5% on average). The municipality offered grants to support the company. In San Francisco and Oakland, the selection of beneficiaries by a welfare programme put in place by the California Social Services Department has been used as the basis and the programme's beneficiaries do not pay registration fees for using shared services.

Lack of access to bank accounts: partnerships between shared mobility systems and banks or credit unions have been put in place to reach unbanked individuals. This is the case of Capital BikeShare in Washington, DC; CitiBike and Ithaca CarShare in New York; and iGO in Chicago. The issue has also been addressed by offering alternative payment modes, e.g. money order systems were used in Buffalo.

Informational barriers: special outreach programmes have been put into place, for instance by Ithaca CarShare with a local community in New York, while in Minneapolis the city introduced an outreach programme in support of bike-sharing.

Profitability barriers: federal, state and local funds have been used to subsidise capital investment in shared mobility or to users directly (although this still remains limited practice). An example is the Job Access and Reverse Commute Program. The funds of this programme from the US Department for Transport were dedicated to supporting capital costs as well as operating costs. While a large share went to formal public transport, the programme also provided significant support to shared vans providing services to low-income populations.*

Increased costs because of liability issues: insurance networks have begun to specialise in covering shared mobility schemes. Non-profit schemes in Denver (eGo) and San Francisco (City CarShare) are, for instance, covered by such an insurance network.

* These funds were transferred to the Moving Ahead for Progress in the 21st Century Act Program, which changed the eligibility criteria; therefore, the programme no longer focuses on improved access to low-income communities.
Source: Kodransky and Lewenstein (2014[56]).

The potential of micro-transit

Micro-transit can be defined as “privately or publicly operated, technology-enabled transit service that typically uses multi-passenger/pooled shuttles or vans to provide on-demand or fixed-schedule services with either dynamic or fixed routing” (SAE International, 2018[57]). While mass transit remains the backbone of shared and high-occupancy mobility, micro-transit can play a key role in developing efficient multimodal transport networks.

If not steered towards shared modes, technology-based mobility can bring negative, rather than positive, outcomes. Technology-based mobility services are often conflated with shared mobility. Crozet (2019[58]) identifies four models of technology-based mobility services: 1) peer-to peer car rental; 2) short-term rental of vehicles managed and owned by a provider; 3) ride-hailing, ride-sourcing, e-hailing (Uber-type services, except Uber pool); and 4) ride-sharing, micro-transit or on-demand public transport.[18] These services' emissions reduction potential varies widely, and analysis suggests that only a wide adoption of the fourth model can materialise into significant carbon dioxide (CO_2,) air pollution and congestion reductions (since none of the first three models effectively tackle low occupancy) (Crozet, 2019[58]). In most countries, however, the third model, i.e. ride-hailing that is not shared, often provided by transportation network companies, has expanded widely and resulted in increased congestion, emissions and low efficiency of road space use. For example, de Bortoli (2020[52]) finds that in Paris, taxis and ride-hailing vehicles were the highest emitting modes per passenger-kilometre, followed by private cars. The increase in total travel resulting from the introduction of these services is, to some extent, a result of a market correction, since in many cities taxi supply was restricted and insufficient. It is, however, also the result of modal shifts from public and active modes towards ride-hailing services (thus, from less emission-intensive to more emission-intensive modes) (Crozet, 2019[58]). Ride-hailing has also resulted in an increase in the vehicle stock (Crozet, 2019[58]).

Micro-transit (the fourth option) can significantly contribute to lowering emissions by increasing vehicle occupancy and improving the efficiency of the public transport network. There is significant potential, in particular in contexts where public transport may have important quality and coverage gaps, for on-demand micro-transit services to play a key role in providing better alternatives to car use. The ITF (2019[53]) argues that these services can incentivise modal shifts from private vehicles and low-occupancy ride-sourcing by “providing higher quality transit services at prices that represent a premium to standard public transport, but a significant discount to ride-sourcing”, also increasing in many cases general load factors (ITF, 2019[53]). Many of these services provide flexible collect and drop-off points that are equidistant from the origins/destinations of the passengers riding them, allow for easy booking, and offer services that cost less than car ownership and use or alternative lower occupancy (e.g. taxis, Uber) alternatives (see Box 5.6).

Experience with on-demand micro-transit is still limited and shows that results depend on the specific local circumstances. For instance, in Mexico City, analysis of an on-demand mini-van service (Jetty)[19] showed that around 50% of trips were previously done by private cars and ride-hailing. Nonetheless, a large share of the remaining trips came from semi-formal (*microbus*) public transport services (Flores-Dewey, 2019[59]). On the one hand, the incumbent *microbuses* are higher occupancy vehicles; on the other, they create congestion by blocking traffic lanes (chasing passengers aggressively and making multiple and often inefficient stops) (OECD, 2015[14]). Jetty services also have better quality and safety standards than incumbent *microbuses*, and use cleaner vehicles (Flores-Dewey, 2019[59]). In some cases (including the Jetty example), new on-demand service companies have integrated incumbent operators as drivers in their services (Flores, 2018[60]). This allows reducing equity concerns that the shift towards a better quality system (and the shift towards cleaner fleets) results in leaving a segment of the population without a livelihood. It also increases feasibility, as in many cases, incumbent operators are well-organised and constitute a powerful group that can oppose change (OECD, 2015[14]).

Paternina Blanco (2020[61]) estimates that if such a trend was generalised in the Latin American region and paratransit (i.e. informal or semi-formal) services became digitalised on-demand shared services, CO_2

emissions from urban passenger transport systems could be almost 40% lower in 2050 than if these services remained in their current state.[20] Reductions would only occur if services were integrated with formal transport services. In this situation, integration would mean higher ridership for public transport services, as well as a reduction in urban congestion thanks to the co-ordination of fleet movements. However, if services were not integrated with formal public transport, the potential would be lost. Instead, emissions could be more than 10% higher by 2050 than if digitalisation had not taken place at all. In such a situation, emissions increases would result from higher congestion due to a lack of fleet co-ordination, as well as from a decrease in public transport ridership brought about by competition. Fleet electrification could increase the positive decarbonisation impacts. If, beyond service integration, policies aimed at supporting paratransit operators into renewing their fleet, by 2050 CO_2 emissions could be almost 70% lower than if paratransit services had not been digitalised, integrated to formal public transport services and electrified.

There are also some interesting examples of on-demand services introduced during the COVID-19 crisis that bring attention to the potential these services have in developing accessible, resilient and highly adaptable transport systems, while also contributing to shifting away from car dependency (Box 5.6).

Box 5.6. The role of shared mobility and on-demand van services in addressing the COVID-19 and climate crisis

Urbvan is a vanpooling, shared mobility company that provides services in a number of cities in Mexico. Before the COVID-19 pandemic, Urbvan's main business model in Mexico City was focused on servicing workers going from central and residential areas (e.g. Polanco, Mixcoac, Naucalpan, La Condesa, etc.) to the main business districts (Santa Fe, Reforma, Interlomas). Commuting from these neighbourhoods to the business districts, especially during peak hours, requires long journeys, even with private vehicles. Most of the residents making these trips own private vehicles and use them to commute during the week. Public transport service options for these trips are limited and dominated by low-quality services (*microbuses*). This is, therefore, not a convenient or comfortable alternative to incite private vehicle users to shift to more sustainable modes of transport. Urbvan has therefore provided a way for this segment of workers to avoid having to commute by car. Similar to numbers calculated by other companies (see the Jetty example above), a survey made on its users revealed that around 51% of Urbvan users would otherwise have commuted by car.

With the COVID-19 health crisis, most workers using Urbvan shifted to teleworking and the company experienced a severe drop in activity. Urbvan decided to change strategy and focus on a different market segment that to date had remained marginal: providing services for companies that in turn offered, or subsidised commuting services for their employees.

Urbvan implemented a number of rigorous hygiene measures, providing customers with sanitary kits, adapting vehicles for social distancing and keeping track of contact between employees beyond the working space (to rapidly signal contact cases). While companies could enforce sanitary measures in work areas, the commuting link constituted an important daily risk. Thus, by purchasing Urbvan services, companies could minimise the risk of an outbreak among their staff and support rapid identification of potential contagion to stop it from spreading. Overall, Urbvan became an important solution for a number of trips that would increase the risk of contagion if they were carried out in other public transport services with limited capacity to offer safe conditions. Furthermore, it also avoids minimising health risks due to overuse of private cars and its negative impacts, including carbon emissions.

Urbvan is now progressively servicing intercity trips, which have significantly increased as teleworking practices expand and as the population moves to other cities and only goes to Mexico City periodically. The question of the impacts of increasing teleworking on land use, transport, and related environmental and social outcomes is a relevant one (see discussion earlier in this chapter). On-demand public transport services could be an important part of a strategy that looks to avoid car dependency and related negative climate and other (e.g. air pollution, inequitable access) impacts.

Sources: (Urbvan, 2020[62]) (UrbVan, 2021[63])

Mainstreaming micro-transit may imply a number of changes in government in terms of regulation and monitoring frameworks. These changes could also facilitate the street and territories redesign discussed in Chapters 3 and 4, and are also important for the regulation of micro-mobility and active shared modes (as discussed above).

First, setting and monitoring minimum service and safety standards is a pre-condition for well-functioning micro-transit services. Authorities may not all have such regulatory power, or governance structures allowing them to regulate micro-transit at the most efficient territorial level (e.g. peripheries rather than just the city centre) (see Box 5.1).

Second, the capacity to set data requirements, and analyse such data to plan and regulate services appropriately, is another condition that may not be met in all countries. Analysis suggests that innovation in terms of public-private partnerships involving data sharing may be required to unlock the benefits of micro-transit (ITF, 2015[64]). International experience suggests that metropolitan transport authorities can play an important role in both regulation and data management and requirement settings (ITF, 2018[23]) (see Chapter 4).

Third, authorities may need to update legal frameworks to remove barriers to micro-transit development. For example, the Mexican Federal Economic Competition Commission (COFECE) recently released an analysis highlighting a number of ways in which the current legislation for intercity passenger services impedes the development of new business models and limits the possibilities that new technologies can bring. Among these barriers are the possibility to propose reduced tariffs when ridership is high, and the need to establish fixed routes and collect/drop-off stations, which impedes services from adapting to traffic conditions and proposing collect and drop-off points that will minimise last-mile travel needs (COFECE, 2019[65]).

Fourth, financial support (e.g. subsidies) could be allocated to micro-transit. Such financial support could facilitate their development in areas where services might have limited profitability but could ensure social value (ITF, 2019[53]). Governments could also consider tax credits for mobility providers indexed to load factors, to incentivise high levels of occupancy. Incentives (e.g. tax breaks) could also be provided to companies that demonstrate a high share of pooling among employees, including shared vehicles (cycling, micro-mobility and public transport) rather than car-pooling exclusively. In this case, setting thresholds that vary depending on location (i.e. higher thresholds for companies located in dense city centres) could be used (Sperling, Pike and Chase, 2018[66]).

Fifth, the reallocation, redesign and pricing of road space (discussed in Chapter 3) can also contribute to increasing the attractiveness of micro-transit. For example, road-pricing instruments differentiated by occupancy levels could make single- or low-occupancy car travel relatively more expensive, and thus less attractive *vis-à-vis* micro-transit (see Chapter 3). Pooled vehicles can also be granted special stop and parking space at specific locations (e.g. airports) (Sperling, Pike and Chase, 2018[66]).[21]

References

Bayliss, K., G. Mattioli and J. Steinberger (2020), "Inequality, poverty and the privatization of essential services: A "systems of provision" study of water, energy and local buses in the UK", *Compilation & Change*, Vol. 25/3-4, pp. 478-500, https://doi.org/10.1177/1024529420964933. [19]

BBC (2021), "Greater Manchester bus network back under public control", BBC News, https://www.bbc.com/news/uk-england-manchester-56523708 (accessed on 21 July 2021). [25]

Bojovic, D., J. Benavides and A. Soret (2020), "What we can learn from birdsong: Mainstreaming teleworking in a post-pandemic world", *Earth System Governance*, Vol. 5, p. 100074, http://dx.doi.org/10.1016/j.esg.2020.100074. [45]

Brown, A. et al. (2020), "Impeding access: The frequency and characteristics of improper scooter, bike, and car parking", *Transportation Research Interdisciplinary Perspectives*, Vol. 4, p. 100099, http://dx.doi.org/10.1016/J.TRIP.2020.100099. [54]

Buck, D. (2012), *Encouraging Equitable Access to Public Bikesharing Systems*. [50]

Buckle, S. et al. (2020), "Addressing the COVID-19 and climate crises: Potential economic recovery pathways and their implications for climate change mitigation, NDCs and broader socio-economic goals", *OECD/IEA Climate Change Expert Group Papers*, No. 2020/04, OECD Publishing, Paris, https://dx.doi.org/10.1787/50abd39c-en. [34]

Cervero, R. (2011), "State roles in providing affordable mass transport services for low-income residents", *International Transport Forum Discussion Papers*, No. 2011/17, OECD Publishing, Paris, https://doi.org/10.1787/5kg9mq4f4627-en. [32]

Cervero, R. and A. Golub (2007), "Informal transport: A global perspective", *Transport Policy*, Vol. 14/6, pp. 445-457, http://dx.doi.org/10.1016/J.TRANPOL.2007.04.011. [18]

COFECE (2019), *Estudio de competencia en el autotransporte federal de pasajeros*, Mexican Federal Economic Competition Commission, Mexico City, https://www.cofece.mx/wp-content/uploads/2019/04/Estudiocompetenciaautotransportefederalpasajeros.pdf. [65]

Crow, D. and A. Millot (2020), "Working from home can save energy and reduce emissions. But how much?", International Energy Agency, Paris, https://www.iea.org/commentaries/working-from-home-can-save-energy-and-reduce-emissions-but-how-much (accessed on 29 July 2020). [42]

Crozet, Y. (2019), "Cars and space consumption: Rethinking the regulation of urban mobility", *International Transport Forum Discussion Papers*, No. 2020/13, OECD Publishing, Paris, https://doi.org/10.1787/8abaa384-en. [58]

de Bortoli, A. (2020), "Are e-scooters good or bad for the environment?", International Transport Forum, Paris, https://www.itf-oecd.org/are-e-scooters-good-or-bad-environment. [52]

Dijkstra, L., H. Poelman and V. Paolo (2019), "The EU-OECD definition of a functional urban area", *OECD Regional Development Working Papers*, No. 2019/11, OECD Publishing, Paris, https://doi.org/10.1787/d58cb34d-en. [10]

Docherty, I., G. Marsden and J. Anable (2018), "The governance of smart mobility", *Transportation Research Part A: Policy and Practice*, Vol. 115, pp. 114-125, http://dx.doi.org/10.1016/j.tra.2017.09.012. [55]

EIT and McKinsey (2019), *Examining the Impact of a Sustainable Electric Micromobility Approach in Europe*, EIT InnoEnergy, Eindhoven, https://www.innoenergy.com/discover-innovative-solutions/reports/micromobility-report (accessed on 22 July 2021). [51]

Flores-Dewey, O. (2019), "App-based collective transport service in Mexico City: A start-up case study", *International Transport Forum Discussion Papers*, No. 2019/01, OECD Publishing, Paris, https://doi.org/10.1787/f2ab80ea-en. [59]

Flores, O. (2018), "¿Mejor transporte? Comencemos por los conductores", *2018*, Jetty, https://www.jetty.mx/update/2018/03/25/trabajo-operadores.html (accessed on 19 July 2021). [60]

GMCA (2021), "Mayor of Greater Manchester makes landmark decision: City-region to be first outside London to have local control over buses", Greater Manchester Combined Authority, https://www.greatermanchester-ca.gov.uk/news/mayor-of-greater-manchester-makes-landmark-decision-city-region-to-be-first-outside-london-to-have-local-control-over-buses (accessed on 21 July 2021). [26]

IEA (2020), "Rail – Analysis", International Energy Agency, Paris, https://www.iea.org/reports/rail (accessed on 25 November 2020). [35]

IISD (2020), "Green stimulus for Finland's transport sector: Sustainable Recovery 2020", International Institute for Sustainable Development, https://www.iisd.org/sustainable-recovery/news/green-stimulus-for-finlands-transport-sector (accessed on 26 March 2021). [36]

ITF (2020), "Safe micromobility", *International Transport Forum Policy Papers*, No. 85, OECD Publishing, Paris, https://dx.doi.org/10.1787/0b98fac1-en. [67]

ITF (2020), *Shared Mobility Simulations for Lyon*, Case-Specific Policy Analysis, International Transport Forum, Paris, https://www.itf-oecd.org/shared-mobility-simulations-lyon. [49]

ITF (2019), "Benchmarking accessibility in cities: Measuring the impact of proximity and transport performance", *International Transport Forum Policy Papers*, No. 68, OECD Publishing, Paris, https://doi.org/10.1787/4b1f722b-en. [7]

ITF (2019), *Regulating App-Based Mobility Services: Summary and Conclusions*, ITF Roundtable Reports, No. 175, OECD Publishing, Paris, https://dx.doi.org/10.1787/94d27a3a-en. [53]

ITF (2018), "Policy directions for establishing a metropolitan transport authority for Korea's Capital Region", *International Transport Forum Policy Papers*, No. 61, OECD Publishing, Paris, https://dx.doi.org/10.1787/8b87cefc-en. [23]

ITF (2018), *The Social Impacts of Road Pricing: Summary and Conclusions*, ITF Roundtable Reports, No. 170, OECD Publishing, Paris, https://dx.doi.org/10.1787/d6d56d2d-en. [29]

ITF (2017), *Income Inequality, Social Inclusion and Mobility*, International Transport Forum, Paris, https://www.itf-oecd.org/sites/default/files/docs/income-inequality-social-inclusion-mobility.pdf. [12]

ITF (2017), *Income Inequality, Social Inclusion and Mobility*, ITF Roundtable Reports, No. 164, OECD Publishing, Paris, https://dx.doi.org/10.1787/g2g7ae77-en. [15]

ITF (2017), *Shared Mobility Simulations for Auckland*, Case-Specific Policy Analysis, International Transport Forum, Paris, https://www.itf-oecd.org/sites/default/files/docs/shared-mobility-simulations-auckland.pdf. [48]

ITF (2017), "Shared mobility simulations for Helsinki", *International Transport Forum Policy Papers*, No. 39, OECD Publishing, Paris, https://doi.org/10.1787/3d340a2a-en. [47]

ITF (2015), "Big data and transport: Understanding and assessing options", *International Transport Forum Policy Papers*, No. 8, OECD Publishing, Paris, https://doi.org/10.1787/5jlwvzdb6r47-en. [64]

ITF (2014), *Valuing Convenience in Public Transport*, ITF Round Tables, No. 156, OECD Publishing, Paris, https://doi.org/10.1787/9789282107683-en. [1]

ITF (forthcoming), *Developing Accessibility Indicators for Latin American Cities*, OECD Publishing, Paris, forthcoming. [8]

Jones, A. (2016), "Transport devolution in the UK: A re-balancing of power", Intelligent Transport, https://www.intelligenttransport.com/transport-articles/19653/transport-devolution-uk (accessed on 21 July 2021). [16]

King, A. (2021), "Greater Manchester leaders back bringing buses under public control", The Meteor, https://themeteor.org/2021/03/24/greater-manchester-leaders-back-bringing-buses-under-public-control (accessed on 23 July 2021). [24]

Kodransky, M. and G. Lewenstein (2014), *Connecting Low-Income People to Opportunity with Shared Mobility*, Institute for Transportation & Development Policy, https://www.itdp.in/wp-content/uploads/2016/06/Shared-Mobility_Full-Report.pdf. [56]

Kumar, A. and O. Agarwal (2013), *Institutional Labyrinth: Designing a Way Out for Improving Urban Transport Services – Lessons from Current Practice*, The World Bank, Washington, DC, https://openknowledge.worldbank.org/handle/10986/17630. [21]

Leahy, P. (2020), "Greens' plan to shift billions to public transport hit by roads budget", The Irish Times, https://www.irishtimes.com/news/politics/greens-plan-to-shift-billions-to-public-transport-hit-by-roads-budget-1.4250798 (accessed on 23 March 2021). [5]

Liao, Y. et al. (2020), "Disparities in travel times between car and transit: Spatiotemporal patterns in cities", *Scientific Reports*, Vol. 10/1, http://dx.doi.org/10.1038/s41598-020-61077-0. [9]

Lin, P. et al. (2006), "Effective teleworking to reduce traffic demand and energy consumption", paper submitted for the 6th Asia-Pacific Transportation Development Conference and the 19th ICTPA Annual Meeting. [43]

London City Hall (2020), "There can be no national recovery without a London recovery", Mayor of London, London, https://www.london.gov.uk/press-releases/mayoral/londons-recovery-vital-for-uks-recovery (accessed on 26 March 2021). [37]

Lozzi, G. et al. (2020), *Research for TRAN Committee – COVID-19 and Urban Mobility: Impacts and Perspectives*, European Parliament, Policy Department for Structural and Cohesion Policies, Brussels, https://www.europarl.europa.eu/RegData/etudes/IDAN/2020/652213/IPOL_IDA%282020%29652213_EN.pdf. [40]

Mattioli, G. et al. (2020), "The political economy of car dependence: A systems of provision approach", *Energy Research & Social Science*, Vol. 66, p. 101486, http://dx.doi.org/10.1016/j.erss.2020.101486. [13]

Moeckel, R. (2017), "Working from home: Modeling the impact of telework on transportation and land use", *Transportation Research Procedia*, Vol. 26, pp. 207-214, http://dx.doi.org/10.1016/j.trpro.2017.07.021. [44]

OECD (2019), *Accelerating Climate Action: Refocusing Policies through a Well-being Lens*, OECD Publishing, Paris, https://dx.doi.org/10.1787/2f4c8c9a-en. [33]

OECD (2015), *OECD Territorial Reviews: Valle de México, Mexico*, OECD Territorial Reviews, OECD Publishing, Paris, https://dx.doi.org/10.1787/9789264245174-en. [14]

Paternina Blanco, J. (2020), *Assessing Future Impacts of Urban Shared Mobility from a Wellbeing Framework: The Case of Latin America*, Specialised Master's dissertation. [61]

Peralta-Quiros, T. and C. Rodríguez Hernández (2016), "Balancing financial sustainability and affordability in public transport: The case of Bogotá, Colombia", *International Transport Forum Discussion Papers*, No. 2016/16, OECD Publishing, Paris, https://doi.org/10.1787/21b96177-en. [31]

Phillipson, B. and S. Gilfillan (2015), "Route masters: The re-regulation of bus services in Tyne and Wear", *Renewal*, Vol. 23/1-2, pp. 17-29, https://renewal.org.uk/wp-content/uploads/2020/09/phillipson_final-1.pdf. [20]

Proost, S. (2018), "Reforming private and public urban transport pricing", *International Transport Forum Discussion Papers*, No. 2018/15, OECD Publishing, Paris, https://doi.org/10.1787/3567dda4-en. [27]

Public Transport Users Association Victoria Australia (2009), "Myth: More money is spent on public transport than on roads", web page, https://www.ptua.org.au/myths/spend (accessed on 23 March 2021). [4]

Ravalet, E. and P. Rérat (2019), "Teleworking: Decreasing mobility or increasing tolerance of commuting distances?", *Built Environment*, Vol. 45/4, pp. 582-602, http://dx.doi.org/10.2148/benv.45.4.582. [41]

SAE International (2018), *Taxonomy and Definitions for Terms Related to Shared Mobility and Enabling Technologies*, SAE International, https://www.sae.org/standards/content/j3163_201809 (accessed on 22 July 2021). [57]

Sánchez-Atondo, A. et al. (2020), "Understanding public transport ridership in developing countries to promote sustainable urban mobility: A case study of Mexicali, Mexico", *Sustainability*, Vol. 12/8, p. 3266, http://dx.doi.org/10.3390/su12083266. [2]

Sohail, M., D. Maunder and S. Cavill (2006), "Effective regulation for sustainable public transport in developing countries", *Transport Policy*, Vol. 13/3, pp. 177-190, http://dx.doi.org/10.1016/J.TRANPOL.2005.11.004. [17]

Sperling, D., S. Pike and R. Chase (2018), "Will the transportation revolutions improve our lives – or make them worse?", in *Three Revolutions*, Island Press/Center for Resource Economics, http://dx.doi.org/10.5822/978-1-61091-906-7_1. [66]

Sterman, J. (2000), *Business Dynamics: Systems Thinking and Modeling for a Complex World*, Irwin/McGraw-Hill, http://jsterman.scripts.mit.edu/Business_Dynamics.html. [6]

Taylor, B. and C. Fink (2013), "Explaining transit ridership: What has the evidence shown?", *Transportation Letters*, Vol. 5/1, pp. 15-26, http://dx.doi.org/10.1179/1942786712z.0000000003. [3]

TfL (2015), *London's Bus Contracting and Tendering Process*, Transport for London, London, http://content.tfl.gov.uk/uploads/forms/lbsl-tendering-and-contracting.pdf. [22]

Thicknesse, E. (2021), "Long-term funding deal for TfL can "fuel" UK recovery, says network boss", CityAM, https://www.cityam.com/long-term-funding-deal-for-tfl-can-fuel-uk-recovery-says-network-boss (accessed on 26 March 2021). [38]

UITP (2020), *Full Free Fare Public Transport: Objectives and Alternatives*, International Association of Public Transport, Brussels, https://cms.uitp.org/wp/wp-content/uploads/2020/09/Policy-Brief-FullFreeFarePT-DEF-web.pdf. [11]

UITP (2020), “Guardians of mobility: From the front lines in Milan, Italy”, International Association of Public Transport, https://www.uitp.org/news/guardians-of-mobility-from-the-front-lines-in-milan-italy (accessed on 24 March 2021). [30]

UITP (2014), *Better Public Transport Fare Policy for More Resilient Funding*, policy brief, International Association of Public Transport, Brussels, https://cms.uitp.org/wp/wp-content/uploads/2020/09/Policy-Brief-FullFreeFarePT-DEF-web.pdf. [28]

UrbVan (2021), *Interview with the UrbVan Head of Public Affairs*. [63]

Urbvan (2020), *Impact Report Urbvan*. [62]

Wardman, M. (2014), *Valuing Convenience in Public Transport*, ITF Round Tables, No. 156, OECD Publishing, Paris, https://doi.org/10.1787/9789282107683-en. [39]

Zenkteler, M. et al. (2019), “Home-based work in cities: In search of an appropriate urban planning response”, *Futures*, p. 102494, http://dx.doi.org/10.1016/j.futures.2019.102494. [46]

Notes

[1] As discussed later on in the chapter, authorities could also improve the provision of public transport in low-density areas by carefully planning networks and retaining a certain level of public control over the services provided (Mattioli et al., 2020[13]).

[2] As it penalises the segments of the population depending on public transport, often low-income households.

[3] In many cases this is exacerbated by a lack of regulatory capacity by governments. See Section 5.2.1.

[4] Transport performance is computed as the ratio of accessible destinations to nearby destinations (ITF, 2019[7]).

[5] See Section 5.2.2 for a discussion on micro-mobility and pedestrians.

[6] The process in each city has been distinct and more or less successful. For instance, in both Bogotá and Chile, competitive tendering has been established, while in Mexico City this step was never taken (OECD, 2015[14]).

[7] Economically speaking, non-earmarked cash transfers could be a superior alternative. Practice has shown that current conditions (e.g. under-priced private vehicle use) could lead to some negative impacts from the use of these funds (at least in the short run). For instance in Bogotá, cash transfers provided with the intention to increase affordability for covering public transport fares were very often used to buy highly polluting, but low-cost, motorbikes, which are also associated with high traffic fatalities (ITF, 2017[15]). Thus, at least until a number of conditions (e.g. correct pricing of private vehicles) are fixed, direct public transport fare subsidies might still be a good alternative, in practice (ITF, 2017[15]).

[8] Competitive tendering is also key to ensuring that subsidies are channelled to bridging the gap between affordability and the cost of quality services rather than covering inefficient operations (ITF, 2017[15]).

[9] Nonetheless, fare-box revenues are still an important source (ITF, 2018[23]). Affordability issues can justify subsidising public transport prices (Cervero, 2011[32]).

[10] The VT is paid as a percentage of the employer's total payroll cost.

[11] A business rate supplement can be applied to existing commercial developments with rateable value above GBP 55 000, charged at 2 pence per pound of rateable value.

[12] A charge levied on the most polluting cars driving through central London.

[13] The impacts of teleworking and new behaviour triggered by the COVID-19 pandemic (discussed later in this chapter) will, of course, need to be acknowledged as peak times, for instance, might now be at different times of the day in many places.

[14] The report provides ways forward for measuring and valuing such elements, as well as for mainstreaming these into policy decisions (e.g. socio-economic appraisals).

[15] This might mean less but longer commuting trips.

[16] The ITF (2020[67]) defines micro-mobility as "the use of vehicles with a mass of less than 350 kg and a design speed of 45 km/h or less."

[17] Based on original data.

[18] On-demand public transport refers to bus-like services that are adaptable to consumer demand in relation to scheduling, route and/or other service elements, while micro-transit refers services using mini-buses and app-based booking.

[19] Jetty implemented an app-based booking system and uses data to adjust routes.

[20] Results stem from an analysis based on the global urban passenger transport model used for the *ITF Transport Outlook 2019*. The *ITF Transport Outlook 2019* focused on potential impacts of various transport innovations for transport activity for all world regions up until 2050, including increased shared mobility. The results for Latin American cities come from an analysis that calibrated the Outlook's urban passenger transport model with additional regional case studies. The analysis was carried out before the COVID-19 pandemic and so does not include changes that could have resulted from it. The analysis was quantitative, and did not consider the political economy of the proposed changes, such as the necessary interactions between public authorities, private entrepreneurs and paratransit operators, required for having the highlighted integration.

[21] Although overall, public transport would need to be the most convenient way to access airports and train stations (OECD, 2015[14]).

6 Innovation and carbon prices for systems redesign

This chapter discusses the untapped potential of systems innovation and how incentives for cleaner vehicles' uptake and carbon prices could be implemented to be more effective and to contribute to wider systems redesign. The chapter also discusses how measurement frameworks overestimate the mitigation potential of policies, biasing decisions towards improved vehicle performance.

Policies fostering innovation and technological change such as incentives for cleaner vehicles' uptake, as well as market-based instruments such as carbon prices play a central role in current climate strategies. While fundamental to achieve mitigation goals, the potential of these instruments to mitigate emissions is not always fulfilled, synergies with other well-being outcomes are often missed, while important trade-offs are also created.

The effectiveness (both for decarbonisation and other benefits) and the feasibility of these instruments could be much larger if these were implemented as part of a wider strategy to foster systems innovation. Failing to do so can instead, importantly lock-in emissions, either by reinforcing the dynamics described in chapters 3-5 (thus off-setting to a great extent any progress in reducing emissions per vehicles); or by failing to create the right conditions for widespread change towards more sustainable choices (often also translating into roll-back of policies like carbon pricing).

This chapter discusses key considerations to avoid that incentives and enabling infrastructure to accelerate the uptake of better vehicle technologies foster car-dependency, as well as the ways in which systemic redesign could help increase the effectiveness and feasibility of carbon pricing . A final section argues that overall, better methodologies for measuring and comparing the impacts of different policies is needed to steer decisions towards untapping the synergies **between innovating at the parts and the systems level, which is crucial** given the scale of the climate challenge.

6.1. The untapped potential of systems innovation

As discussed in chapter 2, **Systems innovation is innovation aimed at transforming the systems' functioning** (Systems Innovation, 2020[1]), and while in some cases requires advanced technologies, it is also often about changes that are not technological. Superblocks in Barcelona, described in Chapter 3, are an example of low-tech systems innovation. Superblocks innovate in the way in which public space is allocated and designed, thus modifying the systems' structure and significantly affecting people's transport modes choices.

Advanced technologies open up enormous opportunities for systems innovation, and many synergies can be created between innovating at the parts and the systems level. For example, GPS technologies and apps today allow people to share vehicles (e.g. bikes) and combine transport modes in ways that were unimaginable just a few decades ago. However, without embedding GPS technology and apps in an attempt to redesign transport and urban systems to shift them away from car-dependency, these technologies have so far led more to the uptake of ride-hailing (e.g. Uber-like non-shared services); without really helping to overcome the challenges to decarbonise the sector (and in some cases making it more challenging). These technologies could instead allow the shift from a system which functioning requires each person to own a car, and where cars have an utilisation rate of 5% in average (Shoup (2005[2]) accessed from Franco (2020[3])), to systems in which a multiplicity of transport modes are available for people to choose and combine according to their needs and have access to cars as a service. In such systems, much smaller car fleets would be needed, which would make achieving high shares of electric vehicles in the short-term more plausible and would entail less potential trade-offs, as less minerals (and thus mining) will be required. In addition a system in which a high number of vehicles are managed as part of a same fleet and where vehicles utilisation rates are higher, can help accelerate vehicle turn over and thus the uptake of cleaner technologies, while also facilitating the uptake of new technologies for better managing the demand for electricity (e.g. vehicle-to-grid (V2G) technologies (Gschwendtner, 2021[4]); also reducing potential pressure on the energy sector. At the same time, such a system can also increase the feasibility and effectiveness of market-based instruments such as carbon pricing by creating better conditions for people to make more sustainable choices; thus reducing the potential distributional negative outcomes and raising acceptability.

Unfortunately, most of these potential synergies remain untapped, and for the contrary, often carbon strategies (following a decoupling logic- see Chapter 2) focus on decarbonising vehicles and correcting pricing, while leaving car-dependency practically intact. The rest of this section discusses policies and charging infrastructure for cleaner vehicles, as well as carbon pricing in the context of system's redesign.

6.1.1. Innovation in parts that advances systems redesign: incentives and charging infrastructure for cleaner vehicles

Both fuel economy standards (targeting vehicle supply) and tax incentives to purchase cleaner vehicles (targeting vehicle demand and influencing supply indirectly) are important instruments to improve the fuel efficiency and emissions performance of the vehicle fleet (Wappelhorst, Mock and Yang, 2018[5]). Vehicle purchase taxes and circulation taxes (one-off or annual charges) are the most common tax incentive mechanisms to encourage the purchase of low-carbon (including electric) vehicles. In some countries, revenues from the purchase taxes of more polluting vehicles are used to grant rebates/subsidies to cleaner vehicles (often referred to as "fee-bate programmes"). In addition, due to price differentials between combustion and electric vehicles,[1] additional incentives may be needed to accelerate their uptake[2], and a number of countries have increasingly made use of these incentives.[3]

Norway is a front-runner in moving forward in electrifying its vehicle fleet and uses a wide range of tax and non-tax incentives for reducing the generalised cost of driving. In 2017, electric vehicles accounted for 39% of all new car sales in Norway, turning the country into the most advanced market for EVs worldwide (IEA, 2020[6]), and Oslo into the "electric vehicle capital" (Holtsmark and Skonhoft, 2014[7]). Between 1992 and 1997, the Norwegian government introduced a registration tax exemption for EVs, free public parking, a reduction in the annual circulation tax and the company car tax, and an exemption from the road toll and ferry charge. A value-added tax exemption for battery electric vehicles also entered into force in 2001. Additionally, since 2005, EVs are allowed to use lanes that are reserved for buses and taxis (Lindberg and Fridstrøm, 2015[8]), and can change their battery for free (Holtsmark and Skonhoft, 2014[7]). A significant part of the combustion engine vehicle tax revenues has been used to support the development of charging infrastructure (IEA, 2020[6]).

The Norwegian case provides two key lessons. First, while packages of incentives can certainly help, mainstreaming incentives into the wider fiscal system is key. The fiscal system in Norway includes a number of CO_2-based related taxes, equivalent to paying a carbon tax higher than EUR 1 250 per tonne (Fridstrøm, 2020[9]). This shows the potential of embedding EV incentives into wider fiscal reforms.

Second, special attention needs to be given so that incentives included in packages do not reinforce car dependency. While the share of EVs has importantly increased, evidence suggests that car travel and ownership in Norway is also being incentivised as a result of the incentive packages (Holtsmark and Skonhoft, 2014[7]). Specifically, allowing EVs to use bus lanes has resulted in more bus congestion, potentially reducing their attractiveness *vis-à-vis* cars, and thus exacerbating rather than helping reverse the erosion of sustainable modes. Exempting EVs from parking fees also locks-in space for cars (instead of other modes and uses) and incentivises their use over active or shared modes. While the replacement of combustion cars with EVs can reduce tail-pipe CO_2 emissions, air pollution and noise,[4] non-exhaust emissions, and other social costs (e.g. road fatalities), inequality of access remains, and may be exacerbated. A bigger EV fleet also exacerbates trade-offs with other environmental impacts, e.g. related to minerals extractions for batteries (Holtsmark and Skonhoft, 2014[7]) (see Chapter 2). EV incentives designed, instead, from a systemic approach, i.e. with careful attention of not exacerbating car dependency, could become more effective in reducing emissions while simultaneously achieve other well-being goals.

Importantly, and adding to the discussion on measurement biases at the end of this chapter, evaluation of incentives for the purchase of cleaner vehicles needs to be compared to other policy and investment options, such as incentives for modal shifts towards active and shared modes, or policies and infrastructure investments fostering the creation of proximity to avoid trips as much as possible. Instead, estimated CO_2 emissions reductions from the introduction of EVs are most often compared to emissions in a scenario in which vehicles remain combustion-based. The measurement reflects the implicit assumption that the number of vehicles is a given (rather than a result of the system's design, as explained in Section 3.1).

Charging infrastructure is also fundamental for the uptake of EVs (Falchetta and Noussan, 2021[10]), and its deployment needs to be significantly accelerated to meet stringent international mitigation targets. The stock of charging infrastructure increased by 40% between 2018 and 2019 (IEA, 2020[6]), with France, Germany, Italy, the Netherlands, Norway, Sweden and the United Kingdom being the countries with the highest installed capacity as of November 2020 (Falchetta and Noussan, 2021[10]). The IEA estimates however that, for instance, the number of charging facilities needs to almost double (to around 20 million) to reach emissions goals in the Sustainable Development Scenario[5] (IEA, 2020[6]).

Policies to accelerate the transition towards car independent systems could reduce charging facility needs, facilitating reaching electrification targets and reducing the costs to do so. For instance, San Francisco aims for a 100% EV fleet by 2030, and a study of infrastructure needs to deliver such goal finds that public charging infrastructure needs could be reduced by 45% if 80% of trips are "non-automobile" (walking, biking, transit); another goal of San Francisco's strategy (SFMTA, 2017[11]) (Figure 6.1). As a result, 2 900 instead of 5 100 public charging stations would be needed by 2030, reducing the required growth rate of installation from 18% to 12%, thus facilitating the strategy's implementation (Hsu, Slowik and Lutsey, 2020[12]).

Figure 6.1. San Francisco modal shift goal by 2030

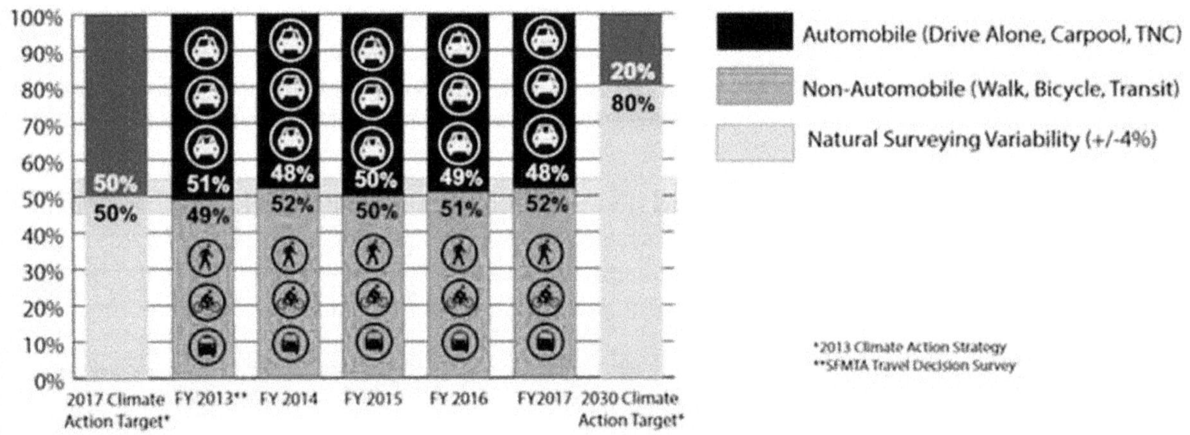

Source: Extracted from SFMTA (2017[11]).

In turn, the deployment of charging infrastructure could foster system redesign. Mobility hubs and charging stations with services for different transport modes can facilitate modal shifts from private cars and reduce car dependency (Transport & Environment, 2020[13]). Mobility hubs are **locations in which sustainable transport modes such as (**e-)bikes, cargo or children's bikes, and e-scooters could be made available (Transport & Environment, 2020[13]). Charging stations with services for different users can, for instance, provide slow chargers for park & ride (i.e. people leaving their car parked to take public transportation, for example at the outskirts of cities), as well as fast charging for long-distance trips, taxis, ride-sharing services and commercial delivery vans (Transport & Environment, 2020[13]). Cities could develop joint energy, transport and telecom plans to find the best locations for developing new hubs and for assessing the needs in terms of charging facilities for existing hubs (Transport & Environment, 2020[13]).

Other actions to facilitate the deployment of charging infrastructure include incorporating charging points' standards into real estate development (e.g. introducing targets for the shares of parking space with charging points) and adding charging stations to existing parking spaces. To reduce on-road parking and traffic and liberate urban space for other uses (e.g. electric micro-mobility), such actions need to go hand-in-hand with the revision of parking space regulation and the removal of minimum parking requirements where these are still in place (as discussed in Chapters 3 and 4). To account for equity considerations, Transport & Environment (2020[13]) recommends targets for the development of charging facilities and shared EV services in low-income areas.

6.1.2. Carbon prices and systems redesign

The most widely used instrument to price carbon emissions in the road sector across OECD countries are fuel excise taxes (OECD, 2019[14]). Fuel excise taxes are considered to be the most efficient policy instrument for promoting behavioural change to reduce carbon emissions via reduced driving, a shift towards fuel-efficient vehicles and the use of more sustainable transport modes (van Dender, 2019[15]).A study in Canada finds as well that carbon pricing has contributed to reduced driving by containing urban sprawl, one of the three dynamics described in this report. The authors find that, on average, a 1% increase in gas prices led to a 0.32% increase in the population in city centres and a 0.60% decrease in low-density housing (Tanguay and Gingras, 2012[16]).

Evidence suggests, however, that carbon pricing alone will not translate into emission reductions at the pace and scale needed, even at high prices (Tvinnereim and Mehling, 2018[17]; Rosenbloom et al., 2020[18]). Rosenbloom et al. (2020[18]) analyse carbon pricing from a systemic perspective and suggest that a complex problem like climate change cannot be solved solely through market instruments, and that climate strategies focused primarily on carbon pricing will not result in the transformative change needed to reach net-zero goals on time. The authors call for policies triggering changes across new vehicle technologies, infrastructure, business models, regulation and city planning (Rosenbloom et al., 2020[18]).

In addition, setting carbon prices has been politically challenging, with public resistance resulting in policy roll-back or stagnation in a number of countries (Douenne and Fabre, 2020[19]) and almost 40% of emissions in road transport priced below central estimates of the carbon price that would be needed by 2030 to decarbonise the economy by mid-century (e.g. EUR 120 by 2030) (OECD, 2021[20])[6]. The impact of fuel prices on people's choice is also low when alternatives to car driving are not available or limited, as illustrated in Figure 6.2 (Geman, 2019[21]).

Figure 6.2. Gasoline prices and vehicle miles travelled in the United States

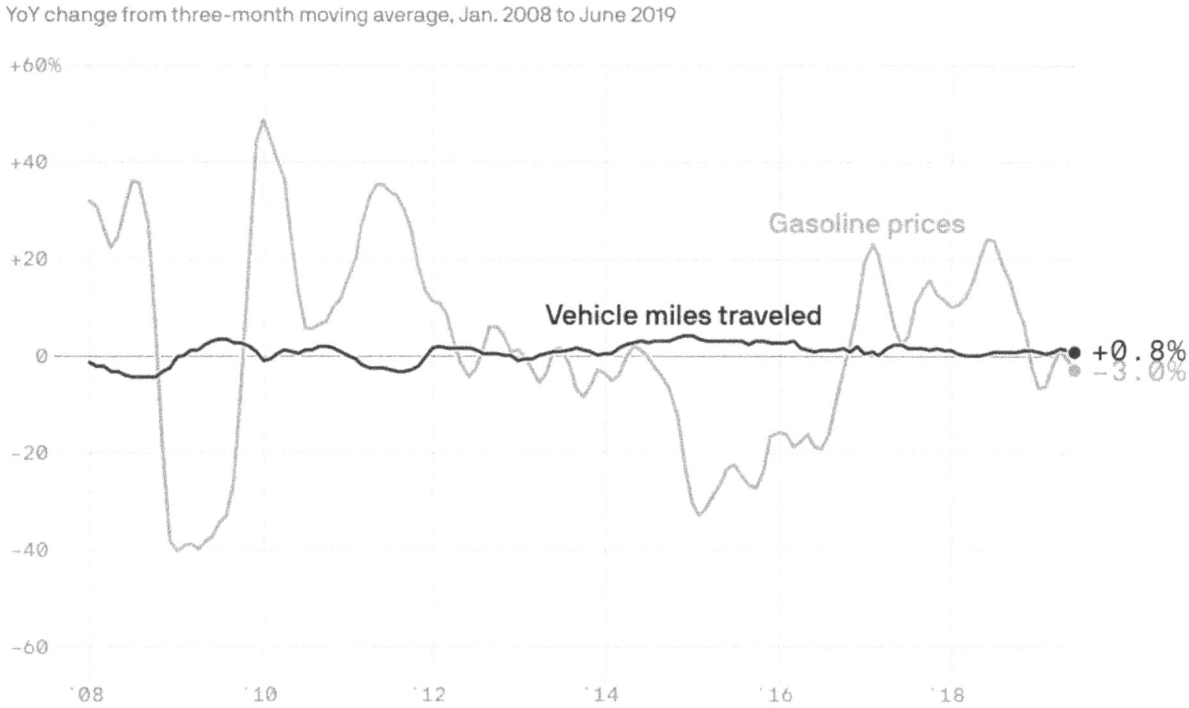

Note: YoY = Year on year.
Source: Geman (2019[21]).

Nonetheless, combining carbon prices with policies contributing to car independence can significantly increase their mitigation potential (Rosenbloom et al., 2020[18]; Kaufman et al., 2020[22]), as well as their acceptance. Behavioural change would be easier, and possible in the first place, if alternatives to car use were available and convenient. The revenue raised by carbon pricing could also help enhance public support and address equity concerns; for instance, through supporting sustainable mobility projects. Policies are also likely to have a higher acceptability if they are framed as part of a larger package with environmental and/or social benefits (rather than being perceived as a revenue collection mechanism), and if communication efforts shed light on policy efforts to, in parallel to pricing, improve access to alternative transport modes and tackle equity considerations (ITF, 2017[23]; 2018[24]).

A number of studies have shown, for instance, that public transport infrastructure can significantly change the elasticity of travel and energy demand (and related greenhouse gas emissions) and increase the responsiveness to carbon pricing in the transport sector. Avner, Rentschler and Hallegatte (2014[25]) estimate that price elasticity of CO_2 emissions from private car travel is twice as high in a region like Paris, with a dense public transport network, than it is in areas without such a dense network. The authors find that the absence of dense public transport systems increases transport emissions while importantly limiting the territory's capacity to mitigate. Similarly, Gillingham and Munk-Nielsen (2019[26]) find that in Denmark, the price elasticity of driving is higher among people that live centrally in urban areas and have the shortest commutes. They highlight that, in contexts where access to public transport is limited (e.g. many cities in the United States), price elasticities are low since there is no easy way to shift away from car use (e.g. due to the absence of commuting trains). Mattioli, Wadud and Lucas (2018[27]) show that in the United Kingdom, low-income households with car-related economic stress (e.g. transport representing a high share of their budget) show the lowest price elasticities to fuel price increases, likely due to a lack of alternatives. The authors develop a vulnerability index to fuel price increases by combining exposure (cost burden of motor fuel), sensitivity (income level) and adaptive capacity (access to alternative transport infrastructure) (Mattioli et al., 2019[28]). Analysis based on this type of index can help identify vulnerable households, infrastructure gaps and necessary compensatory measures, as well as potential acceptability issues related to carbon pricing increases.

6.2. Better measurement for striking a balance between innovation in parts and systems innovation

While improving vehicles' emission performance is important to reduce emissions in the sector, data suggests that efforts to electrify vehicles have been ineffective in reducing emissions at the pace needed, and the potential of such efforts has systematically been overestimated, biasing decision-making. For example, Lamb et al. (2021[29]) find that emission reductions from electrification efforts in the transport sector have largely been offset by emission increase due to growing traffic.

As discussed in Litman (2017[30]), there are important omissions, of both negative and positive impacts, in the way emissions reduction options are evaluated. These omissions can reinforce deeply engrained ideas such as technological optimism and fossil fuel solutionism[7] (see Chapter 2), which in turn bias decision-making towards climate strategies focused on a decoupling logic, i.e. on improving vehicles rather than on focusing on how to reduce traffic volumes (Litman, 2017[30]). The rest of this section discusses two measurement biases that influence policy decisions: the failure to reflect rebound effects from improved vehicle efficiency, and the gap between laboratory and real-world emissions.

Research by Litman (2017[30]) suggests that rebound effects from improved vehicle efficiency are seldom, if at all, included in climate strategies and programmes assessments. This leads to an overestimation of the mitigation potential of improved vehicle efficiency, while also underestimating the importance of systemic policies. Long-term rebound effects range between 15% and 30% (Litman, 2017[30]). For example, a 20% rebound effect means that, everything else equal, a 50% increase in fuel economy will increase travel by 10%; thus energy savings will only be 40% (Litman, 2017[30]). Due to the rebound effect, policies improving vehicle efficiency can also cause other negative impacts such as congestion, accidents, and inefficient use of public space, rarely accounted for in decision-making processes (Litman, 2017[30]). As discussed in Anable (2008[31]), "the rebound effect is not inevitable", but minimising it requires policies that can restrain (and actually reverse) demand increases (such as those discussed in Chapters 3-5).

The growing gap between laboratory and real-world emissions is another barrier for informed policy decisions, which also translates in overestimating the potential of policies focused on improving vehicle technologies. The gap between emission testing and real-life emissions has widened significantly over the years, implying that vehicles are in reality less efficient than what emission testing shows. For example, in Europe, research suggests that the gap has increased from 9% in 2001 to 28% in 2012 and 42% in 2015 (Transport & Environment, 2016[32]), and that, in contrast to what emission tests show, on-road efficiency in Europe stalled between 2012 and 2016 (Transport & Environment, 2016[32]). Transport & Environment (2016[32]) finds that the gap between laboratory and on-road testing could translate into an extra 1.5 billion tonnes of CO_2 emissions in Europe by 2030.

In addition to misinforming policy decisions, the gap between emission testing and real emissions affect car drivers. In Europe, car drivers spend annually EUR 549 more than the cost expected when looking at the fuel economy levels of their vehicles (Transport & Environment, 2016[32]). By 2030, this could add up to a cumulative excess expenditure by European drivers equal to EUR 1 trillion; and an import of around 6 billion extra barrels of oil at the EU level (Transport & Environment, 2016[32]).

The gap is particularly wide for hybrid and plug-in hybrid vehicles (PHEVs) (Transport & Environment, 2016[32]). Studies show that PHEVs' on-road emission levels are significantly higher than the level of emissions that are registered for these vehicles, and higher than the thresholds (e.g. 50 kg CO_2/km in

Europe) that make a vehicle eligible for preferential treatment. For instance, tests on the three most popular and performing PHEVs in Europe reveal that they can emit three to four times more than official levels (Bannion, 2020[33]; Plötz et al., 2020[34]). The gap can be up to 8 times higher for less performant vehicles, and up to 12 times in the case of vehicles designed for geo-fencing, i.e. when the engine is used to recharge the battery. This could for instance be problematic in the case of low-emission zones, as there is an incentive to drive in this mode before entering the LEZ area (Berman, 2020[35]).

Ignoring the wide gap in the case of hybrids and PHEVs has mislead policies in a number of ways. For example, hybrid and PHEVs have become eligible for preferential treatment, often being eligible for tax reductions and other incentives such as super credits for fuel economy standards in Europe. They are also exempted from bans and/or included in EV mandates, which has contributed to boosting their sales (Bannion, 2020[33]), locking in emissions, and reducing climate policy effectiveness (Brand et al., 2020[36]).

Expanding the shift (having already taken place in Europe and Japan) from tests based on theoretical driving (the New European Driving Cycle) to tests based on real driving (the Worldwide Harmonised Light Vehicle Test Procedure) (WLTPfacts.eu, n.d.[37]) is an important step to reducing the widening gap between laboratory and real emissions. The shift towards the Worldwide Harmonised Light Vehicle Test Procedure will influence a number of key policies (e.g. fuel economy and CO_2 emission standards, CO_2-based taxation and labelling) by allowing targets and criteria that better reflect real emissions levels (for more see WLTPfacts.eu (n.d.[37])).

Beyond the type of test, the extensive and increased flexibilities (e.g. wheel and tyre specification, tyre pressure, running temperature, among others) permitted during testing procedures are another key factor underlying an increasing gap. Flexibility has allowed manufacturers to optimise certain testing conditions to achieve lower fuel consumption and CO_2 emissions (European Environment Agency, 2016[38]). For example, in Europe, while the gap between test and on-road emissions would be between 19% and 28% without flexibilities, with flexibilities it reaches on average 38%, and even up to 50% (Transport & Environment, 2016[32]).

To improve measurement, Transport & Environment (2016[32]) calls for the implementation of road testing (with the use of portable emissions monitoring systems) and for regulations to limit discrepancies between laboratory and on-road tests to 10%. On-road test checks will importantly reduce the incentives for relying on flexibilities and can steer innovation towards vehicles that perform well on-road rather than in the laboratory (Transport & Environment, 2016[32]). Along these lines, the 2020-21 European CO_2 and fuel economy standards already incorporated the regular monitoring of on-road emissions data through on-board devices (European Commission, 2020[39]).[8] Other ways forward include: strengthening testing frameworks, bringing attention to good practice, advocating for the establishment of surveillance authorities, introducing independent conformity checks and strengthening testing frameworks, and random testing and intensive audits on car manufacturers' own tests (as already done by the United States' Environmental Protection Agency) (Transport & Environment, 2016[32]).

As a way forward, a better reflection of the rebound effect and real-world emissions are key for more informed policy decisions. Better measurement could help policy makers shift away from technological optimism and fossil fuel solutionism, and better assess the importance of putting systems redesign efforts at the centre of climate strategies.

References

Anable, J. (2008), *The Cost-effectiveness of Carbon Abatement in the Transport Sector*, Campaign for Better Transport, London, https://bettertransport.org.uk/sites/default/files/research-files/Carbon_abatement_research.pdf. [31]

Avner, P., J. Rentschler and S. Hallegatte (2014), "Carbon price efficiency: Lock-in and path dependence in urban forms and transport infrastructure", *Policy Research Working Paper*, World Bank, Washington, DC, https://doi.org/10.1596/1813-9450-6941 (accessed on 29 March 2021). [25]

Bannion, E. (2020), "Plug-in hybrids: Is Europe heading for a new dieselgate?", European Federation for Transport and Environment, Brussels, https://www.transportenvironment.org/publications/plug-hybrids-europe-heading-new-dieselgate (accessed on 10 December 2020). [33]

Berman, B. (2020), "Should plug-in hybrids be forced into EV mode in cities? Fiat tests the tech", Electrek, https://electrek.co/2020/06/03/should-plug-in-hybrids-be-forced-into-ev-mode-in-cities-fiat-tests-the-tech (accessed on 28 July 2021). [35]

Brand, C. et al. (2020), "Road to zero or road to nowhere? Disrupting transport and energy in a zero carbon world", *Energy Policy*, Vol. 139, p. 111334, http://dx.doi.org/10.1016/j.enpol.2020.111334. [36]

Douenne, T. and A. Fabre (2020), *Yellow Vests, Carbon Tax Aversion, and Biased Belifes*, Paris School of Economics, Paris, https://www.parisschoolofeconomics.eu/docs/douenne-thomas/job-market-paper--yellow-vests,-carbon-tax-aversion,-and-biased-beliefs.pdf (accessed on 26 March 2021). [19]

European Commission (2020), *CO_2 emission performance standards for cars and vans | Climate Action*, https://ec.europa.eu/clima/policies/transport/vehicles/regulation_en (accessed on 5 October 2021). [39]

European Environment Agency (2016), "Explaining vehicle emissions: Why do laboratory and road measurements differ?", European Environment Agency, https://www.eea.europa.eu/highlights/explaining-vehicle-emissions (accessed on 26 March 2021). [38]

Falchetta, G. and M. Noussan (2021), "Electric vehicle charging network in Europe: An accessibility and deployment trends analysis", *Transportation Research Part D: Transport and Environment*, Vol. 94, p. 102813, http://dx.doi.org/10.1016/J.TRD.2021.102813. [10]

Franco, S. (2020), "Parking prices and availability, mode choice and urban form", *International Transport Forum Discussion Papers*, No. 2020/03, OECD Publishing, Paris, https://doi.org/10.1787/04ae37c3-en. [3]

Fridstrøm, L. (2020), *The Carbon Price Implicit in the Norwegian Road, Fuel and Vehicle Taxation System*, Norwegian Institute of Transport, Oslo, https://trid.trb.org/view/1752155 (accessed on 26 March 2021). [9]

Geman, B. (2019), “Transportation emissions are a tough nut to crack”, Axios, https://www.axios.com/carbon-pricing-difficult-to-reduce-transportation-emissions-b6cf8a74-6cfe-47ca-9f6e-c5b4d266d96c.html (accessed on 30 August 2021). [21]

Gillingham, K. and A. Munk-Nielsen (2019), “A tale of two tails: Commuting and the fuel price response in driving”, *Journal of Urban Economics*, Vol. 109, pp. 27-40, http://dx.doi.org/10.1016/j.jue.2018.09.007. [26]

Gschwendtner, C. (2021), *Vehicle-to-Grid (V2G) and car sharing: Joining forces to decarbonize electricity and transport?*, https://blogs.ethz.ch/energy/v2g-and-car-sharing-joining-forces/ (accessed on 10 August 2021). [4]

Holtsmark, B. and A. Skonhoft (2014), “The Norwegian support and subsidy policy of electric cars: Should it be adopted by other countries?”, *Environmental Science & Policy*, Vol. 42, pp. 160-168, http://dx.doi.org/10.1016/J.ENVSCI.2014.06.006. [7]

Hsu, C., P. Slowik and N. Lutsey (2020), *City Charging Infrastructure Needs to Reach 100% Electric Vehicles: The Case of San Francisco*, International Council on Clean Transportation, Washington, DC, https://theicct.org/publications/sf-ev-charging-infra-oct2020 (accessed on 2 December 2020). [12]

IEA (2020), *Global EV Outlook 2020: Entering the Decade of Electric Drive?*, OECD Publishing, Paris, https://dx.doi.org/10.1787/d394399e-en. [6]

ITF (2018), “Strategies for mitigating air pollution in Mexico City”, *International Transport Forum Policy Papers*, No. 30, OECD Publishing, Paris, https://doi.org/10.1787/bb049481-en. [24]

ITF (2017), *Income Inequality, Social Inclusion and Mobility*, ITF Roundtable Reports, No. 164, OECD Publishing, Paris, https://doi.org/10.1787/g2g7ae77-en. [23]

Kaufman, N. et al. (2020), “A near-term to net zero alternative to the social cost of carbon for setting carbon prices”, *Nature Climate Change*, Vol. 10/11, pp. 1010-1014, http://dx.doi.org/10.1038/s41558-020-0880-3. [22]

Lamb, W. et al. (2020), “Discourses of climate delay”, *Global Sustainability*, Vol. 3, http://dx.doi.org/10.1017/SUS.2020.13. [40]

Lamb, W. et al. (2021), “A review of trends and drivers of greenhouse gas emissions by sector from 1990 to 2018”, *Environmental Research Letters*, Vol. 16, http://dx.doi.org/10.1088/1748-9326/abee4e. [29]

Lindberg, G. and L. Fridstrøm (2015), “Policy strategies for vehicle electrification”, *International Transport Forum Discussion Papers*, No. 2015/16, OECD Publishing, Paris, https://doi.org/10.1787/5jrvzrldjs8n-en. [8]

Litman, T. (2017), *Smart Transportation Emission Reduction Strategies*, Victoria Transport Policy Institute, Victoria, British Columbia, https://www.vtpi.org/ster.pdf. [30]

Mattioli, G. et al. (2019), “Vulnerability to motor fuel price increases: Socio-spatial patterns in England”, *Journal of Transport Geography*, Vol. 78, pp. 98-114, http://dx.doi.org/10.1016/j.jtrangeo.2019.05.009. [28]

Mattioli, G., Z. Wadud and K. Lucas (2018), “Vulnerability to fuel price increases in the UK: A household level analysis”, *Transportation Research Part A: Policy and Practice*, Vol. 113, pp. 227-242, http://dx.doi.org/10.1016/j.tra.2018.04.002. [27]

OECD (2021), *Effective Carbon Rates 2021: Pricing Carbon Emissions through Taxes and Emissions Trading*, OECD Publishing, Paris, https://dx.doi.org/10.1787/0e8e24f5-en. [20]

OECD (2019), *Taxing Energy Use 2019: Using Taxes for Climate Action*, OECD Publishing, Paris, https://dx.doi.org/10.1787/058ca239-en. [14]

Plötz, P. et al. (2020), *Real-World Usage of Plug-In Hybrid Electric Vehicles Fuel Consumption, Electric Driving, and CO2 Emissions*, International Council on Clean Transportation, https://theicct.org/publications/phev-real-world-usage-sept2020 (accessed on 10 December 2020). [34]

Rosenbloom, D. et al. (2020), “Opinion: Why carbon pricing is not sufficient to mitigate climate change – and how “sustainability transition policy” can help”, *Proceedings of the National Academy of Sciences*, Vol. 117/16, pp. 8664-8668, http://dx.doi.org/10.1073/pnas.2004093117. [18]

SFMTA (2017), *2017 San Francisco Transportation Sector Climate Action Strategy*, San Francisco Municipal Transportation Agency, San Francisco, CA, https://www.sfmta.com/sites/default/files/reports-and-documents/2017/12/12-5-17_item_15_transportation_sector_climate_action_strategy.pdf. [11]

Shoup, D. (2005), “The high cost of free parking”, in *The Twenty-First Century Parking Problem*, https://www.researchgate.net/publication/264967305_The_high_cost_of_free_parking (accessed on 13 August 2021). [2]

Systems Innovation (2020), *Introduction to Systems Innovation*, Systems Innovation, https://www.systemsinnovation.io/post/systems-innovation-guide (accessed on 29 March 2021). [1]

Tanguay, G. and I. Gingras (2012), “Gas price variations and urban sprawl: An empirical analysis of the twelve largest Canadian metropolitan areas”, *Environment and Planning A*, Vol. 44, pp. 1728-1743, http://dx.doi.org/10.1068/a44259. [16]

Transport & Environment (2020), *Recharge EU: How many charge points will EU countries need by 2030*, European Federation for Transport and Environment, Brussels, https://www.transportenvironment.org/discover/recharge-eu-how-many-charge-points-will-eu-countries-need-2030/ (accessed on 2 December 2020). [13]

Transport & Environment (2016), *Mind the Gap 2016*, European Federation for Transport and Environment, Brussels, https://www.transportenvironment.org/publications/mind-gap-2016-report (accessed on 26 March 2021). [32]

Tvinnereim, E. and M. Mehling (2018), “Carbon pricing and deep decarbonisation”, *Energy Policy*, Vol. 121, pp. 185-189, http://dx.doi.org/10.1016/j.enpol.2018.06.020. [17]

van Dender, K. (2019), “Taxing vehicles, fuels, and road use: Opportunities for improving transport tax practice”, *OECD Taxation Working Papers*, No. 44, OECD Publishing, Paris, https://dx.doi.org/10.1787/e7f1d771-en. [15]

Wappelhorst, S., P. Mock and Z. Yang (2018), *Using Vehicle Taxation Policy to Lower Transport Emissions: An Overview for Passenger Cars in Europe*, International Council on Clean Transportation, https://theicct.org/publications/using-vehicle-taxation-policy-lower-transport-emissions (accessed on 26 July 2021). [5]

WLTPfacts.eu (n.d.), "What is WLTP: The Worldwide Harmonised Light Vehicle Test Procedure?", web page, https://www.wltpfacts.eu/what-is-wltp-how-will-it-work (accessed on 26 March 2021). [37]

Notes

[1] Today, a standard medium-size electric vehicle is still 40% more expensive than a comparable (i.e. similar size) internal combustion vehicle (IEA, 2020[6]).

[2] As the price of electric vehicles continues to drop (due to a significant decrease in battery cost (IEA, 2020[6])) and taxes and regulations become more stringent, the need for this type of incentive will probably be reduced, or even eliminated.

[3] In Austria, incentives for the uptake of EVs consist of additional tax reductions and exemptions. France and the United Kingdom have opted for bonus payments and premiums for the purchase of EVs. In France, for example, electric and plug-in hybrid electric vehicles (emitting 20 g/km CO_2 or less) benefit from a EUR 6 000 subsidy under the fee-bate scheme.

[4] Although this might increase road safety problems.

[5] Compared to the increase in a scenario reflecting current and announced policies (Stated Policy Scenario)

[6] Higher price trajectories could contribute to decreasing uncertainty to reach net-zero targets, especially under conditions that make challenges to decarbonise higher, such as low oil prices (Kaufman et al., 2020[22]).

[7] Technological optimism is the idea that the potential to reduce emissions is with technology, most often applied at the level of the element's level, e.g. vehicles. Fossil fuel solutionism is the idea that, as our fuels are becoming more efficient, they are the bridge towards a low-carbon future (Lamb et al., 2020[40]).

[8] Transport & Environment recommends the difference between emissions reported and those from on-board testing to be below 10%.

7 The well-being lens and the post-COVID context: A real-world experience

This chapter places the recommendations in this report in the context of the COVID-19 crisis and its aftermath. It provides examples of measures that were undertaken during the lock-down and post lock-down periods (e.g street re-design) and discusses opportunities and challenges going forward.

The transport sector experienced unprecedented change as a result of the social distancing measures and reduced economic activity triggered by the COVID-19 crisis. With lock-down came important traffic reductions (e.g. passenger surface transport dropped by 50% on average compared to 2019 (Le Quéré et al., 2020[1])), which in turn led to an important temporary[1] reduction in air pollution (e.g. NOx, NO_2, and $PM_{2.5}$ and PM_{10} emissions (Vincendon, 2020[2]; da Silva, 2020[3]; Mahato, Pal and Ghosh, 2020[4])) as well as greenhouse gas emissions (Le Quéré et al., 2020[1]). At the same time, less than proportional improvements in traffic fatalities (ITF, 2020[5]) showed that if not accompanied by proper street redesign and speed regulation (among other complementary actions), a reduction in traffic will not, on its own, solve the road safety challenge (Buckle et al., 2020[6]). The recent COVID-19 crisis has also highlighted the need for decision making in transport to take account of the risks of shocks such as disease outbreaks as well as the (possibly) more frequent disruptions due to, for example, floods and snowstorms.

The health crisis provided a number of lessons and opportunities for advancing in the direction of systemic change (or reversing car-dependency), mainly by facilitating the shift in thinking to reverse induced demand and emphasising the value of active modes. However, it also brought challenges, by adding to the already existing barriers for shifting away from sprawl and making more difficult the mainstreaming of shared modes and trips, which, as has been argued in this report, has an enormous potential to reverse the erosion of sustainable alternatives to car use.

This chapter summarises some of the opportunities and challenges brought about by the COVID-19 crisis. It discusses ways forward to build on the opportunities and overcome the challenges to advance change towards better functioning transport systems.

7.1. The opportunity: Increased awareness of the power of street redesign

The COVID-19 crisis provided interesting lessons and opportunities on the use of active modes of transport and the management and reallocation of public space (Buckle et al., 2020[6]). A number of cities engaged in the reallocation of road space for active transport modes (walking and cycling) and micro-mobility vehicles (such as e-scooters and e-bikes). By doing this they showed that such modes can effectively help to increase the resilience of transport systems by allowing travel in the absence of, or with reduced, public transport services (Schwedhelm et al., 2020[7]; Bert et al., 2020[8]). This has been possible especially in those cities that have created proximity between people and places, and thus where the scope for these modes is greater.

The health crisis also emphasised the opportunity for reallocating space to other uses besides transport. Traffic reductions during confinement made it ever more evident that an over dimensioned amount of public space is occupied by cars. This has led a number of local governments to reassess not only the current allocation of road space between different modes of transport, but also between transport and other uses (e.g. space for car parking vs. space for commercial or recreational activity) (ITF, 2020[9]; Buckle et al., 2020[6]).

Actions during the health crisis also illustrated how short- and long-term goals can be aligned via public space reallocation and redesign (ITF, 2020[9]). Liberating and reallocating space from car use helped cities to better adapt to the need for social distancing. At the same time, these changes have opened opportunities for cities to become more attractive (e.g. allowing to integrate more green space), and fostering economic activity (e.g. expanding available surface area for businesses-such as new terraces) (Perk et al., 2015[10]). Savills (2016[11]) finds that reconfiguring streets can also liberate space for increasing housing supply in central areas (see more in Chapter 3).

(Glaser and Krizek, 2021[12]) reviewed 55 of the United States' largest cities to assess how municipalities' emergency responses could potentially trigger a transition to sustainable urban mobility. The COVID-19 pandemic altered the use of street space in many cities that implemented emergency response measures to allow individuals to walk, bike and travel to and from essential business while keeping a safe distance. "Transition experiments" showcase how alternative systems to vehicle transportation might gain traction due to the conditions created by COVID-19. (Glaser and Krizek, 2021[12]) found that a number of "innovator" cities utilised the pandemic to build street networks and test new forms of streets.

7.2. The challenge: The risk of exacerbating private transport and sprawl

Increased awareness of the effects of street redesign is key to move towards disappearing traffic (the transformational change see Chapter 3). Nonetheless, shifting away from car dependency also requires systems to shift away from sprawled territories towards those that create proximity between people and places (Chapter 4), as well as from eroded towards integrated networks of shared and sustainable modes (Chapter 5).

The COVID crisis has raised important concerns about the viability of cities– especially compact cities – and the mere idea of proximity. Concerns that high densities can be a factor in the rapid spread of viruses such as COVID-19 has raised unease about the desirability of dense and compact urban areas among many groups (Hernandez-Morales, Oroschakoff and Barigazzi, 2020[13]). Although dense environments (as currently designed) may lead to negative consequences such as air pollution or congestion; these environments also have numerous benefits, such as infrastructure investment efficiency, access to a diversity of local services, enabling conditions for technological development and innovation, and low travel costs, energy consumption and greenhouse gas emissions (OECD, 2012[14]).

Lockdown restrictions have also brought to light the disadvantages of restricted living space in cities relative to suburban or rural areas, in particular in cities where green space is limited (Ahmadpoor and Shahab, 2021[15]; SEI, 2020[16]). This has led to the growing belief that large numbers of city dwellers (in particular those in metropolitan areas) will leave the city in the pursuit of more living space and private green spaces (Hernandez-Morales, Oroschakoff and Barigazzi, 2020[13]). This trend is supported by the "normalisation" of teleworking as mainstream practice.

Similarly, concerns over shared mobility for health reasons have meant that public transport and other types of shared services have seen challenges escalate. The perceived risks and fear of contagion translated into major drops in public transport use, leading to the risk of increased car use (ITF, 2020[9]) and importantly damaging the financial health of public transport systems.[2] While individual bicycle and micro-mobility use has increased, shared services using these modes have been in many cases temporarily shut-down or experienced large drops in use (Bert et al., 2020[8]). Shared e-scooter services have been hit the hardest, since unlike some bike-sharing schemes, they do not receive public support (Hawkins, 2020[17]).

7.3. A way forward

The first step to overcoming the increased challenges to advance systemic change is to recognise (and effectively convey the message) that a future based on the systems that we have, is not without challenges. As described above, the "new" COVID-19 context could be seen as one that undermines and renders the recommendations in this report infeasible, since a system based on an increased role of shared – and especially public – transport, and increased proximity and compact development might seem unviable and even undesirable now. However, a closer look at the wider picture, including the lessons learnt from the lockdown and post-confinement periods, sheds light on the fact that a continuation (and further exacerbation) of car dependency will likely increase the tensions between coping with the immediate pressures and achieving the long-term goals of resilience and sustainability.

In terms of climate goals, an increase in the use of cars, due to lower use of public transport or increased sprawl, will further delay emission reductions. In addition increased sprawl can further jeopardise biodiversity and reduce carbon sinks. Both things will increase the risks that not meeting climate goals will entail (e.g. extreme weather events such as droughts and wild fires, etc). Moreover, the intensification of suburban sprawl and car dependency can be conducive to a higher risk of mortality in the case of future pandemics, for example via poor air quality, which has increased mortality rates related to COVID-19 (Grove, 2020[18]) (UN, 2020[19]).

In contrast, the structural changes proposed in this report could help the sector better manage both the near and long-term challenges (including climate change) and recovery packages could be key to accelerating such changes. Importantly, density per se has not been proven to be directly linked to the spread of COVID-19. Some studies in the United States, for instance, show that density was not significantly associated with higher infection rates. On the contrary, denser counties tended to have lower mortality rates (probably due to a higher level of development and better health services) compared to more sprawled counties (OECD, 2020[20]). However, a link between density and a higher risk of contagion was found in urban areas in which density is accompanied by factors such as overcrowding, air pollution, poverty and limited access to services (UN, 2020[19]). Thus, redesigning transport and urban systems in ways that can contribute to solving such issues, is in reality key to increasing resilience.

A priority would be to ensure the continuity of street redesign as a key element of recovery packages, with the aim of triggering wide-scale transformations (such as those planned for Barcelona with Superblocks - see Chapter 3) rather than small pilots in specific places. Moreover, in the view of the challenges discussed above, placing actions discussed in Chapter 4 (to reverse sprawl) and 5 (to reverse the erosion of shared modes) at the centre of recovery packages and plans needs also to be a priority.

Important synergies, between climate and wider well-being and short and long-term goals could be created. For instance, if effectively mainstreamed (by scaling street redesign, among other things), active and micro-mobility modes could become public transport's best allies, attracting an array of short distance trips and thus helping to reduce overcrowding (ITF, 2014[21]). The increase in physical activity from greater active travel could also improve general health and help to reduce the risk of death in the case of contagion of respiratory-related viruses such as COVID-19. Building on virtual solutions such as teleworking can also improve public transport management, if well-co-ordinated with broader transport and land-use policies (Hook et al., 2020[22]) (as discussed in chapter 5). In parallel, other (smaller scale) shared services (e.g. shared bicycles, e-scooters, shared and pool car systems, and on-demand public transport services) with added cleanliness and distancing procedures, could also survive and contribute to relieving pressures on public transport systems while also delivering more equitable access to opportunities (e.g. jobs, education centres). A system that can effectively enhance accessibility, especially for the most vulnerable through the development of multi-modal and sustainable systems, can contribute to reducing "chronic stresses"[3] (e.g. poverty, unemployment) that increase inequalities and undermine the resilience of cities and territories on a daily basis (100 Resilient Cities, n.d.[23]) ; and which have made some cities particularly weak during the health and economic crisis (UN, 2020[24]) (Cohen, 2020[25]).

Moreover, liberating and re-allocating significant space from car use in a systematic way could ensure priority is given to less carbon-intensive and more space efficient transport modes, in addition to having cities that are better prepared for social distancing in situations like the COVID-19 crisis. Space liberated from cars could also help cities become more attractive, healthy and strengthen policies consistent with climate mitigation and adaptation goals. Among other things it would allow for planning of more and better quality green space which can, in turn, further incentivise active travel – (Perk, 2015[26]) help reduce incentives to move further out, and contribute to reducing heat islands. Reconfiguring streets can also importantly liberate space for increasing housing supply in central areas, while making these more attractive (Savills, 2016[27]). Cities could also become more equitable and conducive for economic recovery, since road and public space can also be used to improve both recreational and travel space around housing and be allocated to local economic activity.

Evidence also suggests that recovery packages fostering an increased role of public transport and other sustainable modes could lead to significant jobs opportunities, as experienced in the 2009 recession in certain countries. In 2013 public transport generated almost as many jobs globally (13 million, 2013 figure) as the number of jobs generated by the car industry today (14 million, 2013 figure) (Buckle et al., 2020[6]), Active and shared transport modes could also generate important amounts of jobs if their role was to be expanded. For example, in the United States, investment in public transport have generated 31% more jobs per dollar spent than the construction of roads and bridges, while in Korea, jobs generated by public transport, rail and cycling infrastructure investments accounted for 15% of the total jobs generated by the 2009 recovery package (Buckle et al., 2020[6]). As the International Energy Agency shows, bicycle manufacturing and repair, as well as the investment in infrastructure for pedestrians and cyclists, also have high employment factors. Start-ups could also become a more significant job generator and, as discussed in Chapter 5, micro-mobility could contribute to job creation by bringing almost 1 million jobs annually in Europe between now and 2030 if mainstreamed (Buckle et al., 2020[6]). Job opportunities in the automotive industry will remain crucial, and some transformations in the type of skills needed due to electrification, automation, and new business models for shared mobility services are worthy of attention. For example, recent studies suggest that new economic activities such as fleet operation or software development that automotive manufacturers may carry out could create a significant number of job opportunities.

References

100 Resilient Cities (n.d.), *Urban Resilience - 100 Resilient Cities*, http://100resilientcities.org/resources/#section-1 (accessed on 25 May 2020). [23]

Ahmadpoor, N. and S. Shahab (2021), "Urban form: Realising the value of green space: A planners' perspective on the COVID-19 pandemic", *Town Planning Review*, Vol. 92/1, pp. 49-55, http://dx.doi.org/10.3828/tpr.2020.37. [15]

Bert, J. et al. (2020), "How COVID-19 will shape urban mobility", Boston Consulting Group, https://www.bcg.com/publications/2020/how-covid-19-will-shape-urban-mobility (accessed on 29 July 2020). [8]

Buckle, S. et al. (2020), "Addressing the COVID and climate crises: Potential economic recovery pathways and their implications for climate change mitigation, NDCs and broader socio-economic goals", *OECD/IEA Climate Change Expert Group Papers*, No. 2020/04, OECD Publishing, Paris, https://doi.org/10.1787/50abd39c-en. [6]

Cohen, P. (2020), "Straggling in a Good Economy, and Now Struggling in a Crisis", *The New York Times*, https://www.nytimes.com/2020/04/16/business/economy/coronavirus-economy.html (accessed on 26 March 2021). [25]

da Silva, G. (2020), "COVID-19 drop in pollution to be short-lived", Pursuit, University of Melbourne, https://pursuit.unimelb.edu.au/articles/covid-19-drop-in-pollution-to-be-short-lived (accessed on 20 August 2020). [3]

Glaser, M. and K. Krizek (2021), "Can street-focused emergency response measures trigger a transition to new transport systems? Exploring evidence and lessons from 55 US cities", *Transport Policy*, Vol. 103, pp. 146-155, http://dx.doi.org/10.1016/j.tranpol.2021.01.015. [12]

Grove, M. (2020), "Suburban sprawl increases the risk of future pandemics", ArchDaily, https://www.archdaily.com/943939/suburban-sprawl-increases-the-risk-of-future-pandemics (accessed on 7 October 2020). [18]

Hawkins, A. (2020), "How the novel coronavirus is speeding the scooter apocalypse", The Verge, https://www.theverge.com/2020/5/13/21257307/electric-scooter-bikeshare-covid-19-bird-lime-uber-subsidies (accessed on 29 July 2020). [17]

Hernandez-Morales, A., K. Oroschakoff and J. Barigazzi (2020), "The death of the city", Politico, https://www.politico.eu/article/the-death-of-the-city-coronavirus-towns-cities-retail-transport-pollution-economic-crisis (accessed on 16 March 2021). [13]

Hook, A. et al. (2020), "A systematic review of the energy and climate impacts of teleworking", *Environmental Research Letters*, Vol. 15/9, p. 093003, http://dx.doi.org/10.1088/1748-9326/ab8a84. [22]

ITF (2020), *Re-spacing Our Cities For Resilience*, International Transport Forum, Paris, https://www.itf-oecd.org/sites/default/files/respacing-cities-resilience-covid-19.pdf. [9]

ITF (2020), *Road Safety Annual Report 2020*, OECD Publishing, Paris, https://doi.org/10.1787/f3e48023-en. [5]

ITF (2014), *Valuing Convenience in Public Transport*, ITF Roundtable Reports, No. 156, OECD Publishing, Paris, https://doi.org/10.1787/9789282107683-en. [21]

Le Quéré, C. et al. (2020), "Temporary reduction in daily global CO2 emissions during the COVID-19 forced confinement", *Nature Climate Change*, Vol. 10, pp. 647-653, http://dx.doi.org/10.1038/s41558-020-0797-x. [1]

Mahato, S., S. Pal and K. Ghosh (2020), "Effect of lockdown amid COVID-19 pandemic on air quality of the megacity Delhi, India", *Science of the Total Environment*, Vol. 730, http://dx.doi.org/10.1016/j.scitotenv.2020.139086. [4]

OECD (2020), *Cities Policy Responses*, OECD, Paris, https://read.oecd-ilibrary.org/view/?ref=126_126769-yen45847kf&title=Coronavirus-COVID-19-Cities-Policy-Responses (accessed on 16 March 2021). [20]

OECD (2012), *Compact City Policies: A Comparative Assessment*, OECD Green Growth Studies, OECD Publishing, Paris, https://dx.doi.org/10.1787/9789264167865-en. [14]

Perk, V. (2015), *Capturing the Benefits of Complete Streets*. [26]

Perk, V. et al. (2015), *Capturing the Benefits of Complete Streets*, Florida Department of Transportation, Tallahassee, FL, https://www.nctr.usf.edu/2016/01/capturing-the-benefits-of-complete-streets-2. [10]

Savills (2016), *Completing London's streets*, https://pdf.euro.savills.co.uk/uk/residential---other/completing-london-s-streets-080116.pdf (accessed on 24 March 2021). [27]

Savills (2016), *Completing London's Streets*, Savills, https://pdf.euro.savills.co.uk/uk/residential---other/completing-london-s-streets-080116.pdf. [11]

Schwedhelm, A. et al. (2020), "Biking provides a critical lifeline during the coronavirus crisis", World Resources Institute, https://www.wri.org/insights/biking-provides-critical-lifeline-during-coronavirus-crisis#:~:text=As%20the%20world%20works%20to,%2C%20as%20of%20mid%2DApril.&text=In%20Philadelphia%2C%20cycling%20has%20increased,during%20the%20COVID%2D19%20outbreak (accessed on 25 May 2020). [7]

SEI (2020), "Lockdown highlights the value of green space in cities", Stockholm Environment Institute, https://www.sei.org/perspectives/covid19-value-of-green-space-in-cities (accessed on 16 March 2021). [16]

UITP (2020), "Guardians of mobility: From the front lines in Milan, Italy", web page, UITP, https://www.uitp.org/news/guardians-of-mobility-from-the-front-lines-in-milan-italy (accessed on 26 March 2021). [28]

UN (2020), *COVID-19 in an Urban World*, policy brief, United Nations, New York, NY, https://unsdg.un.org/resources/policy-brief-covid-19-urban-world (accessed on 7 October 2020). [19]

UN (2020), *COVID-19 in an Urban World*, https://www.ohchr.org/Documents/Issues/Housing/SR_housing_COVID-19_Guidance_ (accessed on 7 October 2020). [24]

Vincendon, S. (2020), "Un mois après le déconfinement, la pollution de l'air a fait son retour", BFMTV, https://www.bfmtv.com/environnement/deconfinement-la-pollution-de-l-air-revient-peu-a-peu_AN-202006090099.html (accessed on 20 August 2020). [2]

Notes

[1] Both air pollution and emission levels returned to pre-confinement levels rapidly.

[2] As discussed in Chapter 5, for instance, the expected loss of revenue from fares by the end of 2020 in European public transport systems was EUR 40 billion (UITP, 2020[28]).

[3] "slow moving disasters that weaken the fabric of a city"-(100 Resilient Cities, n.d.)

8 Conclusion

This chapter provides the main conclusions of the report. It summarises the mind-set shifts triggered by the well-being lens process and the way these apply to surface transport and the report's policy recommendations.

As indicated by analysis from the IPCC, policies leading to transformational pathways can lead to net-zero systems *by design* and increase the chances of meeting the Paris Agreement's temperature goal. Identifying such policies is, thus, fundamental.

This report applies the Well-being lens process to the surface transport sector. The process is designed to help policy makers identify transformational policies able to accelerate the transition towards net-zero systems by design, i.e. systems able to improve well-being while requiring less energy and materials and producing fewer emissions.

The Well-being lens process triggers two mind-set shifts, that this report argues are needed to meet net-zero targets on time: i) from means (e.g. GDP) to ends (well-being); and ii) from parts to systems functioning. The first shift allows *envisioning* an increase in well-being (health, equity, etc.) through low-demand systems (rather than considering high demand as a condition for high life quality). For policy-making, this means that managing or reducing demand becomes a policy lever. The second shift sheds light on the importance of *understanding* the systems' dynamics driving unsustainable results. For policy-making, this means focusing climate action on reversing such dynamics and redesigning systems.

For the transport sector the mind-set shifts described above translate into moving: i) from a focus on mobility towards accessibility; and ii) from improving vehicles' performance in car-dependent systems towards transforming the systems' functioning (i.e. a systemic mind-set) so that people can access places with ease without the need to travel long distances for every daily need. This shift in thinking expands the scope of climate action, as policies can now focus on reversing car dependency, rather than just improving vehicles' performance.

Policies with the potential to reverse car dependency include street redesign and improved management of public space, spatial planning focused on creating proximity, and policies to mainstream shared mobility. These are briefly described here below.

The current design of city streets, with excessive and increasing road space granted to cars, fosters induced demand (i.e. increased vehicle ownership and use). Street redesign and improved management of public space can help reverse this trend by reallocating public space and investment to low-carbon and space-efficient modes (e.g. according to Complete Streets' principles) and balancing space use between transport and other uses (i.e. according to place-making principles); leading to *disappearing traffic*. Barcelona's Superblocks are an example of street redesign and reallocation that is planned to transform the whole of the Barcelona Municipality. Parking policy is also crucial to street redesign, and to ensuring public space is managed efficiently and aligned with environmental and social goals (e.g. through parking pricing and regulation). Road pricing can also be a powerful tool, if coupled with street redesign and space reallocation and aimed at the efficient use of space.

Spatial planning aimed at increasing proximity can contain, and eventually reverse, urban sprawl. Most territories are organised around dense inner cities centralising services and job opportunities, surrounded by car-dependent residential areas. New development and urban renewal strategies based on accessibility-based planning frameworks such as the 15-minute city could allow urban areas and their hinterlands to become networks of 15-minute cities in which people can move across the territory, but no longer need to travel long distances to meet their everyday needs. Metropolitan transport authorities provide a strong institutional basis for developing accessibility-based strategic planning at the level of metropolitan areas and regions. Regulations such as minimum parking requirements and traffic-based transport assessments, currently steering new developments towards sprawl, can be substituted by regulation promoting the creation of proximity and compact development (e.g. maximum parking regulations and multimodal assessments).

Policies to accelerate the development of multimodal and sustainable transport networks are fundamental to reverse the erosion of active and shared transport modes. Strengthening public transport networks through increased investment and improved methodologies for determining public transport pricing and planning is key to avoid the often-observed public transport low-cost, low-revenue, low-quality trap. In parallel, support to mainstream shared bicycles and micro-mobility, as well as the expansion of on-demand micro-transit services can significantly increase the attractiveness of these modes (also contributing to providing services that can complement the offer of public transport). This can be done via the use of new technologies and integrated subscription cards (e.g. one account to access all transport services available in the city), regulation that promotes cooperation between government and service providers, and government subsidies in areas where micro-mobility or on-demand services can bring social and environmental benefits but may not be profitable for the private sector. Support to the development of new vehicles (e.g. innovative micro-mobility) and the expansion of services for multipurpose trips (e.g. cargo e-bikes, shared (e-)bikes with baby seats, kids' bikes) could also contribute to making shared mobility more attractive.

There are numerous synergies between the policies described above, focused on redesigning systems, and market-based instruments, such as carbon pricing. Pricing carbon is fundamental for steering sustainable choices, but its effectiveness is limited in car-dependent systems where such choices are not convenient or available, and where carbon prices can generate negative distributional impacts and thus are publicly difficult to implement. For example, evidence suggests that the impact of fuel prices on people's choice is low when alternatives to car driving are not available; and that prices' impact on people's choice increases when public transport infrastructure is available. Carbon pricing and policies focused on accelerating the transition towards car-independent systems are complementary and can, together, lead to more efficient and publicly acceptable policy packages.

Innovation and technological change – both at the parts and systems levels – play a major role in climate strategies aiming at net-zero systems by design. So far, however, policies and finance have focused on innovation at the parts' level (e.g. technologies to improve vehicles' performance or to developing autonomous cars), leaving the potential of systems innovation untapped (including to increase the effectiveness of innovation at the parts' level).

Systems innovation is innovation aimed at transforming the systems' functioning. Superblocks in Barcelona are an example of low-tech systems innovation. Superblocks innovate in the way in which public space is allocated and designed, thus modifying the systems' structure and significantly affecting people's transport modes choices. Advanced technologies open up enormous opportunities for systems innovation. For example, GPS technologies and apps allow to move from a system which functioning requires each person to own a car, to systems in which a multiplicity of transport modes are available for people to choose and combine according to their needs. Coupled with the policies described above, these technologies can significantly, and in a cost-effective manner, reduce traffic volume and emissions, while significantly improving people's daily lives.

Glossary

Accessibility refers to the possibility of accessing places with ease, and is the interaction of mobility and proximity (Silva and Larson, 2018[1]). The notion of accessibility implies that people's well-being does not ultimately depend on how much and how far they can travel, but on the possibility to meet their needs with ease, including by not having to travel long distances, or to travel at all. The creation of proximity is a key objective of accessibility-oriented policies. Accessibility can be measured in a number of ways. Contour-based accessibility measures are one of the most commonly used (and simpler) types of accessibility indicators. They can measure the number of opportunities (e.g. jobs, green spaces, transport stations) which can be reached within a given travel time, distance or cost; or the time/cost (average) required to gain access to a fixed number of opportunities from a given location (ITF, 2017[2]). In some contexts, "connectivity" is used to describe what in this report we define as accessibility, whereas the word "accessibility" is used to describe the ease of access of the population with mobility impairments specifically.

Car independent systems are those in which a bulk of daily activities can be done without a car or a motorcycle. People only move from less emitting and space intensive modes (e.g. active, then micro-mobility and public transport/ micro-transit) to the more emitting and space intensive ones (e.g. cars or motorcycles), as they make less frequent trips. Car and motorcycle use is reserved for those trips that can create more value than the costs they impose to society (i.e. reserved for specific purposes or circumstances); but they are not systematically the most convenient, nor the only, available option in most places. In these systems, distances between people and places are short (there is proximity), and public space is organised in such a way that active and shared modes (including public transport) are the fastest and safest modes for most people (including children) to get to places.

Car dependency is defined as the combination of "high levels of per capita automobile travel, automobile-oriented land-use patterns, and reduced transport alternatives" (Litman, 2002[3]). Throughout this report, the term is used to refer to dependency over cars and other private motorised vehicles such as motorcycles and sport utility vehicle (SUVs). The term also includes the notion of the overuse of private motorised vehicles.

Car overuse refers to the situation in which the harmful consequences of car use are greater than its benefits.

Community severance "describes the effects of transport infrastructure or motorised traffic as a physical or psychological barrier separating one built-up area from another built-up area or open space". It "occurs when transport infrastructure or motorised traffic divides space and people" (Anciaes, Jones and Mindell, 2015[4]). Community severance is also described as the "barrier effect" resulting from transport systems that limit, rather than facilitate, people's mobility (Anciaes, Jones and Mindell, 2015[4]).

Feedback loop. A feedback loop is a non-linear cause-effect relationship. A linear causal relationship is one in which a variable affects a second variable, and the cause-effect chain stops there. In non-linear cause-effect relationships, a variable affects a second variable, which in turn affects the first variable again. The variables feed into each other, leading to circular – rather than linear – cause-effect chains. Feedback loops (i.e. non-linear cause-effect chains) can be reinforcing or balancing. In reinforcing feedback loops, the effect of the first variable alters the second, which feeds back to affect the first variable again, in the same direction. For example, the more eggs, the more chickens, which leads to even more eggs and more chickens. In balancing feedback loops, variables affect each other in opposite directions. For example, the more foxes the less rabbits. The number of rabbits (the food stock of foxes) then affects the number of foxes: the less rabbits, the less foxes. And the less foxes, the more rabbits, as rabbits can reproduce more with less predators. Note that reinforcing feedback loops lead to acceleration, while balancing feedback loops lead to equilibrium. If the results of feedback loops are observed over time, reinforcing feedback loops lead to exponential curves (positive or negative) and balancing feedback loops to cyclical curves.

Incremental change refers to change to the properties of the parts or elements within a system not affecting the system's organisation or functioning (Systems Innovation, 2020[5]).

Induced demand is a key dynamic underlying car dependency and high-emissions transport systems and is the phenomenon by which road expansion increases car traffic (WSP and RAND Europe, 2018[6]).

Leverage points are places to intervene in a system's structure (Meadows, 1999[7]), and are based on the idea that "different types of solutions have different amounts of leverage to change the system" (Hinton, 2021[8]). Low leverage points refer to places where an action generates little change in the system's behaviour and results. High leverage points are places where an action triggers important changes in the system's behaviour and results. The closer to the root causes of a problem, the higher the leverage. For more, see Meadows (1999[7]).

Mobility is used in this report to designate physical movement, which can be measured in terms of vehicle-kilometres, passenger-kilometres (passenger), tonne-kilometres (freight) or number of trips.

Multimodal planning refers to planning that considers various modes (walking, cycling, automobile, public transit, etc.) and connections among modes (Litman, 2020[9]).

Road space management strategies are alternatives to the construction of new road infrastructure. These aim to ensure the enhanced and more efficient utilisation of existing roadways while reducing or eliminating the costs associated with building new roads (Sharma, 2017[10]).

Root cause analysis is a tool aimed at identifying the root causes of problems. The idea behind root cause analysis is that to solve a problem, the root causes need to be identified and solved, as opposed to addressing intermediate causes or "fixing" the problem's symptoms.

Single-use development (and logic) refers to a type of urban development in which each area focuses on a specific land use, e.g. suburbs tend to be residential neighbourhoods, places of interest are often concentrated in city centres or in specific areas (e.g. shopping malls), and offices are clustered in working districts.

System. A system is a set of elements whose interconnections determine its structure and behaviour. Elements are things, people, factories, bikes. **Interconnections** are the way the elements are organised: rules, incentives, sanctions, information.

Systems thinking is a way of thinking that allows us to see systems, rather than just parts.

System dynamics is an approach for understanding the cause-effect relationships that lead systems to behave as they do, and thus produce the results that we observe (e.g. unsustainable levels of emissions, traffic volume increase, etc.) (Sterman, 2002[11]).

Transit-oriented development "is commonly defined as a type of mixed-use urban development within close proximity (walking distance) to mass transit facilities. Transit-oriented development principles are based on organising new development and redevelopment along mass transit corridors that serve as main transport axes, building high-density development along these corridors and fostering mixed land use and jobs." (OECD (2019[12]), based on ITF (2017[2])).

Transformational change refers to change in the way a system is organised and functions (Systems Innovation, 2020[5]).

Urban sprawl is defined as the rapid and scattered expansion of development and is a key dynamic underlying car dependency and high-emissions transport systems.

Well-being. The concept of well-being incorporates aspects such as health, education, security, environmental quality, and political and social rights (OECD, 2019[12]). It goes beyond economic welfare, (i.e. beyond gross domestic product) and comprises both current well-being outcomes and the resources that help sustain these outcomes over time (OECD, 2019[12]). Well-being outcomes are captured in frameworks such as the Sustainable Development Goals and the OECD Well-being Framework (OECD, 2011[13]).

References

Anciaes, P., P. Jones and J. Mindell (2015), "Community severance: Where is it found and at what cost?", *Transport Reviews*, Vol. 36/3, pp. 293-317, http://dx.doi.org/10.1080/01441647.2015.1077286. [4]

Hinton, J. (2021), *Relationship-to-Profit: A Theory of Business, Markets, and Profit for Social Ecological Economics*, Thesis for Degree of Doctor of Philosophy in Sustainability Science and Economics, Stockholm University, http://dx.doi.org/10.13140/RG.2.2.31508.73603 (accessed on 5 July 2021). [8]

ITF (2021), *ITF Transport Outlook 2021*, OECD Publishing, Paris, https://dx.doi.org/10.1787/16826a30-en. [14]

ITF (2017), *Income Inequality, Social Inclusion and Mobility*, ITF Roundtable Reports, No. 164, OECD Publishing, Paris, https://dx.doi.org/10.1787/g2g7ae77-en. [2]

Litman, T. (2020), *Introduction to Multi-modal Transportation Planning: Principles and Practices*, Victoria Transport Policy Institute, Victoria, British Columbia, https://www.vtpi.org/multimodal_planning.pdf. [9]

Litman, T. (2002), *The Costs of Automobile Dependency and the Benefits of Balanced Transportation*, Victoria Transport Policy Institute, Victoria, British Columbia, https://www.vtpi.org/autodep.pdf. [3]

Meadows, D. (1999), *Leverage Points: Places to Intervene in a System*, The Sustainability Institute, Hartland, VT, https://donellameadows.org/wp-content/userfiles/Leverage_Points.pdf (accessed on 16 June 2021). [7]

OECD (2019), *Accelerating Climate Action: Refocusing Policies through a Well-being Lens*, OECD Publishing, Paris, https://dx.doi.org/10.1787/2f4c8c9a-en. [12]

OECD (2011), *How's Life?: Measuring Well-being*, OECD Publishing, Paris, https://dx.doi.org/10.1787/9789264121164-en. [13]

Sharma, S. (2017), "Optimal corridor selection for a road space management strategy: Methodology and tool", *Journal of Advanced Transportation*, Vol. 2017, pp. 1-12, http://dx.doi.org/10.1155/2017/6354690. [10]

Silva, C. and A. Larson (2018), "Challenges for accessibility planning and research in the context of sustainable mobility", *International Transport Forum Discussion Papers*, No. 2018/07, OECD Publishing, Paris, https://doi.org/10.1787/8e37f587-en. [1]

Sterman, J. (2002), "Systems dynamics modeling: Tools for learning in a complex world", *IEEE Engineering Management Review*, Vol. 30/1, pp. 42-52, http://dx.doi.org/10.1109/EMR.2002.1022404. [11]

Systems Innovation (2020), *Introduction to Systems Innovation*, Systems Innovation, https://www.systemsinnovation.io/post/systems-innovation-guide (accessed on 29 March 2021). [5]

WSP and RAND Europe (2018), *Latest Evidence on Induced Travel Demand: An Evidence Review*, UK Department for Transport, London, https://assets.publishing.service.gov.uk/government/uploads/system/uploads/attachment_data/file/762976/latest-evidence-on-induced-travel-demand-an-evidence-review.pdf. [6]

www.ingramcontent.com/pod-product-compliance
Ingram Content Group UK Ltd.
Pitfield, Milton Keynes, MK11 3LW, UK
UKHW051502290926
15471UKWH00008B/1371

9 789264 591448